1700

THE POLKS
OF NORTH CAROLINA
AND TENNESSEE

by
Mrs. Frank M. Angellotti

REPRINT FROM

The New England Historical and Genealogical Register

Volume 77, pp. 133–145, 213–227, 250–270
Volume 78, pp. 33–53, 159–177, 318–330

Reprinted by
James K. Polk Memorial Association
Columbia, Tennessee

Published for

The James K. Polk Memorial Association
Columbia, Tennessee

by

SOUTHERN HISTORICAL PRESS, INC.
P.O. Box 738
Easley, South Carolina 29641-0738

ISBN 0-89308-543-X

CONTENTS

Col. Ezekiel Polk, Dec. 7, 1747-Aug. 31, 1824. *From Evelyn Tate Buchanan.*

PREFACE

Sixty years have passed since "The Polks of North Carolina and Tennessee" appeared in *The New England Historic Genealogical Magazine*. The Genealogy by Mrs. Frank M. Angellotti was at the time, and is even to this day, the most comprehensive compilation on the important Polk family. Not only has the family furnished a President of the United States, but a Bishop of the Episcopal Church, several Confederate generals, and other leaders in the military, political, economic, and cultural life of our country.

The New England Historic Genealogical Society has very kindly allowed the James K. Polk Memorial Association to reprint the genealogy. It has been reproduced in facsimile edition with a full name index and, as an added attraction, a number of photographs have been included.

The James K. Polk Memorial Association was organized in 1924 by Mrs. Rollin P. Grant, the former Saidee Polk Fall, following the death of her mother, Mrs. George William Fall, niece and adopted daughter of the President's widow, Sarah Childress Polk. In 1929 the home of James K. Polk's parents in Columbia, Tennessee, was purchased with funds from the State of Tennessee, Maury County, the City of Columbia, and Mrs. Grant.

The home in Columbia, built by Samuel Polk in 1816, is the only house yet standing, with the exception of the White House, in which Polk lived. It was opened to the public in 1930 and is filled with Polk artifacts.

A museum is housed in the adjoining "Sister's House," so called because two of the President's sisters lived in the house.

The purpose of the Association is to preserve the Polk ancestral home and properties and to perpetuate the memory of the eleventh President of the United States.

In partial fulfillment of this objective, it gives us a great deal of pleasure to present this reprint. There has been a resurgence of interest in genealogy in recent years, perhaps due in part to the celebration of our country's bicentennial. The search for ancestors has become one of the most popular hobbies today. A month seldom passes without an inquiry about Polk family history. We are deeply grateful to Mrs. Angellotti for compiling the genealogy and to the New England Historic Genealogical Society for allowing this reprint to be made.

> Mrs. Charles C. Alexander
> Chairman, Polk Genealogy Committee
>
> Mrs. Horace Rainey
> Mrs. J.L. Whiteside
> Mrs. Phillip Warren

PUBLISHER'S NOTE REGARDING
THE ORIGINAL ADDENDUM SECTION FOUND ON
PAGES 101 AND 102

The publisher would like to call to the reader's attention that the page numbers found under the Additions and Corrections in the Addendum section on page 101 and 102 must be changed, as they are not applicable to this reprinted edition.

The Table below shows the page numbers appearing in the original genealogy, and to the right are their corresponding page numbers found in this reprinted edition.

Page numbers in original edition	This edition
Volume 77, No. 306, pp. 133-145	pp. 1- 13
Volume 77, No. 307, pp. 213-227	pp. 14- 28
Volume 77, No. 308, pp. 250-270	pp. 29- 49
Volume 78, No. 309, pp. 33- 54	pp. 50- 70
Volume 78, No. 310, pp. 159-178	pp. 71- 89
Volume 78, No. 311, pp. 318-330	pp. 90-102

THE POLKS OF NORTH CAROLINA AND TENNESSEE

By Mrs. FRANK M. ANGELLOTTI of San Rafael, Calif.

IT is the purpose of this article to trace the descendants of William[3] Polk of Maryland, who settled in North Carolina about 1750 and through his sons, four of whom were officers in the Revolution, was the ancestor of the distinguished Polk family of North Carolina and Tennessee, to which James Knox Polk, eleventh President of the United States, and Leonidas Polk, Bishop and Confederate General, belonged. A brief account also is given of the first two generations of Polks in America, in order to show the family connections of William Polk of Maryland and North Carolina and his descent from Robert Polk, the immigrant ancestor of the family.

The compiler of the article is indebted to Mr. George Washington Polk of San Antonio, Tex., for the line of his ancestor, Brig. Gen. Thomas Polk (5), and for various researches in the line of Capt. Charles Polk (6), and to Mr. Wilmot Polk Rogers of Berkeley, Calif., for the line of his ancestor, Col. Ezekiel Polk (8). Additions and corrections for this genealogy will be welcome, and should be sent to the compiler.*

*It is not surprising that a family which has furnished a President to the United States, a Bishop-General to the Confederate Army, and many other men who have acquitted themselves well in public office or in military or naval service should have engaged the attention of genealogists, biographers, and historians, and that in consequence a considerable amount of material about Robert Polk of Maryland and his descendants is already in print. Much of this material belongs chiefly to the fields of biography or history, but two genealogies of the family should be mentioned here. The first is found in a series of articles by Miss Mary Winder Garrett, published in 1896–1899 in the *American Historical Magazine* of Nashville, Tenn. (vols. 1, 2, 3, and 4), and the second is a good-sized volume by William Harrison Polk of Lexington, Ky., entitled "Polk Family and Kinsmen," published in 1912. This latter work contains an abundance of genealogical and biographical matter about the Polk family, with many letters and records and with numerous portraits and other illustrations; but the arrangement of the contents is faulty and inconvenient from the genealogist's point of view, it is difficult to separate the genealogical data from the other material, dates of birth, marriage, and death are often lacking, and the book is not free from errors. The articles by Miss Garrett, although much less voluminous and perplexing than the "Polk Family and Kinsmen," also omit many important dates. It seems, therefore, to the compiler of this article and to her collaborators that a genealogy of the Southern Polks, arranged on the REGISTER plan and correcting the errors and supplying the deficiencies of the earlier works, will serve as a useful guide in tracing descent from Robert Polk of Maryland and will be welcomed by all who are interested in the historic families of the United States.

1. CAPT. ROBERT[1] POLLOCK or POLK (as the name became contracted in Maryland), the immigrant ancestor of the Polks of North Carolina and Tennessee, came to America with his family from co. Donegal, Ireland,* probably between 1672 and 1680, when John Polk, his son, registered the earmarks of his cattle, and settled on the Eastern Shore of Maryland. He died between 6 May 1699, when his will (on file at Annapolis, Md.) was dated, and 5 June 1704, when it was proved. He married, before coming to America, MAGDALEN (TASKER) PORTER, who made her will (on file in Somerset Co., Md.) 7 Apr. 1726, daughter of Colonel Tasker of Broomfield Castle, near Londonderry, Ireland, a chancellor of Ireland, and widow of Colonel Porter, in whose regiment, a part of the Parliamentary forces under Cromwell, Robert Pollock served as captain. On the death of Colonel Tasker, Broomfield Castle was left to his elder daughter, Barbara, while Magdalen received another estate of her father's called Moneen, "lying in the Barony of Rafo, County of Donegal, in the Parish of Lyford," near the village of Strabane, Ireland. In her will of 1726 Magdalen left Moneen to her youngest "son Joseph Pollock and the heirs of his body forever." Her will begins "I Magdalen Pollock," but is signed "Magdalen Polk."

Robert Polk and his sons and grandsons received grants of land on the Eastern Shore of Maryland from the Lords Baltimore between 1687 and 1742,† and in 1689 the names of Robert Polk and his son John appear on a list of loyal subjects of Somerset Co., Md., who addressed a letter to King William and Queen Mary.

Children (order of births uncertain):

    i.   JOHN,[2] b. probably in Ireland; d. in 1707; m. (1) JANE ———, who d. 28 Oct. 1700; m. (2) JOANNA KNOX, sister of Nancy (Knox) Owens, the first wife of his brother William. His will has not been found, but a deed from William Kent and his wife to Ephraim Polk recites that John Polk's will was dated 20 Nov. 1702. He had devised Locust Hammock and other lands to William Kent, probably in trust for his (John Polk's) children, and these lands were afterwards conveyed to the two children. In 1708 their uncle, William Polk (2), was appointed their guardian. Children by first wife (births recorded in the church at Monie, Somerset Co., Md.): 1. *William*,[3] b. 11 July 1695; d. in Maryland, probably in 1726, his will being proved 21 Feb. 1726/7; m. his first cousin, Priscilla Roberts, dau. of Francis and Ann (Polk) (1, vii).‡ 2. *Ann (Nancy)*, b. 27 Jan. 1698 [? 1698/9]; m. her first cousin, Edward Roberts, s.

---

*For statements about the ancestry of Capt. Robert Pollock or Polk see Addendum I to this article.

†Some of the grants of land in Maryland issued to Robert Polk, his sons, and his grandsons were: To Robert Polk, 7 Mar. 1687, "Polke's Lott" and "Polk's Folly;" 8 Nov. 1700, "Bally Hack." To Ephraim Polk, 20 Sept. 1700, "Clonmell;" 26 Mar. 1705, "Long Delay;" 27 Mar. 1715, "Chance;" 10 Dec. 1740, "Hogg yard." To James Polk, 1 June 1705, "James Meadow;" 27 Feb. 1728, "Green Pastures;" 30 Nov. 1730, "White Oak Swamp." To William Polk, 10 July 1725, "Moneen" and "Donigal;" 10 Sept. 1725, "Romas;" 6 Mar. 1728, "Richmond;" 4 Nov. 1735 (to William Polk and Thomas Pollitt), "Come by Chance." To Charles Polk, 14 Mar. 1728, "Charles Purchase;" 24 July 1733, "Second Purchase;" 2 Nov. 1730, "Charles Advantage." To David Polk, 14 Oct. 1730 "Plimouth;" 11 Nov. 1742, "Davids Hope." To Joseph Polk, 15 May 1738, "Forlorn Hope Addition." To John Polk, "Dublins Advantage;" 20 Dec. 1741, "John's Venture." To Robert Polk, 7 July 1739, "Margaret's Fancy." In some of these grants the surname is given as Pollock. The total grants from 7 Mar. 1687 to 11 Nov. 1742, so far as known, amounted to 4,152 acres.

‡On a Polk "Tree" of 1849 this William Polk, son of John, is given as the progenitor of the Polk family of North Carolina, and this statement was followed by Miss Mary Winder Garrett in her papers on the Polk family; but a later discovery of records in Maryland and other States shows that the line as given in this article is correct. Cf. Polk's "Polk Family and Kinsmen," p. 207.

of Francis and Ann (Polk) (1, vii). 3. *John,* b. 22 Oct. 1700; d. 29 Oct. 1700.

ii. ROBERT, b. probably in Ireland; d. between 2 Feb. 1726/7, when his will was dated, and 10 May 1727, when it was proved.

iii. DAVID, b. probably in Ireland; living 6 May 1699, when he is mentioned in his father's will; probably d. intestate; probably m. ———— NUTTER, dau. of Christopher.

2. iv. WILLIAM, b. probably in co. Donegal, Ireland, about 1664.

v. JAMES, d. in 1727, as the probate of his will, dated 8 Nov. 1726, shows; m. MARY WILLIAMS, probably sister of his brother Ephraim's wife. He left lands to his sons *David,*[3] *John, James,* and *Henry,* and daughters *Mary, Sarah, Elizabeth, Magdalen, Jane,* and *Anna.*

vi. EPHRAIM, b. probably in Ireland about 1671; d. in Somerset Co., Md., about 1717/18, his widow giving bonds as administratrix of his estate on 19 Mar. 1718 [?1717/18]; m., probably about 1700, ELIZABETH WILLIAMS, probably sister of the wife of his brother James. She m. (2) John Laws, and was living as his wife in 1724. Children: 1. *Magdalen,*[3] b. in 1702. 2. *Charles.* 3. *John.* 4. *Joseph.* 5. *Ephraim.*

vii. ANN, d. probably before 6 May 1699, as she is not mentioned in her father's will of that date; m. (1) FRANCIS ROBERTS, a planter, of Dame's Quarter; m. (2) JOHN RENSHAW, JR., who subsequently joined in her bond concerning the estate of her first husband. Children by first husband (surname *Roberts*): 1. *Edward,* m. his first cousin, Ann Polk (1, i, 2), b. 27 Jan. 1698 [?1698/9], dau. of John and Jane. 2. *Priscilla,* m. her first cousin, William Polk (1, i, 1), b. 11 July 1695, d. in Mary'and, probably in 1726, s. of John and Jane.

viii. MARTHA, b. in Maryland about 1679; m. (1) THOMAS POLLETT of Somerset Co., Md.; m. (2) RICHARD TULL of Dame's Quarter, records showing that she was his wife in 1710.

ix. JOSEPH, b. in Maryland about 1681; d. in 1752, aged 71 years; m. (1) ———— WRIGHT, dau. of Col. Thomas (as is shown by the latter's will of 8 Feb. 1753); m. (2) ————, living when her husband made his will. He did not change his surname to Polk, as his brothers did, but adhered to the older form, Pollock. By his mother's will, dated 7 Apr. 1726, he received the estate called Moneen, in Ireland, and lived in Ireland for several years. Then he evidently disposed of his estate there, and returned to Maryland. His brother Robert, in his will of 2 Feb. 1726/7, devised to him "part of Forlorn Hope . . . and likewise a certain tract of land called Bally Hack," and on 15 May 1738 he acquired from Lord Baltimore land called "Forlorn Hope Addition." In his will, dated 12 Sept. 1751 and proved 10 June 1752, he mentions his son Robert Pollock, his youngest son James Pollock, his eldest daughter Ann Pollock, his son Zephaniah Pollock, and his (the testator's) "beloved wife." Children by first wife: 1. *Robert.*[3] 2. *Ann.* Children, probably by second wife: 3. *Zephaniah.* 4. *James.* Perhaps another daughter or other daughters.

2. WILLIAM[2] POLK (*Robert*[1]), born probably in co. Donegal, Ireland, about 1664, died probably near the end of 1739, as his will was proved 24 Feb. 1739/40. He married first NANCY (KNOX) OWENS, widow, sister of the second wife of his brother John (1, i); and secondly ———— GRAY, widow, probably the mother of Allen Gray, who is mentioned in William Polk's will.

He lived at the old family home, "White Hall," on the Eastern Shore of Maryland. His two older sons are not mentioned in his will, but they probably received their shares in his property and left home after their father's second marriage.

Children by first wife:

i. ELIZABETH,[3] b. about 1695; m. JOHN WILLIAMS of Somerset Co., Md.
Children (surname *Williams*): 1. *Mary*, to whom her father, in
his will, left a tract of 100 acres of land called "Ramoth." 2. *John*,
a captain in the Revolution, d. in 1798. Probably two other sons,
who migrated to the Carolinas.

3. ii. WILLIAM, b. in Maryland, probably at "White Hall," his father's
home, about 1700.

iii. CHARLES, b. probably in 1703; d. between 19 Mar. 1753, when his will
was dated, and 20 June 1753, when it was proved; m., probably in
1735, CHRISTIAN MATSON, sister of Ralph. He built a residence
and trading house at the North Bend of the Potomac River, and
was known there as Charles Polk, the Indian trader. In Gist's
Journal it is stated that his name appears in the list of Indian
traders in 1734. On Major's map of 1737 his name is marked with
the names of four other settlers at the North Bend of the Potomac,
where Hancock, Md., now stands. In the spring of 1780 his son,
Capt. Charles Polk, with his brothers William, Edmond, and
Thomas, and their sister, Mrs. Sarah (Polk) Piety, and her children, travelled from Pittsburgh, Pa., to Kentucky, and settled
there. Delilah (Tyler) Polk, wife of Capt. Charles Polk, was captured by Indians, but was recovered.

Children by second wife:

iv. JAMES, b. 17 May 1719; d. in 1770; m. (1) MARY COTTMAN; m. (2)
BETTY COTTMAN, sister of his first wife. His will was proved in
Apr. 1771, in Frederick Co., Md. He and his descendants remained
in Maryland.

v. DAVID, b. in 1721; d. in 1778; m. BETSEY GILLIS. He lived at "White
Hall," the old homestead of his father and grandfather. He was
commissioned a justice of the peace on 8 Jan. 1763, and became a
Colonial judge for Somerset Co., Md. His children remained in
Maryland, where his eldest son, William, was a judge of the Court
of Appeals. This family became connected by marriage with the
families of Lowe, Jenkins, McLane, Cox, Tilghman, Laws, and
many other prominent families.

vi. JANE, b. in 1723; m. JAMES STRAWBRIDGE.

3. WILLIAM[3] POLK (*William,*[2] *Robert*[1]), born in Maryland, probably at "White Hall," his father's home, about 1700, died in
North Carolina, "west of the Yadkin," about 1753. He
married MARGARET TAYLOR, who survived him.

Apparently he and his brother Charles left home after his
father married for the second time, and William settled in the
vicinity of what is now Carlisle, Pa., a region then a part of
the frontier. Later he and his family moved to Mecklenburg
Co., N. C.

Children, born in Cumberland Co., Pa., near the site of the
present Carlisle:

4. i. WILLIAM.[4]

ii. DEBORAH, m. SAMUEL MCLEARY.

5. iii. THOMAS, b. about 1730.

6. iv. CHARLES, b. 9 July 1732.

v. SUSAN, m. BENJAMIN ALEXANDER. Children (surname *Alexander*):
1. *Charles.* 2. *Thomas.* 3. William, a captain in the Revolution,
called locally "Black Bill." 4. *Susan.* 5. *Benjamin.* 6. *Taylor.*

vi. MARGARET, m. ROBERT MCREE of Mecklenburg Co., N. C. Children
(surname *McRee*): 1. *William.* 2. *Debora.* 3. *James.* 4. *Susan.*
5. *Dinah.* 6. *Margaret.* 7. *Thomas.* 8. *Harriet.* 9. *Rachel.* 10.
William. 11. *Mary.*

7. vii. JOHN, b. probably about 1739.
8. viii. EZEKIEL, b. 7 Dec. 1747.

4. WILLIAM[4] POLK (*William,[3] William,[2] Robert[1]*), born in Cumberland Co., Pa., near the site of the present Carlisle, probably went with his father to North Carolina. He married twice, but the names of his wives and the number of his children are unknown.

Children (order of births uncertain):

   i. THOMAS,[5] b. probably in North Carolina; d. at what is now Gibraltar, N. C., in 1842; m. MARY SHELBY of the Chesterfield (S. C.) district, sister of Reese and Thomas Shelby. He lived first on Watson's Creek, but later removed to Richardson's Creek, settling at the place called Little Mountain. Afterwards the settlement became known as Polk's Mountain, and, in 1880, as Gibraltar. Children: 1. *Shelby,[6]* d. in 1847; m. Winifred Colburn; emigrated to Tennessee in 1813; seven children. 2. *Andrew.* 3. *Thomas.* 4. *Job.* 5. *Hannah.* 6. *Dicy.* 7. *Patsy.* 8. *Mary.* 9. *Elizabeth.*

  ii. JOHN, lived on Crooked Creek, in that part of Anson Co., N. C., which is now Union Co. Later he moved to South Carolina.

 iii. EZEKIEL, of North Carolina, d. in 1791. He was ensign in a regiment of United States Infantry 3 June 1790 (Heitman's Historical Register and Dictionary of the United States Army, vol. 1, p. 796).

Perhaps other children.

5. BRIG. GEN. THOMAS[4] POLK (*William,[3] William,[2] Robert[1]*), born in Cumberland Co., Pa., near the site of the present Carlisle, about 1730, died at Charlotte, N. C., 26 June 1794. He married in 1755 SUSANNA SPRATT, daughter of Thomas, who was probably the first white settler in Mecklenburg Co., N. C.

Thomas Polk was a surveyor, and settled near the site of the present Charlotte, N. C. He was elected to the North Carolina Assembly, and remained a member of that body almost continuously from 1766 to 1776. He was a trustee of Queen's College, the first institution for the education of the young in Charlotte. He was an instigator and signer of the so-called Mecklenburg Declaration of 1775. On 19 Apr. 1776 he was commissioned as colonel in the Continental Line, and was assigned to Colonel Moore's brigade, at Wilmington, N. C. In the spring of 1777 he joined Washington in New Jersey, was assigned to Lord Stirling's division, and was in active service under Washington until 10 Feb. 1778. He commanded the escort of the Liberty Bell, when, Philadelphia being threatened, the Bell was removed to Bethlehem, Pa. In the later years of the Revolution he served in the Southern States, and attained the rank of brigadier general. After the War he lived at his old home in Charlotte, received Lafayette when the latter visited that city, and gave a dinner for him at his home, at which the principal men of the county were entertained. For his services in the Revolution he received a land warrant from the North Carolina Assembly for lands in what was then Davidson County, now the State of Tennessee; he also bought up many land warrants of soldiers from North Carolina in the Continental Line, and went to Tennessee and located them.

The original land warrant for his services was presented to the
State of Tennessee by one of his descendants, George Washington Polk of San Antonio, Tex., and is now preserved in
the State Archives.

Children:

i.   THOMAS,[5] a lieutenant in the Revolution, killed at the Battle of
     Eutaw Springs, S. C., 8 Sept. 1781; d. unm.
9. ii. WILLIAM, b. in Mecklenburg Co., N. C., 9 July 1758.
iii. EZEKIEL, lost at sea.
10. iv. CHARLES, b. near Charlotte, Mecklenburg Co., N. C., about 1762.
v.   MARGARET, m. NATHANIEL ALEXANDER, Governor of North Caro-
     lina from 1805 to 1807. No issue.
vi. MARY, m. DAVID BROWN. Three children, all of whom died in child-
     hood.
vii. MARTHA, m. DR. EPHRAIM BREVARD, a prominent patriot of
     Mecklenburg County, N. C., who served in the Revolution. Child
     (surname *Brevard*): 1. *Mary*, m. —— Dickinson of South Caro-
     lina; she left one child, James Polk, who was lieutenant colonel in
     Butler's regiment in the Mexican War and was mortally wounded
     at the Battle of Churubusco, 20 Aug. 1847.
viii. JAMES, m. —— MOORE, dau. of Colonel Moore. No issue.

6. CAPT. CHARLES[4] POLK (*William,*[3] *William,*[2] *Robert*[1]), born in
Cumberland Co., Pa., near the site of the present Carlisle,
9 July 1732, died in Mecklenburg Co., N. C., 10 Mar. 1821.
He married first, in Mar. 1762, MARY CLARK, born in June
1744, died 8 Oct. 1776; and secondly, 5 Feb. 1782, PHILOPENA
HELMS, born 10 June 1764, died 12 Jan. 1849.

About 1750 he migrated with his parents to North Carolina.
When he grew to manhood, he acquired lands in Mecklenburg Co., and lived there until his death.

He was a lieutenant, 7 June 1766, in Capt. Adam Alexander's
company of militia (the Clear Creek Company), as is proved
by a recorded list of that company. He took an active part in
the Revolution, served in the campaign against the Scotch
Highland Tories, and was captain of the Brunswick Light
Horse. The pension granted his widow for his Revolutionary
services was for "five months' service as Captain of Cavalry,
nine months as Captain of Infantry, and nine months and
nineteen days as Captain of Cavalry." The record also states
that he served under Lieut. Col. William Polk and that he was
a brother of Gen. Thomas and of John and Ezekiel Polk.

His will, recorded in Mecklenburg Co., N. C., names as his
executors his brother-in-law, Rev. Jacob Helms, and his son,
George Washington Polk.

Children by first wife:

i.   PEGGY,[5] b. 25 Dec. 1764; m. WILLIAM FREEMAN, b. 24 June 1765.
ii. JOHN, b. 17 Nov. 1766; m. ESTHER POOL. He migrated to Hardeman
     Co., Tenn.
iii. DEBORAH, b. 10 Dec. 1768; m. GIDEON FREEMAN, b. 12 July 1769.
iv. THOMAS, b. 28 Feb. 1771; m. KEZIAH PRIOR, b. 18 Feb. 1768, d. in
     1842. He migrated to Hardeman Co., Tenn.
11. v. MICHAEL, b. in Mecklenburg Co., N. C., 20 June 1774.
vi. MARY, b. 24 Sept. 1776; m. JOHN BROOKS.

Children by second wife:

12. vii. CHARLES, b. in Mecklenburg Co., N. C., 15 Mar. 1784.
   viii. WILLIAM, b. 10 Apr. 1786. He migrated to Hardeman Co., Tenn., and his later history has not been traced.
   ix. SUSANNA, b. 19 June 1788.
   x. EZEKIEL, b. 9 June 1791. He migrated to Hardeman Co., Tenn.
   xi. MARTHA WASHINGTON, b. 4 May 1794; m. MOSES SHELBY. They moved to Tennessee.
   xii. GEORGE WASHINGTON, b. 18 Sept. 1799; m. 4 Dec. 1823 MARGARET GARMAN, b. 10 May 1804. Children: 1. *Martha,*[6] b. 6 Oct. 1824. 2. *Phebe,* b. 10 June 1826. 3. *Charles H.,* b. 23 Apr. 1828. 4. *Mary S.,* b. 2 Mar. 1830. 5. *John P.,* b. 12 May 1832. 6. *Tabitha,* b. 28 Feb. 1834. 7. *William S.,* b. 18 Feb. 1836. 8. *James,* b. 17 Jan. 1838. 9. *Henry M.,* b. 22 Dec. 1840. 10. *George W.,* b. 27 Sept. 1841; d. 6 June 1851. 11. *Margaret,* b. 3 June 1843. 12. *Alphonso,* b. and d. 11 July 1845.
   xiii. ELEANOR, b. 16 Jan. 1804.

7. CAPT. JOHN[4] POLK (*William,*[3] *William,*[2] *Robert*[1]), born in Cumberland Co., Pa., near the site of the present Carlisle, probably about 1739, died probably early in 1785, as on 9 Sept. of that year the Assembly of North Carolina issued Land Warrant No. 2149 "to the heirs of John Polk" for "1000 acres of land within the limits of the land reserved by law for the officers and soldiers of the Continental line of this State." He married, 2 Oct. 1758, ELEANOR SHELBY, daughter of Gen. Evan.*

John Polk went with his parents to Mecklenburg Co., N. C., about 1750, and in a deed of 1763, on file at Charlotte, he is styled "a planter." His wife "Elloner" joined with him in signing a deed in the same county in 1764. His name is given as the author of a petition in 1765 to the Governor and Council, complaining, with his neighbors, of the acts of the chief agent of the large Selwyn grant, on which they lived. On 7 June 1766 he appears as a member of the Clear Creek Company of militia, commanded by Capt. Adam Alexander, in which his older brother Charles (6) was a lieutenant. By acts of the General Assembly of the Province in 1766, 1771, and 1773, he was made a member of commissions charged with laying out roads to connect the western counties with Wilmington and Brunswick Co. He was an officer in Col. Francis Locke's regiment, which was raised to meet the Loyalists then gathering, and which fought a few days later at the Battle of Ramseur's Mills. At various times he served as captain in the militia of that region, when it was called out by the Committee of Safety.

*Gen. Evan Shelby was born in Carnarvonshire, Wales, about 1720, and died at his home at Sapling Grove, Tenn., 4 Dec. 1794. He came with his parents, Evan and Catherine (Davies) Shelby, to Maryland, where they settled near the North Mountain. He married first Letitia Cox, who died in 1777, aged 54 (tombstone record), and was buried at Charlottesville, Va.; and secondly Isabella Elliott. He lived for a time near Salem, N. C. He was present at Braddock's defeat as a captain of Rangers, was a captain in the French and Indian War that followed, and served throughout the war under General Forbes. After his superior officers had been killed or disabled in the battle with the Indians at Point Pleasant, Va., 10 Oct. 1774, he assumed command in the field and routed the enemy. In 1779 he led a successful expedition against the Chickamaugas. He was made a brigadier general in the Militia of Virginia. For his standing as a man, officer, and statesman see Roosevelt's "Winning of the West." His children were: 1. Eleanor, m. Capt. John Polk (7). 2. Susanna. 3. John. 4. Isaac. 5. Evan. 6. Moses. 7. James. 8. Catherine. Mary Shelby, a kinswoman of Eleanor, m. Col. Adam Alexander.

An affidavit concerning the service of Capt. Charles Polk (6), on file in the Pension Office in Washington, contains a declaration that John Polk was appointed Indian Agent for the Catawba Indians. By the efforts of local officers in North Carolina these Indians were kept friendly during the Revolution, but they were not wards of the Government.*

Children:

13. i.   CHARLES,⁵ b. in Mecklenburg Co., N. C., 18 Jan. 1760.
14. ii.   JOHN, b. probably in Mecklenburg Co., N. C., in 1767.
    iii. SHELBY.
15. iv.   TAYLOR, b. in North Carolina about 1780.
    v.   ELEANOR. Her place in the list of children is uncertain. Perhaps she d. young.

8. COL. EZEKIEL⁴ POLK (*William³, William,² Robert¹*), born in Cumberland Co., Pa., near the site of the present Carlisle, 7 Dec. 1747, died near Bolivar, Hardeman Co., Tenn., 31 Aug. 1824, and was buried in Riverside Cemetery. He married first, in Mecklenburg County, N. C., about 1769, MARY WILSON, who died probably before 1790, daughter of Samuel;† secondly, probably, BESSIE DAVIS, although some say that her name was Polly Campbell; and thirdly, in Maury Co., Tenn., in 1812 or 1813, SOPHIA (NEELY) LENNARD, daughter of James Neely.

He was taken by his parents to Mecklenburg Co., N.C., about 1750, and, when he came to manhood, acquired considerable property there. The official records show that he was clerk of Tryon Co. (now abolished‡), N. C., in 1770–1772. Some time between 1772 and 1775 he moved across the border and settled in York Co., S. C., west of the Catawba River. There, in 1775, he was lieutenant colonel of the Twelfth Regiment of South Carolina Militia, for the New Acquisition District,§ a district largely settled by the overflow from Mecklenburg Co. In 1775 the Provincial Congress of South Carolina established the Council of Safety, and authorized the organization of three regiments of troops; and on 18 June 1775 Ezekiel Polk was made captain of the second company in the regiment commanded by Colonel Thompson, and proceeded to march to Ninety-Six. On 28 July 1775 Captain Polk and his company returned to their homes in York Co., and he became active as lieutenant colonel in the militia of his district; but that his company of Rangers was held intact, although the men were allowed to return to their homes, is clear from a first return of the company, covering the period from 18 June to 7 Oct. 1775,

*For information about the services of John Polk see Colonial Records of North Carolina and State Records of North Carolina.

†Samuel Wilson came into the Mecklenburg region about 1752. He was a man of high education and of considerable wealth, and was visited there by his kinsman, Sir Robert Wilson. His first wife was Mary Winslow, daughter of Moses and Jean (Osbourne). His third wife was Margaret Jack. His daughter Violet married Maj. John Davidson. (History of Mecklenburg County, p. 10, by Dr. J. B. Alexander.)

‡Because of the unpopularity of William Tryon, at one time the royal governor of North Carolina, the General Assembly of North Carolina, in 1779, abolished Tryon County and out of its territory organized two new counties, Lincoln and Rutherford.

§Cf. South Carolina in the Revolution, p. 12.

which shows that its personnel was the same when it was called back into service on 21 Aug. as when it was first recruited in June and July. He was in command of this company of Rangers in the "Snow" campaign against the Tories in the back district. About the time when the British abandoned their attempts to take Charleston, the Indians and Tories on the western frontier began to make raids and to massacre; and Colonel Thomas's regiment of militia, with that of Colonel Neil, of which Ezekiel Polk was lieutenant colonel, was sent against them. In three months the Patriots were victorious, and the troops returned home and were disbanded. After Cornwallis's retreat from Mecklenburg Co., N. C., Captain Polk did not return to York Co., S. C., where his property had been confiscated by the enemy, but made his home on Sugar Creek, in Mecklenburg Co. After Sumter was made brigadier general and was authorized to raise regiments in South Carolina to coöperate with General Greene, one of these regiments was placed under the command of Ezekiel Polk.* From this time to the end of the War he continued to serve under Sumter and in the militia, except for several months in 1781 or 1782 which he spent in Pennsylvania.

Shortly before 1790 he migrated with his family to the Western District, as Tennessee was then called, where he had acquired large tracts of land by the purchase of land warrants from Revolutionary soldiers. In 1790 Governor Blount appointed him justice of the peace in Tennessee Co. In 1806 he was living in Williamson Co., Tenn., as is shown by a deed of gift of 300 acres of land on Carter's Creek to his daughter Matilda, wife of John Campbell. In 1811 he was a member of the grand jury formed to "inquire into the body" of Maury Co., Tenn. In 1820 he moved, with his sons Samuel and William and his sons-in-law Col. Thomas Jones Hardeman and Thomas McNeal and their families, and founded the first white settlement in Hardeman Co., Tenn., which was named for his pioneer son-in-law; and there he died.

Children by first wife:

16. i. THOMAS⁶ (twin), b., probably in Tryon Co., N. C., 5 Dec. 1770.

    ii. MATILDA GOLDEN (twin), b. 5 Dec. 1770, it is supposed, as she is called "twin of Thomas" in early Polk records and his birth date is known to be as here given; d. at Springfield, Mo., 20 Sept. 1853; m. (1) 3 May 1792 JOHN CAMPBELL, b. in Pennsylvania, d. in 1816, being lost on a trading trip (on which cotton and molasses were loaded on barges) down the Mississippi to New Orleans; m. (2) in Maury Co., Tenn., in Dec. 1821, PHILIP JENKINS. In 1835 she and her children migrated from Maury Co., Tenn., to Missouri, and settled near Springfield. Her first husband served in the Revolution as a lieutenant of Artillery in Capt. Mott's company, in the Second North Carolina Regiment, commanded by Charles Lamb. His will is dated 21 Apr. 1816, and he died within two months after that date. Children by first husband (surname *Campbell*):† 1. *Mary*,

---

*Cf. *South Carolina Historical and Genealogical Magazine*, vol. 2, p. 105, and *Year Book, City of Charleston*, 1899, pp. 25, 37, 49.

†In addition to the children whose names are here given, there were other children of this marriage who died young.

b., probably in Mecklenburg Co., N. C., 21 Mar. 1795; m. Joseph Miller; three children, perhaps more. 2. *Robert*, b., probably in Mecklenburg Co., N. C., 5 July 1797; d. at Columbia, Tenn., 1 Dec. 1852; m. his second cousin, Elizabeth Polk (14, v), b. 9 Oct. 1796, d. at Columbia, Tenn., 8 July 1856, dau. of John and Elizabeth (Alderson); on the records of Maury Co., Tenn., this Robert Campbell is called Robert, Jr., to distinguish him from his father's brother, Robert, Sr.; eight children, the seventh of whom, Matilda Jane, b. in Maury Co., Tenn., 10 Sept. 1826, d. at Danville, Ky., 15 June 1894, m. in Maury Co., Tenn., 4 July 1848, Washington Curran Whitthorne, s. of Jarvis and Eliza Joyce (Wisener), who was b. in Marshall Co., Tenn., 19 Apr. 1825, d. at Columbia, Tenn., 21 Sept. 1891, was graduated at East Tennessee University in 1843, studied law at Columbia under Hon. James Knox Polk, was a member of the State Senate, 1855–1858, speaker of the Tennessee House, 1859, a presidential elector, on the Breckinridge ticket, in 1860, adjutant general of the State in the Civil War, and (his disabilities having been removed by act of Congress in 1870) a Democratic representative in the Forty-second and in the five succeeding Congresses (1871–1883), was appointed and subsequently elected United States Senator, as a Democrat, for the unexpired term of Howell E. Jackson, served as senator from 16 Apr. 1886 to 4 Mar. 1887, and was a representative in the Fiftieth and Fifty-first Congresses (1887–1891). 3. *Eliza Eugenia*, b., probably in Mecklenburg Co., N. C., 24 May 1800; d. at Carter's Creek, Tenn., 27 July 1856; m. 8 Jan. 1819 Abden Independence Alexander, b. 4 July 1798, d. 1 Oct. 1868, s. of Eliazer (b. 23 Nov. 1763) and Margaret (Carter) (b. 19 Sept. 1770); eleven children. 4. *Ezekiel Madison*, b. in Mecklenburg Co., N. C., 21 July 1802; d. in Polk Co., Mo., 22 Sept. 1874; m. in Maury Co., Tenn., in 1821, Rebecca Patton Adkins, b. in 1800, d. in 1876; ten children, of whom two, James Madison and Robert Bruce, served in the Confederate Army, the latter dying in that service. 5. *John Polk*, b. in Mecklenburg Co., N. C., 29 Mar. 1804; d. at Tallequah, Indian Territory, 28 May 1852; m. in Maury Co., Tenn., 28 May 1827, Louise Terrill Cheairs, dau. of Nathaniel and Sarah (Hall); he served under General Price in the Mexican War, attaining the rank of major in Colonel Doniphan's regiment; ten children, of whom four served in the Confederate Army, viz., John Nathaniel, a captain in the Thirtieth Mississippi Infantry, Leonidas Adolphus Cadwallader, lieutenant colonel in the Third Missouri Infantry, and Thomas Polk and Samuel Independence, soldiers in the same regiment. 6. *William St. Clair*, b. probably in Maury Co., Tenn., 16 May 1808; d. near Humboldt River, Nev., *en route* to California, 24 July 1852; m. (1) 20 Feb. 1826 Mildred Ann Blackman; m. (2) 7 July 1848 Sarah Nichol; six children (three by each wife), of whom the eldest, Leonidas Caldwell, was a captain and later a colonel in the Confederate Army. 7. *Matilda Golden*, b. in Maury Co., Tenn., 14 Apr. 1809; d. at Springfield, Mo., in Nov. 1870; m. in Maury Co., Tenn., Stephen Blackman; seven children. 8. *Junius Tennessee*, b. in Maury Co., Tenn., 24 June 1812; d. at Springfield, Mo., 16 Mar. 1877; m. at Springfield, 16 May 1832, Mary Ann Blackwell; eleven children. 9. *Caroline Huntley*, b. in Maury Co., Tenn., 14 Mar. 1814; m. —————— Hardeman; no issue. 10. *Samuel Polk*, b. in Maury Co., Tenn., 4 May 1816; d. unm. at Springfield, Mo., 6 July 1835.

17. iii. SAMUEL, b., probably in Tryon Co., N. C., 5 July 1772.
    iv. JOHN, b. probably in York Co., S. C., in 1774, but according to the Polk Tree of 1849 he was younger than his brother William Wilson, who was b. 10 Sept. 1776. The Tree also shows that he had two

daughters. 1. *Olivia Mary,*[6] m. —— Prior, and had three children. 2. *Angelina,* m. —— Crawford.*

18. v. WILLIAM WILSON, b., probably in York Co., S. C., a few miles over the line from Mecklenburg Co., N. C., 10 Sept. 1776.

vi. CLARISSA, b., probably in Mecklenburg Co., N. C., 25 Dec. 1782; d. at Bolivar, Tenn., 8 Dec. 1846; m. in Williamson Co. (later Maury Co.), Tenn., in 1803, COL. THOMAS MCNEAL. † Children (surname *McNeal*): 1. *Ezekiel Polk*, b. in Maury Co., Tenn., 6 Sept. 1804; d. at Bolivar, Tenn., 10 Dec. 1886; m. at Bolivar, in 1835, Anne Williams; one daughter, Priscilla, b. 5 Apr. 1836, d. unm. in 1854. 2. *Mary Eliza*, b. in Maury Co., Tenn., 16 Sept. 1806; d. at Bolivar, Tenn., 10 Sept. 1853; m. in Hardeman Co., Tenn., Mark R. Roberts; she migrated to Fannin Co., Tex., about 1835; fourteen children. 3. *Prudence Tate*, b. in Maury Co., Tenn., 29 Jan. 1809; d. at Bolivar, Tenn., 14 Aug. 1840; m. at Hatchie (now Bolivar), Hardeman Co., Tenn., 9 Sept. 1823, Maj. John Houston Bills, s. of Isaac and Lillias (Houston) and nephew of Gen. Sam Houston of Texas; eight children. 4. *Albert Thomas*, b. in Maury Co., Tenn., 28 Jan. 1811; d. at Coffeeville, Miss., 3 Sept. 1844; m. in 1839 Mary Jane Dunlap, dau. of —— and Mary (Blair); two children. 5. *Jane Frances*, b. 11 May 1813; d. at Prairie Lea, Tex., 25 June 1852; m. at Bolivar, Tenn., 14 Oct., 1829, Dr. David Franklin Brown, b. 17 Mar. 1801, d. 7 Nov. 1869, s. of Dr. Joseph of Giles Co., Tenn.; she was educated at Miss Trumbull's school in Baltimore, Md., moved with her family to Texas in 1838, and settled on the Colorado River about three miles from Bastrop; eight children, of whom Albert Polk was a sergeant in Company A, Fourth Texas Infantry, Hood's brigade in the Confederate Army, was mortally wounded in the Battle of Gaines' Mills, Va., 27 June 1862, and d. unm. at Richmond, Va., 14 Aug. 1862, and Lycurgus McNeal, a member of the same company, d. unm. in camp near Humphries, Va., 27 Dec. 1861. 6. *Samuel L.*, b. in Maury Co., Tenn., 1 Dec. 1815; d. unm. at Nashville, Tenn., 5 Sept. 1871. 7. *Evelina Louisa*, b. in Maury Co., Tenn., 26 July 1818; d. at Bolivar, Tenn., 20 Oct. 1855; m. (1) at Bolivar, in 1837, Erasmus McDowell; m. (2) at Bolivar, in 1841, Dr. George Boddie Peters; seven children by second husband, of whom Thomas McNeal served as second lieutenant of Artillery in the Confederate Army (Capt. Marshall T. Polk's battery, Cheatham's division) and James Arthur, who had entered the United States Naval Academy at Annapolis, Md., in 1860 but had resigned from the Academy in 1861, served in the Confederate Navy and later in the Confederate Army. 8. *William Wallace*, b. in Maury Co., Tenn., 28 Sept. 1821; d. at Lockhart, Tex., 7 Apr. 1870; m. at Bolivar, Tenn., 26 Nov. 1844, Elizabeth Walker Barry; he migrated to Texas soon after his marriage, and settled at Lockhart; two sons.

vii. MARY, b. probably in Mecklenburg Co., N. C., about 1784; d. at Bolivar, Tenn., about 1830; m. in Maury Co., Tenn., about 1814, COL. THOMAS JONES HARDEMAN.‡ Soon after his wife's death Colonel Hardeman, with his children, migrated to Texas, settling near Smithville, Bastrop Co., where his old home, now owned by his youngest daughter, still stands. He took an active part in the war for Texan independence, and later was a member of the Congress of the Republic of Texas. Children (surname *Hardeman*): 1.

---

*A deed on file at Charlotte, Mecklenburg Co., N. C., shows that John Wilson gave land in Burke Co., N. C., to "my sister Mary's son John Polk." Unfortunately the early records of Burke County were destroyed during the Civil War.

†Phelan's History of Tennessee, p. 306, states that the first settlement in Hardeman Co. was made near Hickory Valley by Ezekiel Polk and his sons-in-law, Thomas McNeal and Col. Thomas J. Hardeman, and that the County Court was organized at the house of Thomas McNeal. Maj. John H. Bills and Prudence McNeal were the first couple in this vicinity united in marriage under the laws of civilization.

‡One of the first settlers in Hardeman Co., Tenn. He was a brother of Bailey Hardeman, the first secretary of war of the Republic of Texas.

Thomas Monroe, b. in Maury Co., Tenn., 30 Oct. 1815; d. at Knoxville, Tenn., 14 Sept. 1862, while a member of Hood's brigade in the Confederate Army; m. in Bastrop Co., Tex., 16 Apr. 1843, Susan Anna Burleson, dau. of Joseph; he was educated at Nashville, Tenn., as a lawyer, returned to Texas in 1834, and was in General Burleson's command; four children. 2. *William P.*, b. in Maury Co., Tenn., 4 Nov. 1816; d. at Austin, Tex., 8 Apr. 1898; m. (1) in 1842 Rebecca Amanda Wilson, who d. 15 Oct. 1853; m. (2) at Prairie Lea, Tex., 27 Dec. 1857, Sarah Ann (Hamilton) Reade, who d. 8 Nov. 1869, dau. of John and Ann (Good) Hamilton; m. (3) at Austin, Tex., 5 Feb. 1874, Mary Elizabeth Collins, who d. 13 Mar. 1911; he migrated with his father to Texas about 1830, later served in the Texan Army, and attained the rank of brigadier general in the Confederate Army; he resided in Caldwell Co., Tex., until 1876, when he moved to Austin; two daughters by first wife, five children by second wife. 3. *Owen Bailey*, b. in Maury Co., Tenn., 25 Dec. 1819; d. at Weatherford, Tex., 3 Sept. 1890; m. at Brenham, Tex., 30 Apr. 1849, Sarah Meredith Berry, who d. 6 Sept. 1911; five children. 4. *Mary Ophelia*, b. in Maury Co., Tenn., about 1823; d. at Prairie Lea, Tex.; m. near Bastrop, Tex., 8 June 1841, Dr. James Fentress; her only son, Thomas Hardeman, b. near Bastrop, was killed in the Battle of Val Verde, near Albuquerque, N. Mex., 8 Apr. 1862, while serving in the Fourth Texas Cavalry, Green's brigade, in the Confederate Army. 5. *Leonidas Polk*, b. at Bolivar, Tenn., 26 Mar. 1825; d. at Prairie Lea, Tex., 26 Feb. 1892; m. at Lockhart, Tex., 8 Jan. 1852, Tullius [*sic*] Leonora Hamilton, b. 16 Oct. 1834, d. 8 Jan. 1904, dau. of John A.; he served in the Mexican War, enlisted 4 Feb. 1862 in the Confederate Army, was made second lieutenant, 16 May 1862, in Col. William P. Hardeman's regiment, Green's brigade, and served throughout the war, attaining the rank of captain; three children.

viii. LOUISA, b. probably in Mecklenburg Co., N. C., about 1787; d. at Bolivar, Tenn., 20 Dec. 1869; m. (1) in Maury Co., Tenn., about 1807, CAPT. CHARLES RUFUS NEELY, b. in Virginia about 1787, d. near Tuscumbia, Ala., in 1820; m. (2) in Hardeman Co., Tenn., DR. CLINTON C. COLLIER. Her first husband, Captain Neely, migrated to Tennessee when he was young, and afterwards settled near Tuscumbia, Ala. He attained the rank of captain in the War of 1812. Children by first husband (surname *Neely*): 1. *Rufus Polk*, b. in Maury Co., Tenn., 26 Nov. 1808; died at Bolivar, Tenn., 10 Aug. 1901; m. at Bolivar, 18 May 1829, Elizabeth Lea, dau. of John M. and Catherine (McClyment) of Philadelphia, Pa.; for several years he was register and county clerk of Maury Co.; in 1839, as captain of militia, he led a company to assist in removing the Indians to their new territory; he was a member of the State Legislature, 1839–40, and was brigadier general of the Militia of Tennessee; early in 1861 he was appointed captain of Company B, Fourth Tennessee Infantry, Confederate Army, and in May was made colonel of the regiment; eleven children, b. at Bolivar, of whom Charles Lea was killed in the Battle of Brice Cross Roads, 10 June 1864, while serving in the Confederate Army. 2. *Mary Catherine*, b. in Maury Co., Tenn., 16 Jan. 1811; d. at Austin, Tex., 19 July 1896; m. at Bolivar, Tenn., 29 June 1829, William Woods Atwood, who d. 2 Jan. 1871; six children, of whom Rufus Neely enlisted in 1862 in the Confederate Army, was taken prisoner in Feb. 1862 at the fall of Fort Donelson, Tenn., and d. unm. in a military prison at Chicago, Ill., 7 Mar. 1863. 3. *Adela Clarissa*, m. (1) James Bell; m. (2) Thomas Chambliss; m. (3) Col. John Pope of Memphis, Tenn.; one child by first husband, who d. in infancy. 4. *James Jackson*, m. Fanny Stephens. 5. *Thomas*, m. Sarah Fort; one child, William, d. young; perhaps other children. 6. *Fanny*, d. unm. 7. *William*, d. unm.

Children by third wife:*

19. ix. CHARLES PERRY, b. in Maury Co., Tenn., 27 Oct. 1813.
    x. EUGENIA, b. in Maury Co., Tenn.; d. at Wilburton, Okla., 16 Oct.
       1895; m. in Hardeman Co., Tenn., ALEXANDER NEILSON. Children
       (surname *Neilson*): 1. *Hugh*, d. unm. 2. *Sarah*, d. unm. 3. *William*, d. unm. 4. *Ada*, d. unm. 5 *Charles*, b. at Bolivar, Tenn.; d.
       at Corinth, Miss.; m. at West Point, Miss., Hattie Williams; one
       child, Charles, who d. in infancy. 6. *Sophia*, b. at Bolivar, Tenn.;
       m. at Corinth, Miss., George Cox; no issue. 7. *Benigna Ellen*, b. at
       Bolivar, Tenn., 22 Feb. 1856; m. at Corinth, Miss., 19 Nov. 1873,
       Charles Henry Reed, s. of James Crownover and Mary (Phillips);
       residence, McAlester, Okla.; four daughters.
    xi. BENIGNA, b. in Maury Co., Tenn., 30 July 1816; d. at Memphis,
        Tenn., 27 Jan. 1886; m. in Hardeman Co., Tenn., 18 July 1834,
        WILLIAM HENRY WOOD, s. of Drury and Matilda (Carr). Children
        (surname *Wood*): 1. *Mary Morton*, b. at Bolivar, Tenn., 22 May
        1835; m. at Bolivar, 8 July 1858, Napoleon Hill, s. of Duncan and
        Lillias Olivia (Bills); residence, Memphis, Tenn.; seven children,
        b. at Memphis. 2. *Matilda*, d. in infancy. 3. *James*, d. in infancy.
        4. *Benigna Dunlap*, b. at Bolivar, Tenn., 27 Nov. 1843; m. at
        Memphis, Tenn., 30 July 1866, James Henry Martin, s. of John A.
        and Nancy, captain in the Seventh Tennessee Infantry, Confederate Army; residence, Memphis; nine children.
    xii. EDWIN FITZHUGH, b. in Maury Co., Tenn., 6 May 1818; d. at Bolivar,
         Tenn.; m. at Bolivar, 30 July 1846, OCTAVIA ROWENA JONES, dau.
         of Calvin. Children: 1. *Pauline*,⁶ d. in infancy. 2. *Octavia*, b. at
         Bolivar 10 Mar. 1848; m. at Bolivar, 7 Sept. 1869, Tudor F. Brooks;
         residence, "Mecklen," near Bolivar; no issue.

Rebecca Novaline (Kinnard) Langsdon, dau. of David
Michael and Ophelia Elizabeth (Polk) Kinnard and
wife of Isaac Langsdon. *From Mrs. Robert Oliver,
Columbia, Tenn.*

Ophelia Jane Bills, wife of Horace Moore Polk. *From Alice M. Fitts, Okla. City.*

9. LIEUT. COL. WILLIAM[5] POLK (*Brig. Gen. Thomas,*[4] *William,*[3] *William,*[2] *Robert*[1]), born in Mecklenburg Co., N. C., 9 July 1758, died at Raleigh, N. C., 4 Jan. 1834, and was buried there. He married first, 15 Oct. 1789, GRISELDA GILCHRIST, born at Suffolk, Va., 24 Oct. 1768, died at Willswood, near Charlotte, N. C., 22 Oct: 1799, daughter of Thomas, a Scotch merchant, and Martha (Jones) Gilchrist of Northampton Co., N. C., and granddaughter of Robert Jones, a lawyer of Halifax, N. C.; and secondly, at Raleigh, 1 Jan. 1801, SARAH HAWKINS,

born at Pleasant Hill, Warren Co., N. C., died at Raleigh 10 Dec. 1843, buried beside her husband, daughter of Hon. Philemon[3] and Lucy (Davis).*

He was educated at Queen's College, Charlotte, which he left in Apr. 1775, without finishing the college course, to accept a commission as second lieutenant in Capt. Ezekiel Polk's company, of the Third South Carolina Mounted Infantry, under Col. William Thompson. He commanded several expeditions in South Carolina, and was severely wounded in the left shoulder at Great Cane Brake, 22 Dec. 1775, being rendered unfit for service for eight or nine months. On 26 Nov. 1776, by the North Carolina Provincial Congress at Halifax, he was elected major of the Ninth North Carolina Regiment, a new regiment authorized at that time. Having resigned his commission in the South Carolina Infantry, he joined this regiment at Halifax in Mar. 1777, when the regiments of the State assembled there; and in command of four companies he marched, with this division of the Line, into the Jerseys and joined Washington's Army. He was present at the Battles of the Brandywine and Germantown, and in the latter battle he was shot in the mouth. In Mar. 1778, when the nine North Carolina regiments were consolidated into four, he was left without a command; but, returning to the South, he volunteered in the militia, and served as aide to General Caswell when Gates was defeated at Camden. In the fall and winter of 1780 he was lieutenant colonel of the Fourth Regiment, South Carolina Horse, and fought at Guilford Court House and Eutaw Springs. His total active service amounted to five years and two months.

In 1783 he was appointed by the North Carolina Legislature surveyor general of the "Middle District," now a part of the State of Tennessee, and in that capacity resided at French Lick Fort, on the site of the present city of Nashville. He remained there until 1786, and was elected twice from Davidson County to the North Carolina House of Commons. In 1787 he was elected to the Legislature from his native county, which he represented until President Washington appointed him, in 1791, supervisor of internal revenue for the District of North Carolina. This office he held for seventeen years,

*Philemon[1] Hawkins, the founder of the Hawkins family in America, with his wife, Anna Eleanor (Howard), emigrated to America in 1715 and settled on the James River, in Virginia. He died in 1725, and his widow and her only child, Philemon[2] (1717–1801), moved to North Carolina and resided at the mouth of Six Pounds Creek, Butte Co. Philemon[2] was a member from Butte County of the Provincial Congress, Apr. to Nov. 1776, a colonel in the North Carolina Militia, 1776–1781, and councillor of state from Warren County, 9 May 1783, 19 Nov. 1790, and 2 Jan. 1792. He served under Colonial Governor Tryon, in the Alamance campaign, in 1771, as captain of the Butte Light Horse and aide-de-camp to the Governor. At the Provincial Congress of 1776, at Halifax, N. C., he was made a lieutenant colonel of Cavalry, at the age of sixty. He resigned his seat in the Congress, raised a battalion on his own account, and served his State with distinction. His son, Philemon[3] Hawkins (1752–1833), married Lucy Davis. He served under Governor Tryon in his father's company of the Butte Light Horse against the Regulators, and was a colonel in the Revolutionary Army, a councillor of state from Granville Co., N. C., 26 June 1781, representative from the same county, 1779–80, 1782–1786, and from Warren County, 1787–1789, 1803, 1805, 1806, senator from Warren County, 1807, 1808, 1810, 1811, and a member of the Constitutional Convention, 1789.

until the repeal of the internal revenue laws. He was a trustee
of the University of North Carolina at Chapel Hill, 1790–1834,
a director and afterwards president of the State Bank of North
Carolina, 1811–1819, resigning this office in order to give more
of his personal attention to his extensive landholdings (100,000
acres) in Tennessee, one of the original members of the Order
of the Cincinnati, and a member of the committee appointed
by North Carolina to welcome Lafayette in 1824. In Mar.
1812 President Madison, with the consent of the Senate,
appointed Colonel Polk a brigadier general in the United
States Army, but, being a Federalist and opposed to the
policy of the administration, he declined this commission.
He was a personal friend of Andrew Jackson, and is said to
have furnished him, from his notes as surveyor, with information that enabled Jackson to secure valuable lands in Tennessee. His home was at first at Charlotte, but later he moved
to Raleigh. He outlived all the other field officers of the
North Carolina Line.

Children by first wife:

20. i.   THOMAS GILCHRIST,[6] b. in Mecklenburg Co., N. C., 22 Feb. 1791.
21. ii.   WILLIAM JULIUS, b. in Mecklenburg Co., N. C., 21 Mar. 1793.

Children by second wife:

22. iii. LUCIUS JUNIUS, b. at Raleigh, N. C., 16 Mar. 1802.
    iv.   LUCINDA DAVIS, d. in infancy.
23. v.   LEONIDAS, b. at Raleigh, N. C., 10 Apr. 1806.
    vi.   MARY BROWN, b. at Raleigh, N. C., 28 May 1808; d. 1 Mar. 1835;
          bur. in the cemetery at Raleigh; m. 9 Nov. 1826 HON. GEORGE
          EDMUND BADGER of Newbern and Raleigh, N. C., B.A. (Yale,
          1825, as of 1813), M.A. (ib., 1825), LL.D. (University of North
          Carolina, 1834, Yale, 1848), lawyer, member of the House of
          Commons of North Carolina, 1816, judge of the Superior Court
          of North Carolina, 1820–1825, Secretary of the Navy, 5 Mar.–
          12 Sept. 1841, United States Senator from North Carolina, 1846–
          1855, member of the State Convention of North Carolina, 1861,
          b. at Newbern 13 Apr. 1795, d. at Raleigh 11 May 1865. Children
          (surname Badger): 1. Katherine Mallon, b. at Raleigh 9 Aug. 1827;
          bur. at Fayetteville, N. C.; m. 6 May 1846 William H. Haigh of
          Raleigh; three children. 2. Sally Polk, b. at Raleigh 25 May 1833;
          d. there 19 Dec. 1903; m. in Christ Church, Raleigh, 25 Sept. 1854,
          Montford McGehee of Milton, Caswell Co., of "Woodburn"
          (the family home of the McGehees), Person Co., and of Raleigh,
          N. C., lawyer, who d. 31 Mar. 1895; four children.
    vii. ALEXANDER HAMILTON, b. 10 Sept. 1810; d. unm. 8 Sept. 1830.
    viii. JOHN HAWKINS, d. in childhood.
    ix.   RUFUS KING, b. at Raleigh, N. C., 15 May 1814; d. at Nashville,
          Tenn., 25 Feb. 1843; bur. in St. John's Churchyard, Maury Co.,
          Tenn.; m. at the Forks of the Cypress, near Florence, Ala., 3 Sept.
          1840, Right Rev. Leonidas Polk, Bishop of Louisiana, officiating,
          SARAH MOORE JACKSON, who d. at "Westbrook," Maury Co.,
          Tenn., 11 July 1888, and was bur. beside her husband, dau. of
          James and Sarah (Moore) (McCulloch). Her mother, Mrs. Sarah
          (Moore) (McCulloch) Jackson, was dau. of George Moore, 2d.,
          of South Carolina and his wife, ———— (Watters). Rufus King
          Polk called the land in Maury Co., Tenn., which was allotted to
          him by his father, "Westbrook," and he built his residence there.
          Child: 1. Sally Moore,[7] b. at the Forks of the Cypress 1 Sept.
          1841; m. there, 19 Aug. 1863, her first cousin, Maj. Gen. Lucius

Eugene[7] Polk (51), *q. v.*, b. at Salisbury, N. C., 10 July 1833, d. at "Westbrook" 1 Dec. 1892, s. of William Julius, M.D., and Mary Rebecca A. (Long).

24. x. GEORGE WASHINGTON, b. at Raleigh, N. C., 12 July 1817.

   xi. PHILEMON HAWKINS, d. in infancy.

   xii. SUSAN SPRATT, b. at Raleigh, N. C., 25 May 1822; d. at San Antonio, Tex., 10 July 1909; bur. beside her daughter, Mrs. Sallie Polk (Rayner) Hyman, in the cemetery at Fort Worth, Tex.; m. 12 July 1842 HON. KENNETH RAYNER of Hereford Co., N. C., lawyer, member of the State Constitutional Convention of 1835, member of the North Carolina House of Representatives from Hereford County for seven years, Representative in Congress (as a Whig), 1839–1845, presidential elector on the Taylor and Fillmore ticket in 1848, judge of the Court of Commissioners of the Alabama Claims (by appointment of President Grant), 1874, Solicitor of the United States Treasury, 1877–1884, b. in Bertie Co., N. C., in 1808, d. in Washington, D. C., 4 Mar. 1884, bur. at Raleigh. His father was a clergyman and a soldier of the Revolution. Children (surname *Rayner*): 1. *Sallie Polk*, b. at Raleigh 30 Mar. 1845; d. 10 Feb. 1905; bur. in the cemetery at Fort Worth; m. 13 Nov. 1867 Joseph H. Hyman; six children. 2. *Henry A.*, d. in childhood. 3. *Kenneth*, of Dallas, Tex., b. at Raleigh 1 Aug. 1847; d. at Dallas; m. 16 Dec. 1878 Eugenia Leach; one daughter. 4. *Fanny*, d. in childhood. 5. *Susan Polk*, b. at Raleigh 26 Mar. 1855; m. (1) 28 Apr. 1881 Dr. Arthur Glennan; m. (2) A. L. Silling; m. (3) ——— McMillan; three children by first husband. 6. *William Polk*, b. at Raleigh 10 Dec. 1857; d. *s. p.* at El Paso, Tex.; m. 30 Jan. 1879 Lulu Ragsdale. 7. *Hamilton Polk*, b. at Raleigh about 1859; m. (1) Eliza Nelms; m. (2) Anna W. Armand; one child by first wife. 8. *Mary*, d. young.

25. xiii. ANDREW JACKSON, b. at Raleigh, N. C., 10 Aug. 1824.

   xiv. SARAH, died in infancy.

   xv. CHARLES JUNIUS, d. in infancy.

10. CHARLES[5] POLK (*Brig. Gen. Thomas,[4] William,[3] William,[2] Robert[1]*), born near Charlotte, Mecklenburg Co., N. C., about 1762, died in the same county about 1830. He married, about 1785, MARY ALEXANDER, daughter of Hezekiah, who was one of the patriots of the Revolution and a signer of the Mecklenburg Declaration.

At the early age of thirteen years he ran away from home, joined the Revolutionary Army, and served his country with honor, attaining the rank of first lieutenant in his father's regiment, the Fourth Carolina Line. He represented his county in the Lower House of the North Carolina Assembly in 1793–1795 and in 1800. He is known in local history as "Devil Charley."

Children, born in Mecklenburg Co., N. C.:

26. i. THOMAS INDEPENDENCE,[6] b. 4 July 1786.

27. ii. CHARLES JAMES, b. 15 Dec. 1790.

11. MICHAEL[5] POLK (*Capt. Charles,[4] William,[3] William,[2] Robert[1]*) was born in Mecklenburg Co., N. C., 20 June 1774. He married SUSANNA PRYON, born 26 Mar. 1774.

He moved to Georgia and then to Alabama.

Children:

   i. MICHAEL,[6] m. CYNTHIA HARKNESS, and moved to Arkansas.

   ii. SUSANNA, d. 29 July 1848; m. JOHN RAPE. Children (surname

Rape): 1. *Susan P.*, m. Capt. D. F. Richardson. 2. *Mary E.*, m. Robert Fowler. 3. *W. Clark*, m. Martha Gordon; eight children.

iii. DEBORA, b. 11 Nov. 1811; d. in July 1898; m. in Aug. 1832 DR. JAMES F. LEE of Virginia, who d. 30 July 1879. Children (surname *Lee*): 1. *Cornelia Evelyn*, b. 17 Apr. 1833; d. in Apr. 1890; m. in Feb. 1857 Hilliard J. Wolfe; five children. 2. *Mary* (twin), b. 6 Dec. 1836; m. 22 May 1861 Wilson Austin, who was killed in the Civil War. 3. *Margaret* (twin), b. 6 Dec. 1836; unm. 4. *Irene Debora*, b. 30 Oct. 1837; m. John A. Polk of Mineral Springs, N. C.; two children. 5. *Susanna*, b. 31 Mar. 1843; d. young. 6. *Theresa*, b. 24 Nov. 1845; d. young. 7. *Beatrice*, b. 7 Mar. 1847; m. Alexander Monroe Crowell of Monroe, N. C.; four children. 8. *Virginia*, b. 14 Mar. 1850; m. William Constantine Wolfe of Monroe, N. C.; six children. 9. *Elizabeth Colclough*, b. 11 Dec. 1853; m. 25 Dec. 1873 Rev. Jason C. Moser, a Lutheran minister; four children. 10. *James F.*, b. 10 Nov. 1856; d. in 1858.

iv. MARGARET, d. unm.

28. v. CHARLES CLARK, b. in North Carolina 12 Mar. 1814.

12. CHARLES[5] POLK (*Capt. Charles*,[4] *William*,[3] *William*,[2] *Robert*[1]), born in Mecklenburg Co., N. C., 15 Mar. 1784, died in Union Co., N. C., about 1829. He married ELEANOR SHELBY, daughter of Thomas, who was son of Thomas Shelby, Sr.

He settled on Clear Creek, in that part of Anson Co., N. C., which is now Union Co. After his death his widow, about 1835, removed with her children to Campbell Co., Ga., having disposed of their property in North Carolina to their uncle, George Washington Polk (6, xii).

Children, born in Mecklenburg Co., N. C.:

29. i. EZEKIEL,[6] b. 5 Sept. 1808.

ii. MARY (POLLY), b. 13 Aug. 1810; d. in Douglas Co., Ga., 21 May 1848; m. 18 May 1826 SAMUEL WILSON MCLARTY, the eldest of twelve sons of Alexander McLarty, who emigrated from Scotland to America in 1774. She is buried in the old McLarty burying ground. Children (surname *McLarty*): 1. *Charles Bingley*, b. in North Carolina 27 Nov. 1827; d. unm. 2. *Mary Amanda*, b. in North Carolina 1 July 1829; d. in Georgia 18 July 1906; bur. at Douglasville, Ga.; m. 1 May 1845 Williamson Parks Strickland; twelve children. 3. *John C.*, b. in North Carolina 8 Nov. 1831; d. in Georgia 26 Aug. 1862; m. Mary Hartsfield; three children. 4. *George Washington*, m. Martha Webb; six children. 5. *Hannah*, b. 18 Nov. 1836; d. unm. 11 Mar. 1852. 6. *Samuel Marion*, b. 5 Mar. 1839; d. 20 Aug. 1864. 7. *Sophia Caroline*, b. in Campbell Co., Ga., 6 May 1841; m. Thomas Perkenson, b. 22 Feb. 1834; residence, Villa Rica, Ga. 8. *Harvey Ezekiel*, b. in 1843; d. in 1852. 9. *Martha Jane*, b. in Campbell Co., Ga., 4 Jan. 1846; m. John D. Perkenson, b. 9 Sept. 1843; residence, Austell, Ga.; five children.

iii. HANNAH, b. 1 Aug. 1812; d. at Douglasville, Ga., 27 Aug. 1874; m. ALEXANDER GREEN WADDINGTON, who d. at Douglasville 2 Sept. 1893. Both are buried in Watson Cemetery. Children (surname *Waddington*): 1. *Jane*, b. in Cabarrus Co., N. C.; d. in Paulding Co., Ga.; m. Barnett White; nine children. 2. *Polly Ann*, m. Washington Hawkins; six children. 3. *Martha Elizabeth*, b. in Campbell Co., Ga., 9 Sept. 1834; d. 11 Sept. 1866; m. in 1853 Francis Marion Stewart, b. 23 May 1832, d. in Douglas Co., Ga., 26 Dec. 1871; eight children. 4. *Amanda*, b. 11 Aug. 1837; m. 1 Sept. 1859 George Stewart, b. 13 Feb. 1838, d. at Douglasville 11 June 1914; eight children. 5. *Alexander*, b. 17 May 1839; d. at Douglasville 10 July 1890; m. Louisa Blanchard; four children. 6. *Charles William*, of Atlanta, Ga., b. in Campbell Co., Ga., in

1843; m. Jennie Watson; four children. 7. *Campie*, b. in 1849;
d. 20 July 1917; m. Samuel McBrayer, b. 22 July 1847; eight
children. 8. *Catherine*, m. William Roach; resides near Fort
Worth, Tex.; six children.
30. iv. CHARLES SHELBY, b. 14 May 1814.

13. CHARLES[5] POLK (*Capt. John,*[4] *William,*[3] *William,*[2] *Robert*[1]), born
in Mecklenburg Co., N. C., 18 Jan. 1760, died in San Augustine
Co., Tex., 16 Oct. 1848, "aged 89." He married in North
Carolina MARGARET BAXTER, who died in San Augustine Co.
22 June 1840, "aged 70."
He moved first to Tennessee, and settled in the western
part of the State. After his son Alfred migrated to Texas,
he followed, about 1839, settled in San Augustine Co., and
lived there until his death. In a pension declaration on file
in Washington, made by him under the Act of Congress of
1832, he states that he served at various times during the
Revolution in the North Carolina troops under Captains
James Jack, John Polk (his father), Charles Polk (his uncle),
Oliver Wiley, and Fletcher, and Colonels Adam Alexander
and Thomas Polk (his uncle), and that he also served in a
mounted spy company for five months and twenty-eight
days in 1814. He is called in many old family records "Civil
Charley Polk," probably to distinguish him from his cousin,
Charles Polk (10), son of Brig. Gen. Thomas Polk, who was
called "Devil Charley."
Children:

    i. JANE,[6] m. (1) JOHN POTTS; m. (2) DR. —— FOWLER. After her
first marriage she moved from Tennessee to Alabama, and after
her second marriage she moved to Mississippi. Child by first
husband (surname *Potts*): 1. *Missoni*, m. (1) Thomas McQuarler;
m. (2) Christopher Butchee; two children by second husband.
31. ii. JOHN, b., probably in Mecklenburg Co., N. C., about 1782.
    iii. ANDREW, m. MARTHA KIMBALL. They moved from Tennessee to
Missouri, and later settled in Cherokee Co., Tex. Child: 1. *Minnie*,[7]
m. James Anderson, a lawyer of high standing at Waco, Tex.
32. iv. WILLIAM KNOX, b. probably in Mecklenburg Co., N. C.
    v. CYNTHIA SPRINGS, b., probably in western Tennessee, 25 Feb. 1801;
d. in San Augustine Co., Tex., 25 or 28 Aug. 1885; m., probably in
Tipton Co., Tenn., 28 Oct. 1825, her first cousin, JOHN POLK (36),
q. v., b., probably in the Greenbrier District of Virginia, 25 Oct.
1798, d. in Madison Co., Tex., 14 Feb. 1864, s. of John and
Elizabeth (Alderson).
    vi. CHARLES, m. ELIZABETH HAYNE. He migrated with his father to San
Augustine Co., Tex., in 1839, and later moved to Leon Co., Tex.
    vii. ISAAC SHELBY, d. young.
33. viii. ALFRED, b. in Stewart Co., Tenn., 15 Dec. 1808.

14. JOHN[5] POLK (*Capt. John,*[4] *William,*[3] *William,*[2] *Robert*[1]), born
probably in Mecklenburg Co., N. C., in 1767, died at his
home on Carter's Creek, near Columbia, Maury Co., Tenn., 24
May 1845. He married first ELIZABETH ALDERSON (or OLDSON,
as some authorities give it), born probably in 1766, died 24
Nov. 1829;* and secondly MRS. REBECCA BRIGGS, widow.

*The tomb of John Polk and his first wife still stands on the land of the homestead on Carter's
Creek. On one side are the words: "In Memory of John Polk, died May 24 1845 aged 78."
On the other side is the inscription: "In memory of Elizabeth Polk, died Nov. 24, 1829 aged 63."

He lived for a while after his father's death in the Greenbrier District of western Virginia, and an old history of that region mentions him and his wife Elizabeth, calling him "Devil John" and telling of his fighting as a mere boy in the Revolution. In this locality lived the Moores, Walkers (his brother Taylor married here Jency Walker), Campbells, McPheterses, and Spottiswoods. About 1806 he migrated to Tennessee; and there is a deed on file in Maury Co., dated 25 Dec. 1806, from Col. Ezekiel⁴ Polk (8) to "my nephew John Polk," conveying to the latter 170 acres of land in Maury Co. He lived until his death at this home on Carter's Creek. On 28 Aug. 1828 he signed a deed, recorded in Maury Co., conveying certain lands to his sons John and Evan Shelby "for the love and affection" he bore them. In his will, on file in Maury Co., he mentions his wife Rebecca and his children Benjamin, deceased, Nancy Kirby, Elizabeth Campbell, Robert, and F. A. [Franklin Armstead], who was his father's executor.

Children by first wife, born probably in the Greenbrier District of western Virginia:

34. i.   BENJAMIN D. A.,⁶ b. 1 Jan. 1790.
    ii.   NANCY, m. before 1845 ETHELBERT KIRBY, who d. in Jan. 1878.
35. iii. EVAN SHELBY, b. 16 Dec. 1791.
    iv.   ROBERT, b. probably in 1792; d. 4 Aug. 1840; m. MELVINA PORTER. Two of his children were devisees under his father's will. As Ensign Robert Polk of the Tennessee Militia in the War of 1812 he is mentioned in Buell's "History of Andrew Jackson," vol. 2. pp. 26, 27, 31, 317; and after the War he was appointed an Indian agent.
    v.   ELIZABETH, b. 9 Oct. 1796; d. at Columbia, Tenn., 8 July 1856; m. her second cousin, ROBERT CAMPBELL (8, ii, 2), b., probably in Mecklenburg Co., N. C., 5 July 1797, d. at Columbia, Tenn., 1 Dec. 1852, s. of John and Matilda Golden (Polk). Eight children (*vide supra*, 8, ii, 2).
36. vi.   JOHN, b. 25 Oct. 1798.
37. vii. FRANKLIN ARMSTEAD, b. 10 Apr. 1804.

15. TAYLOR⁵ POLK (*Capt. John,⁴ William,³ William,² Robert¹*), born in North Carolina about 1780, died in Polk Co., Ark., 11 Dec. 1824. He married, 1 Nov. 1798,* JENCY WALKER, who died at "The Wilds," in the Valley of the Ouachita, Ark., 3 Dec. 1814, daughter of Tandy.†

*Taylor Polk was married when he was but seventeen years old, and boasted that he "stood six feet two in his stockings" at that age.

†Tandy Walker was a great-grandson of John Walker of Wigtown, Scotland, who married in Scotland, 7 Jan. 1702, Jane Rutherford, daughter of Rev. John, one of the "Border Rutherfords," living on the Tweed. This John Walker sailed from Strangford Lough, Ireland, in May 1726, landed in Maryland 2 Aug. 1726, and settled in Chester Co., Pa., where he died in Sept. 1734 and his widow died in 1738. Both are buried at Nottingham meeting house, in Chester Co. Most of his family of eleven children settled in Rockbridge Co., Va., and in adjoining counties, Walker's Creek in Rockbridge Co. taking its name from them. John Walker, the immigrant ancestor of the family, had a son named John, and the latter's son John, of the third generation of the American family, married Nancy Tandy, whose surname reappears as the Christian name of her son, Tandy Walker. In some genealogies this son is called Alexander Walker, probably because "Tandy" was mistaken for "Sandy," a common nickname for Alexander. In the Virginia census of 1782 and in that of 1790 Tandy Walker is recorded as the head of a family of nine whites and seven slaves, in Mecklenburg Co. His brother, William Walker, was stolen by the Indians in the Green-

Taylor Polk and his wife went from North Carolina to Tennessee and lived for a time in Davidson Co., whence they migrated, with their children, in 1808 to the Valley of the Ouachita, not far from Hot Springs, Ark. They named their home there "The Wilds." They were one of the earliest American families to take up their residence in Arkansas, after the acquisition of the vast Louisiana region by the United States in 1803.

Children, all born near Nashville, Davidson Co., Tenn., except the last two, who were born at "The Wilds," Montgomery Co., Ark.:

    i.   BENJAMIN,[6] b. in 1799; d. in Texas in 1847; m. in Arkansas PEGGY BOATRIGHT. He moved to Texas in 1836. Children (order of births uncertain): 1. *Jency*.[7] 2. *Benjamin*. 3. *James*. 4. *Charles*. 5. *William*. 6. *Richard*. 7. *Priscilla*. There may have been another child, *Martha*. Most of the children died in childhood, but Benjamin left issue.

38. ii.   TAYLOR, b. in 1800.
39. iii.   JAMES, b. in 1801.
40. iv.   CUMBERLAND, b. 7 Aug. 1803.
    v.   WILLIAM, b. in 1805; d. in Arkansas; m. (1) ——— GRIFFITH; m. (2) ——— GRIFFITH, a cousin of his first wife. Child by first wife: 1. *Levi*,[7] who served in the Confederate Army. Child by second wife: 2. *Cumberland*, killed in battle in Arkansas while serving in the Confederate Army.
    vi.   JENCY, b. in 1810; d. in Oklahoma in 1897; m. in Arkansas MITCHELL ANDERSON, s. of James* and brother of Prudence Anderson, who m. Taylor Polk, 2d (38). Children (surname *Anderson*): 1. *Fanny*. 2. *James*. 3. *Mitchell*. 4. *Benjamin*. 5. *Abraham*. 6. *Eliza*. 7. *Stacy*. 8. *Jane*. 9. *Henry*. 10. *Taylor*. Several (perhaps five) of the sons of Mitchell and Jency (Polk) Anderson were killed in Arkansas, while serving in the Confederate Army.

41. vii.   ALFRED, b. 3 Sept. 1814.

16. THOMAS[5] POLK (*Col. Ezekiel*,[4] *William*,[3] *William*,[2] *Robert*[1]), born probably in Tryon Co., N. C., 5 Dec. 1770, died in Robertson Co., Tenn., 1 Nov. 1814. He married, 25 Dec. 1794, ABIGAIL IRVIN, who d. 8 Mar. 1823.

He migrated with his father to middle Tennessee about 1790.

Children, born probably in Robertson Co., Tenn.:

    i.   MARY W. (? WILSON),[6] b. 28 Oct. 1795; probably m. twice, and had issue.
    ii.   EZEKIEL, b. 23 Oct. 1797; d. in childhood.
42. iii.   JAMES IRVIN, b. 29 Oct. 1799.
    iv.   CLARISSA ADALINE, b. 27 Feb. 1802; d. 4 Apr. 1879; m. JOHN H.

brier District of Virginia about 1771, the story being related in the histories of that region. Tandy Walker's children were: 1. Jency, who married Taylor Polk (15). 2. Joel. 3. Tandy, 2d. 4. Sylvester. Tandy Walker, 2d, was at St. Stephens, Ala., in 1803. His wife, who was Mary Mayes of Virginia, was a Methodist of the Tombigbee circuit (cf. West's History of Methodism in Alabama); and his daughter, Sarah Newstep, born at St. Stephens 8 Nov. 1803 and baptized there in 1815, married in 1820 Cassius Reynolds. Tandy Walker, 2d, was an Indian trader and scout, and served under General Claiborne. In 1814, having been ordered, with Captain Erwine, to scout ahead of the Mississippi Volunteers in the Creek Indian country, he was ambushed and wounded, and on this account he was awarded a pension, 4 Sept. 1838. He died in 1843, and was buried on the edge of what is known as Walker's Prairie, near Newbern, Ala. His son, Dr. Tandy Walker, 3d, a physician at Moulton, Ala., represented Lawrence County in the Alabama Legislature, 1838-1843, and was a brilliant, popular, and much-loved man. (Cf. Garrett's Public Men of Alabama.)

*James Anderson went from North Carolina to Missouri and from there moved to Arkansas. His children were: 1. Henry. 2. Mitchell. 3. Sarah. 4. Prudence.

ARNOLD. Children (surname *Arnold*): 1. *Thomas Polk*, b. 31 Dec. 1824; d. 14 Apr. 1879; m. Susan Josephine Parr; nine children. 2. *Emily*, m. ——— Johnson of New Orleans, La. 3. *Jane*, m. ——— Pate. 4. *Cattie*, m. ——— Birch. 5. *Rufus*. 6. *Jim*. 7. *Richard K.*

43. v. THOMAS JEFFERSON, b. 22 Apr. 1805.

vi. SUSANNA AMELIA CAROLINE, b. 26 Mar. 1808; m. JESSE DARDEN. Children (surname *Darden*): 1. *Jake*. 2. *Richard*. 3. *Emily*. Probably others.

vii. LECIE NORWOOD, b. 4 June 1810; m. LUCIUS LENNARD. Children (surname *Lennard*): 1. *Lucius*. 2. *Eliza*. Perhaps others.

viii. LOUISA BLOUNT, b. 17 May 1812; probably d. in infancy, although some accounts say that she m. Nicholas Whitehead and had issue.

17. SAMUEL[5] POLK (*Col. Ezekiel,[4] William,[3] William,[2] Robert[1]*), born, probably in Tryon Co., N. C., 5 July 1772, died in Maury Co., Tenn., 5 Nov. 1827. He married at Hopewell Church, Mecklenburg Co., N. C., 25 Dec. 1794, JANE KNOX, daughter of James of Iredell Co., N. C., a captain in the Revolution.

He migrated with his father to Tennessee in the autumn of 1806, and settled in the rich valley of the Duck River, a tributary of the Tennessee River, in the region which was organized the following year as Maury County. There he became in time a prosperous farmer and also increased his fortune by following the occupation of surveyor. He acted also as agent for his cousin, Lieut. Col. William Polk (9), in the care of the latter's extensive landholdings in Tennessee.

Children:

i. HON. JAMES KNOX,[6] A.B. (University of North Carolina, 1818), A.M. (*ib.*, 1822), LL.D. (*ib.*, 1845), eleventh President of the United States, b. near Little Sugar Creek, Mecklenburg Co., N. C., 2 Nov. 1795;* d. *s.p.* at his home, Polk Place, in Nashville, Tenn., 15 June 1849; bur. in the garden of Polk Place, but in 1893 his body and that of his wife were removed to the grounds of the State Capitol; m. 1 Jan. 1824 SARAH CHILDRESS, b. near Murfreesboro, Rutherford Co., Tenn., 4 Sept. 1803, d. at Nashville, 14 Aug. 1891, dau. of. Joel, a prosperous farmer, and his wife Elizabeth. In 1806, when he was a boy of about eleven years, he accompanied his parents to Tennessee, where he was brought up on his father's farm, and, as he grew older, helped his father in its management. He often went with his father on his surveying expeditions, which sometimes kept them away from home for weeks. He was fond of study and of reading, and took a great interest in his father's mathematical calculations. He attended school, and had made much progress in the English branches, when ill health forced him to give up his studies. He then entered the service of a merchant; but he disliked business, after a few weeks was allowed to return home, and in July 1813 was placed under a private tutor, and was prepared for college. In 1815 he entered the University of North Carolina as a sophomore, and was graduated there in 1818, being recognized as the first scholar in classics and in mathematics and having the honor of delivering the Latin salutatory oration. In 1819 he entered the law office of Hon. Felix Grundy of Nashville, the leader of the Tennessee bar, who had already been chief justice of the Supreme Court of Kentucky and a Representative in Congress from Tennessee and was later to become a United States Senator and Attorney Genera!

*On 2 Nov. 1846 President Polk noted in his diary: "This is my birthday. According to the entry in my father's family Bible I was born on the 2d. day of Nov. 1795 and my mother has told me that the event occurred as near as she could tell about 12 o'clock, meridian, of that day."

of the United States; and, while studying law, he gained the friendship of Andrew Jackson. In 1820 he was admitted to the Tennessee bar, and began practice at Columbia, the county seat of Maury Co., where he soon became eminent in his profession. He served in the Tennessee House of Representatives, 1823–1825, represented the Sixth Tennessee District in Congress (as a Democrat) for seven successive terms, 1825–1839, being Speaker of the House of Representatives from 7 Dec. 1835 on, and was elected Governor of Tennessee in 1839. He was defeated in his campaigns for reëlection as Governor in 1841 and 1843; but in 1844, at the Democratic National Convention in Baltimore, after being mentioned first as a candidate for the nomination for Vice President of the United States, he was brought forward as a "dark horse" and nominated as the Democratic candidate for the Presidency. In the election that followed Mr. Polk was successful, receiving 170 electoral votes to 105 cast for his famous Whig opponent, Henry Clay. The great achievements of his administration as President, 1845–1849, and his own personal share in them are discussed and described *in extenso* in various histories of the United States and in a number of special works relating to his career and policies. In domestic affairs the outstanding events of these four years were the final establishment of the Independent Treasury system (1846) and the passage of the Walker Tariff Act of 1846, in foreign affairs the settlement by treaty of the Oregon boundary dispute with Great Britain (1846), the annexation of Texas (1845), and the Mexican War (1846–1848). President Polk declined to be a candidate for a second presidential term; and after leaving office, with health seriously impaired, retired to his home in Nashville, where he died a few months later. His wife, who survived him for forty-two years, residing at Polk Place in Nashville, had been educated in a Moravian school at Salem, N. C., and was a gracious and stately lady, of excellent taste in dress, of wide reading, and of much conversational ability. She performed her duties as mistress of the White House with conscientious austerity, but was, nevertheless, very popular in Washington society. She became a communicant of the Presbyterian Church in 1834.

ii. JANE MARIA, b. in Mecklenburg Co., N. C., 14 Jan. 1798; d. at Columbia, Tenn., 11 Oct. 1876; m. in Maury Co., Tenn., 24 Feb. 1813, JAMES WALKER.* Children, b. at Columbia (surname *Walker*): 1. *Samuel Polk*, b. 26 Jan. 1814; d. at Memphis, Tenn., 5 Nov. 1870; m. in Maury Co., Tenn., 22 Oct. 1834, Eleanor T. Wormley; eleven or more children, of whom James was a Confederate soldier and was killed in the Battle of Belmont (Mo.), 7 Nov. 1861. 2. *James Hayes*, b. 4 May 1816; d. *s.p.* at Columbia 27 May 1902; m. at Corinth, Miss., 18 May 1869, Sophy Davis. 3. *Joseph Knox*, b. 19 July 1818; d. at Memphis, Tenn., 21 Dec. 1863; m. at Lynchburg, Va., 2 Dec. 1841, Augusta T. Tabb. He was private secretary to his uncle, President Polk, 1845–1849, and colonel of the Second Tennessee Infantry, Confederate Army; nine children. 4. *Jane Clarissa*, b. 7 Oct. 1820; d. at Columbia 27 Nov.1899; m. at Columbia, 21 June 1842, Isaac Newton Barnett; five children. 5. *Mary Eliza*, b. 8 Mar. 1823; d. at Memphis, Tenn., 2 Nov. 1900; m. at Columbia, 12 July 1842, William Sanford Pickett, s. of James and Nancy (Smith); eight children. 6. *Sarah Naomi*, b. 20 Feb. 1825; d. at Nashville, Tenn., 5 Mar. 1916; m. at Columbia, 7 Jan. 1847, John Burton Green, s. of Thomas Jefferson and Fanny (Burton); six children. 7. *Annie Maria*, b. 8 Apr. 1827; m. at Columbia, 26 Dec. 1854, Lemuel M. Phillips; one child, who d. in infancy. 8. *Lucius Marshall*, b.

---

*He was a descendant of John Walker of Wigtown, Scotland, who married Jane Rutherford in 1702 and emigrated to America in 1726, and whose descendants settled on Walker's Creek, Rockbridge Co., Va. *Vide supra*, p. 219, second footnote.

18 Oct. 1829; d. at Little Rock, Ark., 6 Sept. 1863; m. at Charlottesville, Va., 23 Nov. 1856, Celestine Garth, dau. of William and Elizabeth (Martin); he was graduated at the United States Military Academy, West Point, N. Y., in 1850, attained the rank of major in the Confederate Army, and was mortally wounded at Little Rock, 5 Sept. 1863, in a duel with Brigadier General Marmaduke; two children. 9. *Andrew Jackson*, b. 9 July 1834; d. at Indianapolis, Ind., 16 June 1910; m. in Carroll Parish, La., 8 Apr. 1856, Susan Willcox Watts, dau. of Thomas and Susan (Willcox); four children. 10. *Ophelia Lazinska*, b. 10 June 1837; d. 11 May 1839. 11. *Leonidas Polk*, b. 15 Sept. 1839; d. 19 Aug. 1840.

iii. LYDIA ELIZA, b. in Mecklenburg Co., N. C., 17 Feb. 1800; d. in Haywood Co., Tenn., 29 May 1864; m. (1) in Maury Co., Tenn., 5 Aug. 1817, SILAS WILLIAM CALDWELL; m. (2) EDWARD RICHMOND, widower. Children by first husband (surname *Caldwell*): 1. *Samuel Polk*, b. at Columbia, Tenn., 20 June 1818; d. at Denmark, Tenn., 5 Dec. 1885; m. at Denmark, 15 May 1855, his second cousin, Sarah Jane Taylor (18, i, 4), b. at Huntingdon, Tenn., 15 Aug. 1839, d. at Jackson, Tenn., 9 Dec. 1909, dau. of Abner and Laura Weston (Polk); twelve children. 2. *James Montgomery*, b. in Haywood Co., Tenn., 28 May 1828; d. in Haywood Co. 13 Dec. 1868; m. Edmonia Richmond, dau. of his stepfather, Edward Richmond, by a former wife; three children.

iv. FRANKLIN EZEKIEL, b. in Mecklenburg Co., N. C., 23 Aug. 1802; d. unm. at Columbia, Tenn., 21 Jan. 1831.

44. v. MARSHALL TATE, b. in Mecklenburg Co., N. C., 17 Jan. 1805.

vi. JOHN LEE, b. in Maury Co., Tenn., 23 Mar. 1807; d. unm. at Columbia, Tenn., 28 Sept. 1831.

vii. NAOMI TATE, b. in Maury Co., Tenn., 2 July 1809; d. at Memphis, Tenn., 6 Aug. 1836; m. at Columbia, Tenn., 18 Aug. 1825, ADLAI O. HARRIS. Children (surname *Harris*): 1. *Amelia*. 2. *Maria*. 3. *Laura*. 4. *Malvina.*

viii. OPHELIA CLARISSA, b. in Maury Co., Tenn., 6 Sept. 1812; d. at Columbia, Tenn., 18 Apr. 1851; m. at Columbia, 24 Sept. 1829, JOHN B. HAYS. Children (surname *Hays*): 1. *Jane Virginia*, b. 11 Sept. 1830; d. 20 Sept. 1857; m. at Columbia, Tenn., 26 Dec. 1854, E. F. Lee; one child. 2. *Maria Naomi*, b. at Columbia, Tenn., 28 Nov. 1838; d. at Helena, Ark.; m. at Columbia, 18 Dec. 1864, William E. Moore; two children.

45. ix. WILLIAM HAWKINS, b. in Maury Co., Tenn., 24 May 1815.

x. SAMUEL WILSON, b. in Maury Co., Tenn., 17 Oct. 1817; d. unm. at Columbia, Tenn., 24 Feb. 1839.

18. WILLIAM WILSON[5] POLK (*Col. Ezekiel*,[4] *William*,[3] *William*,[2] *Robert*[1]), born, probably in York Co., S. C., a few miles over the line from Mecklenburg Co., N. C.,* 10 Sept. 1776, died at Walnut Bend, Phillips Co., Ark., 8 Oct. 1848. He married ELIZABETH DODD.

He received a liberal education, spent the first few years of his manhood in teaching school, and then became a planter. In 1820, with his father and others, he helped to establish the first white settlement in Hardeman Co., Tenn., where he remained until about 1828, when he crossed the Mississippi River and settled at Walnut Bend, Ark. He owned one of the largest plantations in the Mississippi Valley, the United States Census of 1840 crediting him with being the largest producer of corn in the United States. Although nicknamed

*There is a tradition that William Wilson Polk was born in Mecklenburg Co., N. C., and it is possible that his mother was at the home of her parents when his birth took place.

"Stingy Bill," he financed the campaign of his nephew, James Knox Polk, for the Presidency.

Children:

i. LAURA WESTON,[6] b. in Maury Co., Tenn., 2 Feb. 1805; d. in Madison Co., Tenn., 20 July 1879; m. (1) CHATMAN MANLY; m. (2) ABNER TAYLOR. Children by first husband (surname *Manly*): 1. *William Burton*, b. at Duck Hill, Miss., 12 Aug. 1823; d. near Jackson, Tenn., 20 May 1875; m. at Pleasant Hill, Tenn., 5 Oct. 1850, Eliza Jane Johnson, dau. of Harrison and Jemima (Scruggs); ten children. 2. *Clarissa*, b. at New Castle, Tenn., 23 Apr. 1824; d. at Denmark, Tenn., 22 Aug. 1854; m. at New Castle John Lewis Taylor, s. of John Adam and Frances (Reiley); two children. 3. *Ann Elizabeth*, b. at New Castle, Tenn., 3 Aug. 1828; d. at Denmark, Tenn., 12 Jan. 1903; m. in Carroll Co., Tenn., in Feb. 1848, Frank Taylor; three children. Children by second husband (surname *Taylor*): 4. *Sarah Jane*, b. at Huntingdon, Tenn., 15 Aug. 1839; d. at Jackson, Tenn., 9 Dec. 1909; m. at Denmark, Tenn., 15 May 1855, her second cousin, Samuel Polk Caldwell (17, iii, 1), b. at Columbia, Tenn., 20 June 1818, d. at Denmark 5 Dec. 1885, s. of Silas William and Lydia Eliza (Polk); twelve children. 5. *Andrew*, b. at Denmark, Tenn., 10 Mar. 1842; d. there 29 Jan. 1894; m. there, 15 Sept. 1870, Susan Alexander Utley, dau. of Paris Turner and Susan Carter (Alexander); seven children. 6. *Rebecca Williams*, b. at Denmark, Tenn., 15 Mar. 1845; d. there 18 Nov. 1889; m. there, 15 May 1873, her brother-in-law, Robert Henry French, s. of William Mason and Sarah Hyacinth (Robertson) and widower of her sister, Mary Eliza (Taylor) French (*vide infra*); six children. 7. *Mary Eliza*, b. near Denmark, Tenn., 17 Jan. 1848; d. *s.p.* near Denmark 29 Mar. 1869; m. Robert Henry French, s. of William Mason and Sarah Hyacinth (Robertson), who survived her and m. her sister, Rebecca Williams Taylor (*vide supra*). 8. *Olivia Polk*, b. near Denmark, Tenn., 17 July 1850; d. *s.p.* at Medon, Tenn., 1 May 1881; m. in Jan. 1881 George W. Swink.

ii. CLARISSA, b. in Maury Co., Tenn., 5 Aug. 1806; d. at Bailey, Tenn., 30 Aug. 1844; m. at Bolivar, Tenn., 24 June 1824, ANDREW TAYLOR. Children (surname *Taylor*): 1. *William Polk*, b. 3 Jan., 1825; d. in 1835. 2. *Jane Elizabeth*, b. 30 Dec. 1826; d. in 1835. 3. *Abner Cunningham*, b. 20 Aug. 1827; d. in 1838. 4. *Isaac*, b. at Bolivar 22 Feb. 1830; d. in May 1862; m. at Collierville, Tenn., probably 10 June 1851, Eliza Martin Talley, dau. of Martin and Emily (Holland); he enlisted 10 Mar. 1861 in Co. D, Thirty-eighth Tennessee Infantry, Confederate Army, was captured at the Battle of Shiloh, 7 Apr. 1862, and died in a Federal military prison in May 1862; three children. 5. *Benjamin Franklin*, b. 4 July 1831; d. before 1839. 6. *John Jackson*, b. 30 Apr. 1833; d. about 1837. 7. *Olivia Berry*, b. 30 Mar. 1835; d. in 1839. 8. *Laura Thressia*, b. at Bolivar 15 Dec. 1837; d. at Bailey 21 June 1872; m. at Bailey, 25 Mar. 1856, Charles Robert Davis; five children. 9. *Mary Caroline*, b. at Bolivar 2 Oct. 1839; m. at Bailey, 15 Mar. 1860, Dr. Benjamin Winchester Lauderdale, s. of Samuel Holmes and Mary H. (Winchester); eleven children. 10. *Thomas Le Roy*, of Bailey, b. at Bolivar 24 July 1842; m. at Bailey, 3 July 1867, Annie M. Lauderdale, dau. of Frank and Mary (Duty); he enlisted 15 May 1861 in Co. C, Fourth Tennessee Infantry, Confederate Army, and served four years, being wounded three times; four children, b. at Bailey. 11. *Clarissa Sarah*, b. 6 Aug. 1844; d. at Red Banks, Miss., 11 Aug. 1885; m. (1) at Bailey, 26 Jan. 1870, James M. Northcross; m. (2) at Forest Hill, Tenn., 11 Aug. 1885, H. L. Bradford; three children by first husband, of whom Andrew Taylor enlisted at Nashville, Tenn., 12 May 1898, in Co. F, Second Tennessee Volunteer Infantry, for service in the War with Spain, and d. at Camp Alger, Va., 1 Aug. 1898.

iii. MARY WILSON, b. in Maury Co., Tenn., 21 July 1808; d. at Memphis, Tenn., 13 July 1871; m. in Hardeman Co., Tenn., 27 Dec. 1834, WARDLOW HOWARD, s. of Thomas. Children (surname *Howard*):* 1. *William Thomas*, b. at Memphis 26 Mar. 1836; d. at Rochester, N. Y., 24 Jan. 1869; m. at Memphis, 1 Jan. 1859, Amelia Hungerford, dau. of Lafayette; they had issue. 2. *Nicholas*, b. 14 Aug. 1838; d. 15 Oct. 1840. 3. *Charles*, d. in childhood. 4. *Louisa*, b. 24 July 1843; d. 20 Aug. 1843. 5. *Joseph Kent*, b. 23 Nov. 1846; d. 28 Feb. 1848. 6. *Sallie Kent*, b. 8 July 1848; m. (1) at Memphis, 2 Feb. 1869, John Marshall Hewitt; m. (2) at Marianna, Ark., 25 Apr. 1895, James Bolivar Grove; one child by first husband. 7. *Jackson Polk*, b. 14 Aug. 1850; d. 23 Dec. 1854. 8. *Laura*, b. 8 Oct. 1854; d. at Marianna, Ark., 6 Nov. 1903; m. at Marianna, 20 Oct. 1880, Robert Handcock; six children, all of whom d. unm. 9. *Elizabeth Taylor*, b. at La Grange, Tenn., 23 Feb. 1856; d. at Memphis 12 Nov. 1905; m. at Jackson, Tenn., 13 Nov. 1875, Ripley Gates; two children. 10. *Olivia*, b. 18 Oct. 1856 [*sic*]; d. 28 July 1857. 11. *Mary Wardlow*, b. at Memphis 24 Dec. 1864 [*sic*]; m. at Marianna, Ark., 6 Dec. 1882, Dr. Volney Edward Sumpter; residence, Brinkley, Ark.; seven children.

iv. CAROLINE, b. probably in Maury Co., Tenn.; d. in Fayette Co., Tenn., 27 Nov. 1829; m., probably in Phillips Co., Ark., 20 Jan. 1829, JOHN WIRT. Children, b. in Fayette Co. (surname *Wirt*): 1. *Catherine* (twin), b. 27 Nov. 1829; d. in Fayette Co. 7 Apr. 1884; m. Dr. William J. Cannon; two children. 2. *Caroline* (twin), b. 27 Nov. 1829; d. unm.

v. OLIVIA MARBURY, b. in Maury Co., Tenn., 13 July 1811; d. at Springfield, Mo., 18 July 1850; m. in Hardeman Co., Tenn., 12 Apr. 1831, DANIEL DORSEY BERRY, b. at Baltimore, Md., 16 July 1805, d. 9 Oct. 1862, s. of Benjamin and Elizabeth (Dorsey). They migrated to Greene Co., Mo., in 1831, and settled on the site of the present city of Springfield. Children (surname *Berry*): 1. *Elizabeth Dodd*,† b. in Hardeman Co., Tenn.,‡ 9 July 1833; m. (1) at Springfield, Mo., 5 Aug. 1851, her second cousin, Leonidas Caldwell Campbell, later a captain and a colonel in the Confederate Army, eldest child of William St. Clair (8, ii, 6) and Mildred Ann (Blackman); m. (2) at Walnut Bend, Phillips (now Lee) Co., Ark., 15 Oct. 1868, George Martin Jones, b. in Shelby Co., Tenn., 19 Oct. 1836, s. of Henry Tandy and Mary Edwards (Waller) Jones and grandson of Capt. James Jones of Giles Co., Tenn.; five children by first husband and three children by second husband. 2. *Laura Juliette*, b. at Springfield, Mo., 10 Jan. 1835; d. at Columbia, Mo., 12 July 1882; m. at Columbia, 9 June 1868, John Thilo Fyfer, b. in Quebec, Canada, 3 Feb. 1835, d. at Columbia 6 June 1907, s. of John Michel and Fredericka (Dietrick); he migrated to Orange Co., Va., and in 1856 to Columbia, Mo.; five children, b. at Columbia. 3. *William Polk*, b. in 1837; d. in 1838. 4. *Clarissa C.*,§ b. at Springfield, Mo., 21 May 1838; d. at Columbia, Mo., 27 Dec. 1916; m. at Springfield, 10 Aug. 1854, Joseph Samuel Moss, b. in Logan Co., Ky., 31 Jan. 1831, d. at Columbia 26 Aug. 1898, s. of Joseph and Sallie (Chastain); he settled at Columbia in 1865, was for twenty-five years secretary

*The birth dates of the children of Wardlow and Mary Wilson (Polk) Howard have been taken from Bible records, but evidently those of the last two children are incorrect.— EDITOR.

†Some accounts of the family give no middle name. Others claim that she was named for her grandmother, Elizabeth Dodd. The Berry family records give her birth date as 4 July, but the Campbell family records give it as 5 July.

‡This is inconsistent with the fact that the family moved to Missouri in 1831, unless her mother returned to the old family home in Tennessee.

§The record furnished by members of the family gives her name as Clara, but it is here given as it appears in the Polk Tree of 1849.

of the Christian College Board, and was curator at the State University, 1886–1889; seven children. 5. *John Thomas*, b. at Springfield, Mo., 4 Dec. 1839; d. at Terrell, Tex., 14 Apr. 1901; m. at Columbia, Tenn., 4 Nov. 1872, Ellen Dupuy McKinney, dau. of Thomas and Jane (Dupuy); he served in the Missouri Cavalry, in the Confederate Army, and migrated to Lamar Co., Tex., in 1870; four children, b. in Paris, Tex. 6. *William Benjamin*, of Paris, Tex., b. at Springfield, Mo., 3 May 1841; m. at Roxton, Lamar Co., Tex., 23 Mar. 1882, Mary J. Gordon; he enlisted in 1861 in Capt. Leonidas Caldwell Campbell's company, Third Missouri Cavalry, Confederate Army, was transferred in 1863 to Marmaduke's brigade battery, in the Trans-Mississippi Department, was commissioned captain of Artillery in 1865, was surrendered at Memphis, Tenn., 2 June 1865 and was paroled, migrated to Lamar Co., Tex., in 1879, and was elected brigadier general of the United Confederate Veterans in 1905; six children. 7. *Daniel Dorsey*, b. at Springfield, Mo., 18 Oct. 1842; d. at Springfield 21 Mar. 1915; m. at Columbia, Mo., 6 Nov. 1866, Elizabeth Selby Matthews, dau. of Lawrence and Louisa (Ball); three children, b. at Columbia. 8. *Olivia Polk*, b. at Springfield, Mo., in Aug. 1844; d. in Phillips Co., Ark. in 1877; m. in Phillips Co., Ark., 14 Nov. 1866, J. Ferdinand Rodgers; one daughter, Mary, who d. in infancy. 9. *Mary Eliza*, b. at Springfield, Mo., 4 Mar. 1846; d. *s.p.* at Columbia, Mo., 14 Oct. 1870; m. 21 Dec. 1869 Arthur Walker McAlister. 10. *Louise Matilda*, b. 16 Sept. 1847; d. at Paris, Tex., 3 Dec. 1903; m. (1) in Phillips Co., Ark., 15 Apr. 1867, John J. Clayton; m. (2) in 1877 Frank B. Rodgers; one son by first husband, two children by second husband. 11. *Christiana Thressia*, b. 8 Feb. 1850; d. in Aug. 1851.

46. vi.   JOHN JACKSON, b. in Maury Co., Tenn., 5 Sept. 1813.
47. vii.   THOMAS MARLBOROUGH, b. near Columbia, Maury Co., Tenn., 11 Sept. 1815.
    viii.   SOPHIA.*
    ix.   LOUISA.*
    x.   SARAH ROACH, b. in Hardeman Co., Tenn., in 1821; d. at New Castle, Tenn., in Feb. 1902; m. in Hardeman Co. JOSEPH KENT. Children (surname *Kent*): 1. *Joseph Jackson*, b. at Walnut Bend, Ark., in 1847; d. unm. at Whiteville, Tenn., 13 Mar. 1914. 2. *Olivia Polk*, b. at Walnut Bend, Ark., in Aug. 1854; d. at New Castle, Tenn., 25 Mar. 1890; m. at New Castle, 24 Dec. 1874, James Weston Bass; one daughter.

19. CHARLES PERRY[5] POLK (*Col. Ezekiel,[4] William,[3] William,[2] Robert[1]*), born in Maury Co., Tenn., 27 Oct. 1813, died at Corinth, Miss., 27 Oct. 1893. He married at Bolivar, Tenn., 8 Oct. 1835, ELLEN MATILDA FITZHUGH, daughter of Edmund Burdette and Eliza (Roberts).

He attained to the rank of colonel in the Confederate Army. Children, all except the last one born at Bolivar, Tenn.:

    i.   CHARLES EDWIN,[6] b. 30 Apr. 1838; d. at Corinth, Miss., 7 Nov. 1867; m. at Leighton, Ala., in June 1856, CORNELIA FAIRCLOTH. Children: 1. *Clara,[7]* m. ——— Lane. 2. *Perry.* 3. *Ellen.*
    ii.   JAMES KNOX, b. 27 Dec. 1840; d. *s.p.*; m. ELLEN ELAM.
    iii.   ANN ELIZA, b. 9 June 1843; d. at Jackson, Tenn., 27 May 1873; m. M. L. VESEY. Child (surname *Vesey*): 1. *Ellen Elizabeth*, b. 17 Nov. 1869; m. (1) at Memphis, Tenn., 6 Feb. 1888, George Henry McLeod, who d. at Gomez Palacio, Mexico, 4 Apr. 1906; m. (2) at Amarillo, Tex., 16 June 1908, S. W. Riggan; residence, Cimarron, N. Mex.; five children.
    iv.   EUGENIA, b. 15 Feb. 1846; m. at Corinth, Miss., 9 Feb. 1869, DAVID

*The record is not clear as to this child. If there was such a child, she died very young.

JACOB HYNEMAN, s. of Robert Jesse and Elizabeth (Surratt). They reside at Corinth. Children (surname *Hyneman*): 1. *Annie Lucy*, b. 25 Nov. 1869; d. at St. Maurice, La., 23 Sept. 1890; m. at Corinth, 30 Oct. 1888, Dr. Green Croft Chandler, s. of Green Collier and Martha (Croft); one daughter. 2. *Eugenia*, b. at Corinth 23 Feb. 1872; m. there, 11 Sept. 1896, Robert Cowden Armstrong, s. of Clinton Adolphus and Margaret (Kercheval); residence, Lewisburg, Tenn.; no children. 3. *Nina May*, b. at Corinth 12 May 1874; m. there, 2 June 1898, Frank Sanders Elgin, s. of Charles Patton and Fashion (Duncan); residence, Memphis, Tenn.; two children. 4. *Maggie*, b. at Corinth 8 Nov. 1876; m. there, 6 June 1899, Roy Leighton Young, s. of Tandy Key and Mary (Hoyle); residence, Corinth; three children, b. at Corinth. 5. *Ellen Elizabeth*, b. 20 June 1879; d. unm. 31 Mar. 1907.

v.   PERRY, b. 11 Sept. 1848; d. unm.
vi. WILLIAM WOOD, b. 10 Dec. 1850; d. at Jackson, Tenn.; m. at Crawford, Miss., PATTIE WHEELOCK.
vii. SAMUEL WALKER, b. at Kossuth, Miss., 16 Oct. 1854; living unm. at Glen, Miss.

Evan Shelby Polk, son of John and Elizabeth (Alderson) Polk.
From Valaree Hassell, Oklahoma City.

20. BRIG. GEN. THOMAS GILCHRIST[6] POLK (*Lieut. Col. William,*[5] *Brig. Gen. Thomas,*[4] *William,*[3] *William,*[2] *Robert*[1]), A.B. (University of North Carolina, 1809), A.M. (*ib.*, 1816), born in Mecklenburg Co., N. C., 22 Feb. 1791, died at Holly Springs, Miss., 16 Mar. 1869. He married at Salisbury, N. C., 20 Oct. 1812, MARY ELOISE TROTTER, daughter of Richard.

He entered the University of North Carolina, where he was graduated in 1809, and later studied law at the law school at Litchfield, Conn., where he was graduated in 1813. Soon afterwards he began the practice of his profession. He was a prominent member of the Lower House of the North Carolina Legislature from Mecklenburg County, 1823–1825, and from Rowan County, 1829–1832, an unsuccessful candidate for governor in 1833, and a State senator in 1835–36. He was also a brigadier general in the State Militia. On the visit of Lafayette to North Carolina he commanded the troops that met him at the State line. In 1838 he moved to a plantation at La Grange, Tenn., and soon afterwards moved from Tennessee to Holly Springs, Miss., where he resided until his death. In politics he was a Whig, and in 1844 actively supported Henry Clay for the Presidency against his own kinsman, James Knox Polk (17, i).

Children:

i. JANE,[7] d. *s.p.*; m. DR. ——— BOUCHELLE.
ii. MARY ADELAIDE, b. about 1818; m. in 1844 HON. GEORGE DAVIS of Wilmington, N. C., s. of Thomas and Mary (Moore).* Children (surname *Davis*): 1. *Jane*, d. in infancy. 2. *Junius*, b. 17 June 1845; d. at Wilmington 11 Apr. 1916; m. (1) 19 Jan. 1874 Mary Orme Walker, who d. 6 Nov. 1893, dau. of Thomas D. and Mary Vance; m. (2) Mary Walker Cowan, dau. of Col. Robert of Wilmington; in 1863 he enlisted in the Confederate Army, and served until the end of the War; after the War he practised law, being associated with his father; he was an honorary member of the Society of the Cincinnati; seven children by first wife and three children by second wife. 3. *Mary*. 4. *Emily Polk*, b. at Wilmington, N. C.; m. John E. Crow; five children. 5. *Louis Poisson*, d. unm. 6. *Isabel Eagles*, b. in Wilmington; m. Spencer Shotter; one daughter. 7. *Meta Alexander*, b. in Wilmington; m. George Rountree; five children.
48. iii. WILLIAM, b. at Salisbury, N. C., 17 Nov. 1821.
iv. EMILY, d. unm.
v. THOMAS, d. young.
vi. RICHARD, d. young.
vii. GILBERT, d. young.

*Mary Moore was a daughter of George and Mary (Ashe) Moore, granddaughter of old "King" Roger Moore, and great-granddaughter of the first Gov. James Moore of South Carolina. Her mother, Mary Ashe, was a daughter of John Baptiste Ashe and sister of Gov. Samuel Ashe and Gen. John Ashe.

21. WILLIAM JULIUS[6] POLK (*Lieut. Col. William,*[5] *Brig. Gen. Thomas,*[4] *William,*[3] *William,*[2] *Robert*[1]), A.B. (University of North Carolina, 1813), A.M. (*ib.*, 1816), M.D. (Philadelphia Medical University), born in Mecklenburg Co., N. C., 21 Mar. 1793, died at "Buena Vista," his home, in the suburbs of Columbia, Tenn., 27 June 1860. He married, 1 June 1818, his second cousin, MARY REBECCA A. LONG,* daughter of Lunsford and Rebecca Edwards (Jones).†

After being graduated at the University of North Carolina, he studied medicine at the Philadelphia Medical University, where he was admitted to the degree of Doctor of Medicine. He settled first at Fayetteville, N. C., and began to practise medicine there; but soon afterwards he became a planter in Mecklenburg Co., and in 1836 he moved to Tennessee, where he established himself on his plantation in Maury Co., north of Duck River. A year later he moved to Columbia, Tenn., where his residence in the western suburbs was called "Buena Vista." There he lived until his death. He was a member of the Protestant Episcopal Church, and was at one time president of the Columbia branch of the Bank of Tennessee.

Children:

    i.   GRISELDA GILCHRIST,[7] b. at "Mount Gallant," Northampton Co., N. C., 8 Mar. 1819; d. 7 Apr. 1901; bur. in Cave Hill Cemetery, Louisville, Ky.; m. 4 June 1844 HON. RUSSELL HOUSTON, lawyer, who for many years was chief counsel of the Louisville & Nashville Railroad Company. They resided at Columbia and Nashville, Tenn., and later at Louisville. Children (surname *Houston*): 1. *Mary Russell*, m. Lytle Buchanan; no issue. 2. *Louise Ross*, d. in childhood. 3. *Allen Polk*, b. at Columbia 1 Sept. 1851; m. 27 Nov. 1878 Mattie Belle Schreve (Shreve) of Louisville; residence, Chicago, Ill.; six children. 4. *Lucia Eugene*, b. at Columbia in 1854; m. at Louisville, 30 Oct. 1877, George H. Hull;

---

*Mary Rebecca A. Long was a granddaughter of Col. Nicholas Long, the founder of the Long family in Halifax Co., N. C. He was a wealthy planter on the Roanoke, and his home, "Quanky," was a centre of both social and military activities. When Washington visited the Carolinas, he and his staff were guests for several days at that hospitable mansion. He married (1) Mary Reynolds of Virginia, and (2) 24 Aug. 1761 Mary McKinney, daughter of John. Children by first wife: 1. Gabriel. 2. Anne, married William Martin. Children by second wife: 3. Nicholas, a soldier of the Revolution. 4. Mary, married Bassett Steth of Virginia. 5. Richard, married Bessie Pasture. 6. Lunsford, married Rebecca Edwards Jones. 7. Martha, married Gen. William Gregory. 8. George Washington. 9. John Joseph, married Frances Quintard. 10. Lemuel McKinney, married Mary Amis.

†Rebecca Edwards Jones was a daughter of Gen. Allen Jones of "Mount Gallant," at the head of Roanoke Falls, in Northampton Co., N. C., who was born 24 Dec. 1739 and was educated at Eton. He was a delegate from Northampton County to the First Provincial Congress at Newbern, N. C., 25 Apr. 1774. He was a brigadier general in the Halifax District of North Carolina, and in 1779 he was selected as a delegate to the Continental Congress at Philadelphia, but declined to serve, because he feared that the National Government would destroy the independence of the States. He married (1) 21 Jan. 1762 Mary Haynes, and (2) Rebecca Edwards, daughter of Col. Nicholas Edwards, whose wife was Jane (Eaton) Haynes, widow of Anthony Haynes. Children by first wife: 1. Sarah, married Gen. William R. Davie. 2. Martha, married (1) James W. Green, (2) Judge John Sitgreaves, and (3) Dr. Thomas Hall. 3. Mary, married Gen. Thomas Eaton. Children by second wife: 4. Rebecca Edwards, married Lunsford Long and had issue: 1. *Rebecca Edwards Long*, married her cousin, Col. Cadwallader Jones. 2. *Mary Rebecca A. Long*, married her second cousin, Dr. William Julius Polk. In the museum at Washington's Headquarters, Morristown, N. J., there is a punch bowl, to which is attached a card bearing the following legend: "A punch bowl owned by George Washington. It was given by him to Mrs. Allen Jones of North Carolina."

residence, Tuxedo Park, N. Y.; five children.* 5. *Elise*, b. at Nashville in 1858; m. (1) at Louisville, 10 Oct. 1883, Joseph Ferrell; m. (2) 12 Mar. 1908 Theodore Presser of Germantown, Pa.; two children by first husband.

49. ii. ALLEN JONES, b. at Farmville, N. C., 5 Mar. 1824.
50. iii. THOMAS GILCHRIST, b. in Mecklenburg Co., N. C., 25 Dec. 1825.
    iv. MARY JONES, b. at Salisbury, N. C., 28 Nov. 1831; d. at Nashville, Tenn., 2 Dec. 1919; bur. in St. John's Churchyard, Maury Co., Tenn.; m. JOSEPH GERALD BRANCH of Arkansas. Children (surname *Branch*): 1. *Mary Polk*, b. at "Buena Vista," near Columbia, Tenn.; m. 16 June 1885 Dr. Charles Winn; no issue. 2. *Laurence*, unm. 3. *Lucia Eugenia*, b. at Columbia, Tenn.; m. 11 Dec. 1888 J. William Howard of Maury Co.; two sons.
51. v.   LUCIUS EUGENE, b. at Salisbury, N. C., 10 July 1833.
52. vi. CADWALLADER LONG, b. at Columbia, Tenn., 16 Oct. 1837.
53. vii. RUFUS JULIUS, b. in Maury Co., Tenn., 30 July 1843.

22. HON. LUCIUS JUNIUS[6] POLK (*Lieut. Col. William,*[5] *Brig. Gen. Thomas,*[4] *William,*[3] *William,*[2] *Robert*[1]), A.B. (University of North Carolina, 1822), A.M. (*ib.*, 1844), born at Raleigh, N. C., 16 Mar. 1802, died in Maury Co., Tenn., 3 Oct. 1870, and is buried in St. John's Churchyard, near Hamilton Place, Columbia, Tenn. He married first, in the White House, Washington, D. C., 10 Apr. 1832, Rev. Dr. Hawby officiating, MARY ANN EASTIN, who died 1 Aug. 1847, oldest daughter of William Eastin and his wife Rachel (Donelson), who was a granddaughter of Col. John[2] Donelson, one of the early pioneers of Tennessee;† and secondly, at the home of her father, 15 Sept.

*Griselda Houston Hull, eldest child of George H. and Lucia Eugenia (Houston) Hull, was born at Louisville, Ky., 22 Aug. 1878, and married at Tuxedo Park, N. Y., 25 May 1905, Hon. Richmond Pearson Hobson, LL.D. (Southern University, 1906), born at Greensboro, Ala., 17 Aug. 1870, son of James Marcellus and Sarah Croom (Pearson) Hobson. Mr. Hobson attended the Southern University, 1882–1885, the United States Naval Academy at Annapolis, Md., where he was graduated in 1889, and two schools in France, the École National Supérieur des Mines and the École d'Application du Génie Maritime (at which he was graduated). He served in the United States Navy until Feb. 1903; in the War with Spain he was a lieutenant attached to the fleet under Rear Admiral Sampson, that blockaded Santiago, where the Spanish fleet had taken refuge; and he volunteered for the dangerous duty of sinking the collier *Merrimac* at the entrance to Santiago Harbor, in an attempt to prevent the exit of the Spanish ships. He was captured with his men by the Spaniards, and was held as a prisoner at Santiago for more than a month (3 June–6 July 1898). After resigning from the Navy he was elected in 1904, on the Democratic ticket, as a presidential elector at large in Alabama, and served later as a Democratic Representative from Alabama in the United States Congress for four terms (1907–1915). He has been prominent as a lecturer and writer, especially on naval topics and on national prohibition, of which he has been an earnest advocate. He resides at Los Angeles, Calif. Children, born in Washington, D. C.: 1. Richmond Pearson, Jr., b. 27 Nov. 1907. 2. Lucia, b. 7 July 1909. 3. George Hull, b. 29 Sept. 1910.

†The progenitor of the Donelson family in America was John[1] Donelson, a native of London, England, who emigrated to America in 1670 and settled first at Norfolk, Va. He married, about 1717, Catherine Davies, daughter of David Davies of Summit Bridge, New Castle Co., Del., and sister of Rev. Samuel Davies, A.M., a Presbyterian clergyman, who in 1759 was elected and installed as president of the College of New Jersey (now Princeton University). John[2] Donelson (John[1]), born on the Delaware River about 1718, married Rachel Stokeley of Accomac Co., Va. He was a surveyor, and moved to Pittsylvania Co., Va., where he took out a patent for 200 acres of land, 25 Nov. 1744. He was a vestryman of Camden Parish, a justice of the peace of Pittsylvania County, a colonel of the militia in 1767, and head of the county militia. He represented Pittsylvania County in the House of Burgesses, 1767–1774, and was repeatedly appointed a commissioner to treat with the Indians. In 1779 he moved with his family to Tennessee, where he was one of the early settlers of Nashville and was murdered by Indians or white desperadoes in the autumn of 1785. He had twelve children, of whom the fourth, Rachel, became the wife of Andrew Jackson, President of the United States. Among other prominent members of the family were Andrew Jackson Donelson, private secretary to President Jackson, United States chargé d'affaires to the Republic of Texas, and envoy extraordinary and minister plenipotentiary to Prussia and to the German Confederation, Andrew Jackson Donelson, Jr., a graduate of the United States Military Academy at West Point and an officer in the Confederate Army, Earl van Dorn, a general in the Confederate Army, and Donelson Caffery, United States Senator from Louisiana.

1853, Rev. Dr. Edgar officiating, MRS. ANNE (ERWIN) POPE, daughter of Col. Andrew Erwin of Wartrace, Bedford Co., Tenn.

After completing his college course at the University of North Carolina, he moved to Tennessee about 1823, and settled on his plantation in Maury Co., on the waters of Carter's Creek. Subsequently he and his three brothers, Leonidas, Rufus King, and George Washington, received from their father four tracts of land of about 1300 acres each, lying in a body six or eight miles west of Columbia, Tenn., on the Mount Pleasant turnpike. Where the tracts of land met, these brothers built, on a lot of 6 acres which they gave to the diocese, St. John's Church (Protestant Episcopal), whose churchyard became the family burying ground.* He represented his county in the Upper House of the State Legislature several times, served as adjutant general of the State, and was the second Eminent Commander of the Grand Commandery of Masons in Tennessee.

Children by first wife, born at Hamilton Place, Maury Co., Tenn.:

i. SARAH RACHEL,[7] b. 24 Jan. 1833; d. at Nashville, Tenn., 12 June 1905; bur. in St. John's Churchyard; m. 24 Apr. 1855, Right Rev. James H. Otey, Bishop of Tennessee, officiating, ROBIN AP CADWALLADER JONES, b. 18 Jan. 1826, mortally wounded at Brandy Station, Va., 9 June 1863, while serving in the Confederate Army, s. of Col. Cadwallader and Rebecca Edwards (Long) of "West Hill," Orange Co., N. C. Robin ap Cadwallader Jones moved from North Carolina to the York District, S. C., in 1859. At the beginning of the Civil War he raised and equipped a company of Cavalry, which was attached to the First South Carolina Regiment, of Gen. Wade Hampton's brigade, and he was killed in this service. Children (surname *Jones*): 1. *Mary Polk*, b. at Hillsboro, N. C., 18 Jan. 1856; d. at Nashville, Tenn., 20 Dec. 1893; bur. in Zion Church Cemetery, Maury Co.; m. 18 Jan. 1877 Duncan Brown Cooper; five children. 2. *Rebecca Edwards*, b. 16 Jan. 1857; unm. 3. *Robin ap Robin*, b. 18 Feb. 1859; unm.; member of the Society of the Cincinnati. 4. *Sarah Polk*, b. at Hillsboro, N. C., 10 Oct. 1860; m. 27 June 1888 James C. Bradford of Nashville, Tenn.; two children.† 5. *Lucy Cadwallader*, b. at Hillsboro, N. C., 3 Feb. 1862; m. at Nashville, Tenn., in 1888, Stanley Bell Herndon; residence, Mobile, Ala.; four children.

ii. MARY BROWN, b. 25 Mar. 1835; d. at Hamilton Place 27 Mar. 1890; bur. in St. John's Churchyard; m. at St. John's Church, Ashwood, 2 Sept. 1858, Rev. James Hildebrand, Rector, officiating, HENRY CLAY YEATMAN of Nashville, Tenn., who d. 1 Aug. 1910, and is bur. beside his wife. Children (surname *Yeatman*): 1. *Mary Eastin*, b. at Hamilton Place 25 May 1861; d. *s.p.* 10 Jan. 1917; m. at Hamilton Place, 7 Aug. 1897, Maj. Thomas S. Webb of Knoxville, Tenn. 2. *Henry Clay*, b. 2 Mar. 1866; d. unm. 7 Aug.

*This church was consecrated on Sunday, 4 Sept. 1842, by Bishop Otey of Tennessee, Bishop Leonidas Polk (23) and other clergymen participating in the ceremony.

†Sarah Polk Bradford, one of the two children of James C. and Sarah Polk (Jones) Bradford, married (1) Alfred Thomas Shaughnessy of Montreal, Canada, who was killed in action in the World War in Mar. 1916, while serving in Flanders as a captain in the Sixtieth Canadian Regiment; married (2) at St. Peter's, Eton Square, London, England, 15 Nov. 1920, Capt. Pier Legh, youngest son of Baron Newton and equerry to the Prince of Wales. Children by first husband (surname *Shaughnessy*): 1. Elizabeth, b. at Montreal 28 Jan. 1913. 2. Thomas Bradford, b. at Montreal 14 Jan. 1915. 3. Alfred Thomas (posthumous), b. in London 19 May 1916.

1897; bur. in St. John's Churchyard. 3. *Russell Houston*, b. 25
Apr. 1869; d. unm. 26 Apr. 1893; bur. in St. John's Churchyard.
4. *Trezevant Player*, b. at Hamilton Place, 13 Oct. 1871; m. at
Ewell Farm, Maury Co., Tenn., 11 June 1913, Mary Wharton,
dau. of William and Mary (Currey) of Nashville; three children.
5. *Jennie Bell*, b. at Hamilton Place 3 Mar. 1875; unm. 6. *Lucia
Polk*, b. at Hamilton Place 7 Aug. 1877; d. unm. 2 May 1908;
bur. in St. John's Churchyard.

iii.　EMILY DONELSON, b. 29 Mar. 1837; d. at Nashville, Tenn., 22 Dec.
1892; m. at Hamilton Place, 13 Nov. 1860, JOSEPH MINNICK
WILLIAMS of Nashville, a descendant of the Shelby family of
Tennessee, who d. 18 Dec. 1899. Children (surname *Williams*):
1. *Emily Polk*, d. in infancy. 2. *Henry Yeatman*, b. at Hamilton
Place 29 Mar. 1863; m. at Nashville, 8 Mar. 1894, Louise Pitcher;
residence, San Antonio, Tex.; no issue. 3. *Joseph Minnick*, lawyer,
b. at "Planta Place," Maury Co., Tenn., 18 Feb. 1866; m. at
Shawnee, Okla., 17 Mar. 1913, Clara B. Turner; residence, Altus,
Okla. 4. *Lucius Polk*, b. in Nov. 1867; unm. 5. *Nannie M.*, b. in
1870; d. unm. 9 Apr. 1890. 6. *Eliza Polk*, b. in Apr. 1872; d. unm.
3 July 1891. 7. *Priscilla Shelby*, b. at "Planta Place," Maury Co.,
Tenn., 4 Jan. 1878; m. 7 Mar. 1901 George S. Briggs; residence,
Norfolk, Va.; one child.

iv.　MAJ. WILLIAM, b. 1 Feb. 1839; d. *s.p.* at Memphis, Tenn., 5 Apr.
1906; bur. in St. John's Churchyard; m. REBECCA MAYES of
Columbia, Tenn., who is bur. beside her husband. At the outbreak
of the Civil War William Polk enlisted as a private in Capt. D. F.
Wade's company, which was recruited in Maury Co. and was
attached to the Third Tennessee Regiment, Confederate Army,
commanded by Col. John C. Brown. He was appointed sergeant
major of the regiment. At the fall of Fort Donelson the regiment
surrendered, with other troops, to the Federal forces under General
Grant: but he escaped capture, as he had been wounded and
removed from the field. In the reorganization of the Tennessee
regiments, after an exchange of prisoners, he was transferred
to the Forty-eighth Tennessee Infantry, was chosen adjutant
of the regiment, and was later promoted to be major. The regiment
was at the bombardment of Port Hudson, La., saw service at
Dalton, Ga., Mobile, Ala., New Hope Church, Pine Mountain,
Kenesaw Mountain, Peach Creek, Atlanta, and in all the engagements of General Hood's Tennessee campaign except that at
Franklin, and was surrendered at Bentonville, N. C., in the spring
of 1865. Major Polk never missed a battle in which his regiment
fought, and was on duty constantly until the surrender. Returning
home, he engaged in farming and stock raising for several years
and afterwards in cotton planting in Mississippi. He was a member
of the Society of the Cincinnati.

v.　ELIZA EASTIN, b. 5 Apr. 1841; d. unm. 3 July 1897.

vi.　FRANCES ANNE, b. 4 Aug. 1844; d. 26 Mar. 1912; bur. at Lexington,
Va., beside her husband; m. at Hamilton Place, 29 Nov. 1866,
COL. EDWARD DILLON of Virginia, an officer of the old Army and a
distinguished Confederate soldier. They resided at Indian Rock
and Lexington, Va. Children (surname *Dillon*): 1. *James Royall*,
b. 2 Sept. 1869; d. at Mineral Wells, Tex., 14 May 1914; bur. at
Lexington. 2 *Edward*, b. at Buchanan, Va., 19 Oct. 1871; m;
6 Oct. 1896 Susan Strachan Pendleton; residence, Indian Rock.
five children. 3 *Lucius Polk*, b. at Indian Rock 8 June 1873;
m. 25 Apr. 1899 Mary Evelyn Morton; residence, Indian Rock;
five children. 4. *John Cunningham*, b. at Indian Rock 17 May
1875; m. 18 Jan. 1911 Mae McClung Childress; residence, Norfolk,
Va.; in the World War he was assistant Federal food administrator
for Virginia and was stationed at Richmond; no issue. 5. *Eliza
Polk*, b. at Indian Rock 30 July 1878; m. 4 Apr. 1907 Robert Scott
Spillman; residence, Charleston, W. Va.; three children. 6. *Frances*

Polk, b. 20 Jan. 1880; in the World War she was attached to the American Committee for Devastated France and was stationed in Paris, and later she was in charge of a Red Cross canteen unit on the Western Front. 7. *Francis Cunningham*, mining engineer, b. at Indian Rock 17 Sept. 1885; m. at Talca, Chile, in 1918, Maria Parada, of Chilian parentage; in the World War he served as a chemist in the Ordnance Department, United States Army, at Saltville, Va.

vii. SUSAN REBECCA (twin), b. 7 July 1847; d. at Pass Christian, Miss., 19 Feb. 1922; bur. in St. John's Churchyard; m. at Hamilton Place, 11 Sept. 1866, MAJ. CAMPBELL BROWN, who d. 30 Aug. 1893 and is bur. in St. John's Churchyard. Children (surname *Brown*): 1. *Lucius Polk*, captain, Sanitary Corps, United States Army, b. at Hamilton Place 1 Aug. 1867; m. (1) 30 Jan. 1895 Jessie Roberts of Nashville, Tenn.; m. (2) 12 Dec. 1903 Susan Massie of Virginia; he is director of the Bureau of Food Inspection, New York Department of Health; residence, Staten Island, N. Y.; one son by first wife and three children by second wife. 2. *Dr. Richard Ewell*, b. at Nashville, Tenn., 12 Jan. 1870; d. in New York City 14 June 1919; bur. at Southampton, Long Island, N. Y.; m. 10 Sept. 1901 Marion Lee of New York City; he was a physician in New York City; three children. 3. *George Campbell*, b. 25 Sept. 1871; d. 23 Jan. 1912; bur. in St. John's Churchyard. 4. *Percy* (twin), b. at Elwell Farm, Maury Co., Tenn., 6 Apr. 1874; m. 6 Aug. 1907 Gertrude Plunkett of Nashville, Tenn.; residence, Elwell Farm; three children. 5. *Lizinska* (twin), b. at Elwell Farm, Maury Co., Tenn., 6 Apr. 1874; d. 28 Aug. 1899; bur. in St. John's Churchyard.

54. viii. GEORGE WASHINGTON (twin), b. 7 July 1847.

Children by second wife, born at Hamilton Place, Maury Co., Tenn.:

55. ix. LUCIUS JUNIUS, b. 14 Aug. 1854.
    x.   ELVIRA JULIETTE, b. 5 Sept. 1856; d. at Nashville, Tenn., 8 May 1923; bur. in St. John's Churchyard; m. 13 Jan. 1881 HORACE STEPHENS COOPER of Columbia, Tenn. Child (surname *Cooper*): 1. *Horace Polk*, b. 2 Jan. 1887; unm.

23. RIGHT REV. AND LIEUT. GEN. LEONIDAS[6] POLK (*Lieut. Col. William,*[5] *Brig. Gen. Thomas,*[4] *William,*[3] *William,*[2] *Robert*[1]), S.T.D. (Columbia College, 1838), LL.D., born at Raleigh N. C., 10 Apr. 1806, was killed, by a fragment of bursting shell, on Pine Mountain, near Marietta, Ga., 14 June 1864, while reconnoitring in the field with his staff. He married, 6 May 1830, FRANCES A. DEVEREUX, who died 16 Apr. 1875 and is buried at Augusta, Ga., beside her husband, daughter of John Devereux of The Ferns, co. Wexford, Ireland, and of The Roanoke and Raleigh, N. C., and his wife, Frances (Pollok).*

He received his early education in the schools of Raleigh, and entered the University of North Carolina in 1821; but, having been appointed a cadet in the United States Military Academy at West Point, he entered there in June 1823, was graduated 4 July 1827, and was brevetted a second lieutenant of Artillery. Shortly afterwards, however, in the following December, he resigned from the Army, and on 4 Nov. 1828

_____

*Frances A. Devereux, wife of Leonidas Polk, was a great-granddaughter of Thomas Pollok of Balgra, Scotland, president of the Colony of North Carolina and major general of the Colonial forces. She was also a descendant of Rev. Jonathan Edwards, his sixth daughter, Eunice, being her grandmother. On the death of her mother she inherited 400 slaves.

began his studies for the Protestant Episcopal ministry in the seminary at Alexandria, Va. He was ordained to the diaconate at Richmond, Va., 9 Apr. 1830, and was made a priest in May 1831. He was assistant in the Monumental Church at Richmond, but found it necessary in Aug. 1831, to go to Europe for the benefit of his health. In 1832 he returned to the United States, and in Apr. 1833, with his young wife, he left North Carolina and went to his brother Lucius's plantation in Maury Co., Tenn., where he arrived on 15 May of that year. He became rector of St. Peter's Church, Columbia, Tenn., in that year, served as a clerical deputy to the General Convention of the Protestant Episcopal Church in 1834, and in 1835 was made a member of the Standing Committee of the Diocese. He began to build a home on the lands allotted to him by his father, and this mansion, which was finished in 1837, was called Ashwood Hall. In 1838 he was elected and consecrated Missionary Bishop of Arkansas and the Indian territory south of latitude 36° 30′, with provisional charge of the Dioceses of Alabama, Mississippi, and Louisiana and the missions in the Republic of Texas. Later he bought a sugar plantation near Thibodaux, La., which he called Leighton, and to which he moved his family. In 1841 he resigned his missionary jurisdiction and his provisional charges, and was elected and confirmed Bishop of Louisiana. In 1854 he sold his plantation and moved with his family to New Orleans, where they remained until the outbreak of the Civil War. In 1856 and the years immediately following he was engaged, with other Southern bishops, in founding the University of the South, which was opened at Sewanee, Tenn., after the Civil War.

A Southerner by birth, education, and feeling, a large landowner, and a slaveholder, Bishop Polk was a zealous advocate of the doctrine of secession, and on 25 June 1861 he was commissioned a major general in the Confederate Army. In the early years of the War he held important commands in the Mississippi Valley, led the Confederate forces in the Battle of Belmont, 7 Nov. 1861, and commanded a corps the next year at Shiloh and Corinth. He took part in the Battle of Perryville, and was promoted to the rank of lieutenant general in Oct. 1862. He participated in the bloody battle at Murfreesboro, and commanded the Confederate right wing at Chickamauga. Being blamed by General Bragg for the escape of the Federal Army from annihilation in that battle, he was relieved of his command, and later, having declined President Davis's offer of reinstatement, was ordered to take charge of a camp of Confederate prisoners who had been paroled. In Dec. 1863 he was placed over the Department of Alabama, Mississippi, and East Louisiana, where he redeemed his reputation, and was ordered to unite his command with the army of Gen. Joseph E. Johnston, who was opposing Sherman's march into Georgia. He took part in the chief battles of this campaign, until he was killed by an enemy shell near Kenesaw Mountain,

Ga. His remains were taken to Augusta, Ga., and with simple ceremony were interred beneath the chancel window in the rear of St. Paul's Church. In 1902 a monument to his memory was erected to mark the spot where he fell. A biography entitled "Leonidas Polk, Bishop and General," in two volumes, by his son, Dr. William Mecklenburg Polk, was published in 1893, and a new edition of this work appeared in 1915.

Children:

56. i.   ALEXANDER HAMILTON,[7] b. at Richmond, Va., 27 Jan. 1831.
   ii.   FRANCES DEVEREUX, b. at "Elderwood," Maury Co., Tenn., 27 Nov. 1835; d. 15 Mar. 1884; m. at St. John's Church, Maury Co., 27 Nov. 1866, PEYTON H. SKIPWITH. They resided at Oxford, Miss. Children (surname *Skipwith*): 1. *Kate*, b. 18 Sept. 1867; unm. 2. *Frank*, b. 10 Oct. 1872; unm.
   iii. KATHERINE, b. at Ashwood Hall, Maury Co., Tenn., 16 Aug. 1838; d. 8 Feb. 1916; m. 14 Dec. 1858 WILLIAM D. GALE, who d. at Nashville, Tenn., 30 Jan. 1888 and is bur. beside his wife in Mount Olivet Cemetery. Children (surname *Gale*): 1. *Frances*, b. near Nashville 1 Apr. 1860; m. 30 Apr. 1895 Frank W. Ring, who d. 17 July 1896 and is bur. at Portland, Me.; she resides near Nashville; no children. 2. *William Dudley*, b. on the Yazoo River, in Mississippi, 22 Apr. 1861; m. 18 Jan. 1894 Meta Ora Jackson; he is in the insurance business at Nashville; two children. 3. *Katherine*, b. near Jackson, Miss., 29 Aug. 1862; d. unm. at Nashville 24 Nov. 1889; bur. in Mount Olivet Cemetery. 4. *Leonide*, b. at Asheville, N. C., 10 May 1864; d. unm. at Nashville 16 Sept. 1890; bur. in Mount Olivet Cemetery. 5. *Josephine*, b. 22 Jan. 1867; d. 13 Nov. 1876. 6. *Ethel*, b. 19 Nov. 1869; d. 13 June 1870.
   iv.   SARAH H., b. about 1840; m. FRANCIS DANIEL BLAKE of South Carolina. They reside at Asheville, N. C. Child (surname *Blake*): 1. *Francis Polk*, b. 1 June 1872; d. aged about 20 years.
   v.   SUSAN R., b. at Raleigh, N. C., 16 Apr. 1842; m. 21 June 1870 DR. JOSEPH JONES of New Orleans, La., who d. 16 Feb. 1896. Residence, New Orleans. Children (surname *Jones*): 1. *Fanny*, b. 18 May 1871; unm. 2. *Hamilton Polk*, physician, b. 26 Oct. 1872; m. 25 June 1901 Caroline E. Merrick; residence, New Orleans; in the World War he was major, Medical Division Base Hospital, Fort Bliss, El Paso, Tex. 3. *Laura Maxwell*, b. 26 Aug. 1876; d. at Springside, Chestnut Hill, Philadelphia, Pa., 17 Mar. 1917; bur. in White Marsh Cemetery.
   vi.   ELIZABETH DEVEREUX, b. 29 June 1843; d. at New Orleans, La., 14 Nov. 1918; m. 27 Apr. 1864 COL. WILLIAM E. HUGER, b. at Spring Hill, Ala., 27 Apr. 1841, d. in New York City 3 July 1901; residence, New Orleans. Children (surname *Huger*): 1. *Leonide*, d. in infancy. 2. *Frances Devereux* (twin), b. at New Orleans 24 Mar. 1867; m. 10 Jan. 1895 Henry Richardson Labouisse; residence, New Orleans; three sons. 3. *Emily Hamilton* (twin), b. 24 Mar. 1867; unm.; head nurse in the Read Memorial Hospital, Washington, D. C., and head supervisor of the Reconstruction Hospital. 4. *John Middleton*, cotton broker, b. at New Orleans 1 May 1868; d. 7 May 1912; m. 18 Dec. 1900 Louise Woeste; residence, New Orleans; two children. 5. *Lucia Polk*, b. at New Orleans 29 Oct. 1870; m. 31 Jan. 1894 Joseph Hardie; residence, Dallas, Tex.; two children. 6. *Arthur Middleton*, cotton buyer, b. at New Orleans 26 Aug. 1878; m. 24 Apr. 1903 Lillie Charbounet; residence, New Orleans; one daughter. 7. *William Elliott*, b. 22 Oct. 1882; unm.
57. vii. WILLIAM MECKLENBURG, b. at Ashwood Hall, Maury Co., Tenn., 15 Aug. 1844.
   viii. LUCIA, b. at Leighton Plantation, La., 22 Oct. 1848; m. 8 Jan. 1870

EDWARD CHAPMAN of New Orleans, who d. there 19 Mar. 1883. She resides at Chestnut Hill, Philadelphia, Pa. No issue.

24. GEORGE WASHINGTON[6] POLK (*Lieut. Col. William,[5] Brig. Gen. Thomas,[4] William,[3] William,[2] Robert[1]*), born at Raleigh, N. C., 12 July 1817, died at the rectory of St. John's Church, Maury Co., Tenn., 8 Jan. 1892, and is buried in St. John's Churchyard. He married, at the residence of Mrs. Mary Hilliard, near Franklin, N. C., 24 Nov. 1840, SALLIE L. HILLIARD, who died 2 July 1894.

He was a student at the University of North Carolina, 1833–1837. About 1839 or 1840 he removed from North Carolina to Maury Co., Tenn., and settled on the tract of land allotted to him by his father, which he called "Rattle and Snap," the name bestowed on the original tract. He built his home some distance from the turnpike, and later built a handsome residence near the highway.

Children:

58. i. JAMES HILLIARD,[7] b. in Maury Co., Tenn., 8 Jan. 1842.
59. ii. RUFUS KING, b. at "Rattle and Snap," Maury Co., Tenn., 31 Oct. 1843.
   iii. SALLIE HAWKINS, b. 18 June 1845; d. unm. at Fort Worth, Tex., 18 Nov. 1914; bur. in St. John's Churchyard, Maury Co., Tenn.
   iv. MARY MURFREE, b. at "Rattle and Snap," Maury Co., Tenn., 25 June 1847; m. 29 Nov. 1870 JUDGE JULIUS J. DU BOSE of Memphis, Tenn. She resided at Memphis, Tenn., and at Berkeley and San Francisco, Calif. Children (surname *Du Bose*): 1. *Juliet Brevard*, d. in infancy. 2. *Tascar Polk*, b. in Maury Co., Tenn., 4 Jan. 1873; m. (1) in July 1905 Carrie Van Horn Culbert; m. (2) 14 Feb. 1911 Louise Myrtle Haskin; one daughter by second wife. 3. *Mary Hilliard*, b. at Memphis 26 Dec. 1875; in the World War she was head nurse in charge of the United States Naval Hospital, Brooklyn, N. Y., and later was stationed at the United States Hospital at Brest, France. 4. *Alfred Bishop*, b. 30 Sept. 1877; d. 23 Apr. 1892; bur. in Elmwood Cemetery, Memphis. 5. *Jessie McIver*, b. at Memphis 24 Nov. 1879; m. 15 July 1913 Daniel Edwin Newell; one son. 6. *George Washington*, b. at Memphis 4 July 1881; m. 29 Sept. 1915 Harriet Jane Guernsey; residence, Stockton, Calif.; in the World War he was major in the Ordnance Department, United States Army, and served with the American Expeditionary Forces in France. 7. *Sarah Camilla*, b. at Memphis 17 June 1884; m. 22 Dec. 1903 George Trowbridge Hackley of Los Angeles, Calif., lawyer, who d. in 1914; no issue. 8. *Julius Jesse*, b. 18 Aug. 1889; in the World War he was a private in the Signal Reserve Corps, United States Air Service, at Fort Omaha, Nebr.
   v. GEORGE BREVARD MECKLENBURG, b. 15 Dec. 1848; d. unm. at New Orleans, La., 25 Dec. 1877; bur. in St. John's Churchyard, Maury Co., Tenn.
   vi. SUSAN SPRATT, b. at "Rattle and Snap," Maury Co., Tenn., 23 June 1851; m. 7 Mar. 1877 JAMES YEATMAN PLAYER of St. Louis, Mo. Residence, St. Louis. Children (surname *Player*), b. in St. Louis: 1. *Susan Polk*, d. in infancy. 2. *George Polk*, b. 21 Jan. 1880; m. 17 June 1902 Eva Frank Lemmon of St. Louis; residence, Jefferson City, Mo.; in the World War he was first lieutenant, Signal Corps, with the American Expeditionary Forces in France. 3. *James Yeatman*, b. 30 Mar. 1882; m. 1 Nov. 1911 Lucile N. Harris of San Antonio, Tex.; residence, San Antonio; one daughter. 4. *Susan Trezevant*, b. 8 Aug. 1884; m. 12 Jan. 1907 William

Preston Graves; residence, St. Louis; one daughter. 5 *Thomas Trezevant*, inspector of transportation, Texas Division, Southern Pacific Railroad, b. 7 Sept. 1886; m. 22 Feb. 1916 Carita Green of Houston, Tex., dau. of Samuel; residence, Houston. 6. *Sally Hilliard*, b. 28 Mar. 1889.

    vii. Lucius Junius, b. 21 Apr. 1853; unm.

60. viii. Isaac Hilliard, b. at "Rattle and Snap," Maury Co., Tenn., 8 Aug. 1854.

    ix. Leonidas, d. in childhood.

    x. William Hawkins, b. at "Rattle and Snap," Maury Co., Tenn., 27 Jan. 1859; d. 26 Mar. 1896; bur. at Riverside, Calif.; m. Mabel Vanderbogart. Child: 1. *Anna Leah.*[8]

    xi. Caroline, b. at "Rattle and Snap," Maury Co., Tenn., 26 June 1861; m. (1) her first cousin, Isaac Hilliard; m. (2) Joseph H. Horton. No issue.

25. Andrew Jackson[6] Polk (*Lieut. Col. William,*[5] *Brig. Gen. Thomas,*[4] *William,*[3] *William,*[2] *Robert*[1]), born at Raleigh, N. C., 10 Aug. 1824, died at Vevey, Switzerland, 10 Mar. 1867, and is buried beside his wife in the Protestant cemetery there. He married at Nashville, Tenn., 14 Jan. 1846, Right Rev. James H. Otey, Bishop of Tennessee, officiating, Rebecca Van Leer.

He was a student at the University of North Carolina, 1840–41. He acquired of his brother, Bishop Leonidas Polk (23), his plantation in Maury Co., Tenn., with the house called Ashwood Hall, which he remodelled and made into one of the finest homes in Tennessee.

During the Civil War he made a fortune, when the ships laden with his cotton succeeded in running the blockade of the Southern ports. He was a captain in the Confederate Army, and after the War he lived abroad until his death.

Children:

    i. Antoinette Van Leer,[7] b. at Nashville 27 Oct. 1847; d. at her home, the Château de la Basse Motte, Châteauneuf de Bretagne, Department of the Ille-et-Vilaine, France, 3 Feb. 1919; m. 1 Dec. 1877 General Baron Athanase de Charette de la Contrée, who d. at the Château de la Basse Motte 10 Oct. 1911. He was of an old and noble family of Nantes, France, descended from Guillaume de Charette, Seigneur de la Thomassière et Trevignac, 1398, and was a grandnephew of François Athanase de Charette, a knight of the Military Order of St. Louis, who served at Yorktown in the French Navy under the Count de Grasse, was general in chief of the Catholic and Royal armies in the Vendée, commanded the celebrated Vendéan Corps, and was shot at Nantes by the Republicans, 29 Mar. 1796. The mother of General Baron Athanase de Charette was Louise Marie Charlotte, dau. of H. R. H. Charles, Duke of Berry, s. of King Charles X of France. General Baron de Charette served as ordnance officer of the Duke of Modena, was lieutenant colonel and commander of the Pontifical Zouaves, served in the Legion of the West in the Franco-German War of 1870–71, was made a general of brigade, and in the struggle with the Paris Commune commanded the troops that carried the barrier of the Rue Saint-Antoine and thereby opened Paris. He was elected an honorary member of the North Carolina Society of the Cincinnati in 1909. The marriage of Antoinette Van Leer Polk and General Baron de Charette was a great event, the beauty of the bride and the high family and fine physique of the groom making them a marked couple. Child (surname *de Charette*): 1. *Antoine Polk Van Leer*, b. in Paris, France, 3 July 1880; m. in

St. Patrick's Cathedral, New York City, 11 Nov. 1909, Susanne Henning of Louisville, Ky., dau. of John and Susan (Thornton); in the World War he served in the Tank Corps in the French Army, and was wounded on the Western Front; his daughter, Susanne, was b. in Paris 12 Apr. 1915.

ii. HON. VAN LEER, b. at Ashwood Hall, Maury Co., Tenn. 9 July 1856; d. at Memphis, Tenn., 19 Dec. 1907; m. in New York City, 20 Feb. 1907, MRS. DOROTHY KITCHINE BODINE. He was educated at Sillig's School at Vevey, Switzerland, and at Rugby, England, and spent most of his youth abroad. He returned to the United States and occupied himself with looking after the family affairs. He was elected from Maury County to the Senate of Tennessee, was appointed consul general of the United States at Calcutta, India, by President Cleveland, and was appointed by President Roosevelt in 1906 one of the six commissioners of the United States at the Pan-American Congress at Rio de Janeiro, Brazil. At the time of his death he was editor of the *Weekly News and Scimitar* of Memphis.

iii. REBECCA, b. at Nashville, Tenn., 26 Aug. 1858. She lived most of her life abroad, making her home with her sister, Madame de Charette.

26. THOMAS INDEPENDENCE[6] POLK (*Charles,*[5] *Brig. Gen. Thomas,*[4] *William,*[3] *William,*[2] *Robert*[1]), born in Mecklenburg Co., N. C., 4 July 1786, died in Louisiana 4 Sept. 1863, and was buried at Bastrop, La. He married, 14 July 1808, SARAH ISHAM MOORE, daughter of Col. Isham Moore of the Sumter District of South Carolina.

He resided for many years in Mecklenburg Co., N. C., but spent his winters in South Carolina, where he had a plantation, to which he moved his family in 1827. As colonel of a regiment of volunteers in South Carolina in 1832, at the time of the Nullification controversy, he offered his services in defense of that State when he thought that it would be invaded by the Federal forces. In 1836 he moved to Fayette Co., Tenn., where he inherited a large tract of land from his father, on which he settled. He finally moved in 1855 to Louisiana, and lived there until his death.

Children, born in Mecklenburg Co., N. C.:

61. i. CHARLES BINGLEY,[7] b. 23 Sept. 1809.

ii. MARY ANN, b. 11 Apr. 1811; d. 5 Mar. 1865; bur. with her husband at Bastrop, La.; m. 1 May 1832 JUDGE JOHN J. POTTS. They resided in Morehouse Parish, La. Children (surname *Potts*): 1. *Thomas,* b. at La Grange, Tenn., 9 Jan. 1838; d. in Louisiana 16 June 1904; m. 29 Sept. 1865 Lucy Lanier; resided in Honduras, Central America; one son, who d. in infancy. 2. *William N.,* b. at La Grange, Tenn., 9 Mar. 1841; m. 9 Mar. 1871 Sumner Aiken Hudson; residence, Monroe, La.; two children. 3. *Horace B.,* d. in childhood. 4. *Edgar Nelson,* b. at La Grange, Tenn., 17 Oct. 1843; d. 24 Jan. 1910; bur. at Bastrop, La.; m. 24 Dec. 1872 Miss F. F. Helmich; they reside in Morehouse Parish, La.; four children, b. in Morehouse Parish. 5. *Mary Octavia,* b. 4 Mar. 1859.

62. iii. THOMAS RICHARD, b. about 1813.

63. iv. HORACE MOORE, b. 11 Oct. 1819.

v. EMMA OCTAVIA, b. about 1821; m. at La Grange, Tenn., about 1847, DR. ROBERT MATTHEWS BOUCHELLE. Child (surname *Bouchelle*): 1. *Robert Julian,* b. at La Grange, Tenn., 14 Dec. 1848; m. at Columbia, Mo., 3 Dec. 1874, Virginia Hord Bradford, who d. 30 Dec. 1904; residence, Columbia; six children.

vi. NEWTON NAPOLEON, d. in infancy.

27. CHARLES JAMES[6] POLK (*Charles,*[5] *Brig. Gen. Thomas,*[4] *William,*[3] *William,*[2] *Robert*[1]), born in Mecklenburg Co., N. C., 15 Dec. 1790, died at La Grange, Tenn., 15 Oct. 1837. He married, 24 Oct. 1824, MARTHA HICKS JAMES, dau. of Taliaferro and Frances (Hicks), born 27 Dec. 1804, died 24 June 1846.
Children:

   i.   MARY E.,[7] b. 22 Nov. 1825; d. 5 Aug. 1887; m. 8 Apr. 1846 DOUGLAS R. HUNT, who d. in 1866. Children (surname *Hunt*): 1. *Ella Douglas,* b. 1 Jan. 1847; m. James R. Hull, who d. 13 Sept. 1896; residence, Beaumont, Tex. 2. *Lillian,* d. in childhood. 3. *John Melnotte.* 4. *Douglas K.* 5. *James,* d. in childhood. 6. *Effie,* b. in 1857; m. in 1872 Daniel S. Hawley. 7. *Walter Hamilton,* b. 30 Nov. 1859; m. 10 Jan. 1887 Emma Belle Blaylock.

   ii. FRANCES J., b. 4 July 1827; m. 13 Feb. 1852 JUDGE DRURY W. FIELDS. Children (surname *Fields*): 1. *Edmund Douglas,* d. young. 2. *Jennie,* d. young. 3. *Caspar.* 4. *Drury W.* 5. *William.* 6. *Leonidas.*

   iii. SARAH HENRIETTA, b. in the Sumter District, S. C., 27 Dec. 1829; d. at Memphis, Tenn., 25 May 1897; m. (1) at La Grange, Tenn., 12 Apr. 1847, ALEXANDER HAMILTON AVERY, b. at Buffalo, N. Y., 31 Mar. 1823, d. 8 May 1859, s. of Ebenezer Root and Harriet (Goodwin); m. (2) at Memphis HAMIL BOWEN, b. in Smith Co., Va., 10 Feb. 1818, d. at Memphis 26 May 1872. Her first husband removed, following his marriage, to Memphis, where he founded the *Memphis Whig.* Children by first husband (surname *Avery*): 1. *Walter Hamilton,* b. 21 Apr. 1849; d. 13 July 1869. 2. *Charles Polk,* d. in childhood. 3. *Norman Le Noir,* b. at Memphis 1 Jan. 1853; d. at Mineral Wells, Tex., 9 Sept. 1907; m. at Memphis, 3 Nov. 1875, Minnie Fisher Pullen, b. at Richmond, Va., 25 Dec. 1856, dau. of Benjamin King and Minerva Anner (Smith); he controlled large mercantile interests in Arkansas, Tennessee, Louisiana, and Texas. 4. *Herbert,* d. in infancy. 5. *Lora Belle,* b. 8 Apr. 1857; d. 16 Oct. 1878. Children by second husband (surname *Bowen*): 6. *Henrietta Polk,* b. at Memphis 5 May 1866; m. 18 Sept. 1882 Leonard Warren Redford, b. at Memphis 21 July 1862, s. of Moncure Warren and Lucy Jane (Holmes). 7. *Effie Douglas,* d. young.

   iv. THOMAS JAMES, d. in childhood.

   v. MARGARET EMMA, b. 9 Apr. 1832; m. THOMAS ALLEN of La Grange, Tenn. Two children.

   vi. CHARLES TALIAFERRO, b. 30 June 1834; m. MRS. BELLE HUGHES. Child: 1. *Dow.*[8]

  vii. MARTHA REBECCA, d. in childhood.

28. CHARLES CLARK[6] POLK (*Michael,*[5] *Capt. Charles,*[4] *William,*[3] *William,*[2] *Robert*[1]), born in North Carolina 12 Mar. 1814, died at Alexander City, Ala., 3 Oct. 1888. He married first, in North Carolina, MARY STILWELL; secondly, in Georgia, PHOEBE WOLF; and thirdly, in Alabama, in 1860, JANE ELIZABETH MORRIS, who was born in South Carolina 7 Mar. 1821 and died 26 Nov. 1901.
He removed from North Carolina to Georgia and thence to Alabama.
Children by first wife:

64. i. THOMAS MARSHALL,[7] b. in North Carolina 20 Mar. 1837.

   ii. SUSAN ELIZABETH, b. in North Carolina 8 July 1839; d. 14 Aug. 1900; m. SAMUEL TURNER RAY. Children (surname *Ray*): 1. *Marshall Gaines,* b. 5 Oct. 1858; d. in Aug. 1889; m. in 1881 Ann Crenshaw. 2. *George W.,* b. 14 May 1860; d. in childhood

3. *Mary Jane*, b. 21 Sept. 1863 [sic]. 4. *Mary Louisa*, b. 15 May 1864; m. in Sept. 1879 John Garbough. 5. *Tabitha Belle*, b. 8 June 1869; m. 3 May 1885 Robert Russell. 6. *Ann Elizabeth*, b. 27 Oct. 1871; d. 5 Oct. 1908; m. William Neighbors. 7. *Ida Cornelia*, b. 26 Oct. 1874; d. young.

iii. TABITHA JOSEPHINE, b. in North Carolina 13 Apr. 1841; d. 22 Oct. 1884; m. (1) ANDREW HANCOCK; m. (2) CHARLES CONNOR. Child by first husband (surname *Hancock*): 1. *Andrew Jackson*.

iv. CORNELIA JANE, b. in Georgia in Mar. 1844; m. (1) about 1860 WESLEY HANCOCK; m. (2) about 1865 WILLIAM McLEOD. Child by first husband (surname *Hancock*): 1. *Jefferson*. Children by second husband (surname *McLeod*): 2. *Elizabeth*, m. Calvin McKinnon. 3. *James*, m. ——— Hatley. 4. *Catherine*, m. ——— Blair. 5. *Charles*, d. young. 6. *Michael Sanders*.

v. JAMES KNOX, b. in Georgia 7 Jan. 1846; m. (1) ——— CHESSIRE; m. (2) MARY JORDAN. Child by first wife: 1. *Jimmie Belle,*[8] m. Henry Brockman of Atlanta, Ga.

Children by second wife:

65. vi. MICHAEL SANDERS, b. near McDonough, Ga., 12 Dec. 1848.
vii. JOHN HALE, b. 8 Apr. 1851.
66. viii. CHARLES CLARK, b. at Tallapoosa, Ga., 13 June 1856.

Child by third wife:

ix. EMMA M., b. 15 Sept. 1861; m. 15 Nov. 1876 HENRY WILLIS PEARSON. Residence, Alexander City, Ala. Children (surname *Pearson*): 1. *Ida Florence*, b. 29 July 1877. 2. *Clara Clyde*, b. 7 Mar. 1879. 3. *Charles Lewis*, b. 28 June 1881. 4. *Janie*, b. 1 July 1883. 5. *A child*, b. 30 Aug. 1884. 6. *Henry Willis*, b. 15 Jan. 1885 [sic]. 7. *George Washington*, b. 27 Nov. 1889. 8. *Walter*, b. 3 Aug. 1890. 9. *Walter Washington*, b. 7 Nov. 1891. 10. *John Hale*, b. 10 Oct. 1894. 11. *Mary Emma*, b. 30 Dec. 1897. 12. *Leroy Morris*, b. 11 Oct. 1900. 13. *A child*, b. 12 Mar. 1902. 14. *Ruth Elizabeth*, b. 13 Dec. 1903.

29. EZEKIEL[6] POLK (*Charles,*[5] *Capt. Charles,*[4] *William,*[3] *William,*[2] *Robert*[1]), born in Mecklenburg Co., N. C., 5 Sept. 1808, died in Douglas Co., Ga., 6 June 1886. He married, in Oct. 1828, MALISSA JANE WEDDINGTON, born 3 June 1809, died at Winston, Ga., 19 Feb. 1893, daughter of William and Polly (McLarty). Both are buried at Douglasville, Ga.

Children:

i. MARY ELLEN,[7] b. in Cabarrus Co., N. C., in 1829; d. in Douglas Co., Ga.; m. WESLEY CLONTS. Children (surname *Clonts*): 1. *Jane*, b. in Campbell Co., Ga.; m. Isham King; four children. 2. *Thomas*, m. ——— Foote; no issue. 3. *Charles Asbury*, m. (1) Fanny King; m. (2) Mary Johnson; four children by first wife and three children by second wife.

ii. HANNAH ELIZABETH, b. in Cabarrus Co., N. C., 28 Jan. 1832; d. at Douglasville, Ga., 13 June 1914; m. ISAAC McKELVEY of Georgia. Children (surname *McKelvey*): 1. *Charles Pinckney*, b. in Campbell Co., Ga.; lived and d. at Douglasville, Ga.; m. in 1870 Sarah Bobo; six children. 2. *William Thomas*, b. in Campbell Co., Ga.; m. Frances Bobo; five children. 3. *John*, b. in Campbell Co., Ga., 25 Aug. 1854; m. Savilla Winn, b. 27 Nov. 1859; residence, Joppa, Ala. 4. *Jane*, m. Charles Peavey; two children. 5. *Ezekiel A.*, m. Lulu Phillips; two children. 6. *Ann*, m. Peck Vandergrift; no issue. 7. *George*, d. young. 8. *Lude*, unm. 9. *Ira* (a daughter), unm. 10. *Flora*.

iii. SARAH EVELYN, b. in Campbell Co., Ga., 8 May 1834; m. JOHN HENRY WINN. Residence, Winston, Ga. Children (surname

Winn): 1. *Mary Ann*, m. Ludie Entrekin; nine children. 2. *William Clark*, m. Emma Hartzfield; eight children. 3. *Charles Wesley*, b. in Campbell Co., Ga.; d. at Winston in 1921; m. (1) Bettie Kennedy; m. (2) Julia Ward; one son by first wife and four children by second wife. 4. *Henry Oscar*, m. Mary Entrekin; four children. 5. *Jennie Drusilla*, b. 5 Feb. 1861; m. 13 May 1875 George Entrekin; two children. 6. *Dr. John Thomas*, b. in Campbell Co., Ga., 6 June 1866; m. Aurora McClellan Raney; six children.

67. iv. CHARLES MARION, b. in Campbell Co., Ga., in 1836.
    v. NANCY, b. in 1841; d. unm.
    vi. WILLIAM HALE, b. in Campbell Co., Ga., 1 June 1843; d. *s.p.* at Tazewell, Tenn., while in the Confederate service; m. GEORGIA DARNELL.
    vii. MARTHA ANN, b. in Campbell Co., Ga.; m. JOHN THOMAS FEELY. Residence, Douglasville, Ga. Children (surname *Feely*): 1. *William*, b. 8 Aug. 1867. 2. *Oscar*, b. 25 Aug. 1870; d. 5 Oct. 1898. 3. *John Thomas*, b. 11 Nov. 1872; m. 13 Aug. 1894 his second cousin, Kitty Morris (30, i, 2); eight children. 4. *Mollie*, b. 26 Mar. 1874. 5. *Fayette*, b. 14 Nov. 1877; m. 24 Sept. 1905 Lizzie Hunt. 6. *Minnie*, b. 23 June 1880; d. 17 Apr. 1916; m. 27 Dec. 1905 Stephen Baggett; one daughter.
    viii. AMANDA PAULINE, b. in Campbell Co., Ga., 6 June 1850; m. (1) in 1870 WILLIAM DAVID McGUIRE, who d. 30 Oct. 1884; m. (2) WILLIAM TAYLOR. Children by first husband (surname *McGuire*): 1. *Charles Polk*, b. in Douglas Co., Ga., 29 Nov. 1871; m. 12 Oct. 1904 Fannie Jobe, b. at Columbus, Miss., 19 Oct. 1880; three children. 2. *Joel Seaborn*, b. in Douglas Co., Ga., 11 Feb. 1874; m. 20 Jan. 1904 Lena Sayer; no issue. 3. *Mary Jane*, b. in Douglas Co., Ga., 9 Sept. 1876; m. Leonard Couch; three children. 4. *Maggie Evelyn*, b. in Douglas Co., Ga., 22 Sept. 1879; m. in Nov. 1904 Esker Henderson; one son. 5. *Edna Mae*, b. in Douglasville, Ga., 22 Oct. 1882; m. in July 1900 Thomas Virgil Lee; five children.
    ix. MARGARET VIANA, b. in Campbell Co., Ga., 30 Sept. 1853 [*sic*]; m. (1) 9 Apr. 1866 JAMES MELMETH DARNELL; m. (2) 6 June 1883 NICHOLAS JACKSON NEELY. Residence, Villa Rica, Ga. Children by first husband (surname *Darnell*): 1. *William Leonidas*, b. in Campbell Co., Ga., 8 Nov. 1867; m. (1) Minnie McGuire; m. (2) in Dec. 1918 Mrs. Hattie Ward; residence, Atlanta, Ga.; six children by first wife. 2. *Robert Young*, b. 4 June 1870; m. Winnie Grubbs; residence, Mussel Shoals, Ala.; one son. 3. *Alonzo Ezekiel*, b. in 1873; m. Ora Dorsett; eight children. 4. *Auzora*. Children by second husband (surname *Neely*): 5. *Haiden*, m. Mary Butler; five children. 6. *Myrtle*, m. Arthur Cole; ten children. 7. *Bertha Amanda*, m. Robert Cole; one child. 8. *Nicholas Jackson*, m. Clemmie Puckett; no issue.

30. CHARLES SHELBY[6] POLK (*Charles*,[5] *Capt. Charles*,[4] *William*,[3] *William*,[2] *Robert*[1]), born in Mecklenburg Co., N. C., 14 May 1814, died in Douglas Co., Ga., 10 July 1879. He married KATIE McLARTY, born in North Carolina in 1817, died in Douglas Co., Ga., in 1905, daughter of James and Sarah Ellen (Shelby).*

Children:

    i. SARAH E.,[7] b. in Campbell Co., Ga., 16 Apr. 1843; d. 22 Oct. 1909; m. JAMES MORRIS, who d. 19 June 1903. They resided in Douglas Co., Ga. Children (surname *Morris*): 1. *Hattie*, m. Mantell Vansant; six children. 2. *Kitty*, m. 13 Sept. 1894 her second

*Sarah Ellen Shelby was a daughter of Thomas and Sarah (Helms) Shelby. Her father, Thomas Shelby, was a son of Moses Shelby and Isobel, his wife, whose will of 1776 is on file at Charlotte, N. C.

cousin, John Thomas Feely (29, vii, 3), b. 11 Nov. 1872, s. of John Thomas and Martha Ann (Polk); eight children. 3. *Nola*, unm. 4. *Nellie*, m. her second cousin once removed, Charles Wesley Winn, s. of Charles Wesley (29, iii, 3) and Bettie (Kennedy); one daughter. 5. *Minnie*, m. John Kemp; eight children.

    ii. JAMES E., b. in Campbell Co., Ga., in 1845; d. unm. 7 Nov. 1888.
68. iii. CHARLES THOMAS, b. in Campbell Co., Ga., 23 Nov. 1850.
    iv. KATE, b. in Campbell Co., Ga.; m. JOHN GUY MAXWELL. Residence, Douglasville, Ga. Children (surname *Maxwell*): 1. *Pauline*, m. Benjamin Morris; four children. 2. *Anna*, m. James Van Davette, Jr.; one son. 3. *Cornelia*, m. Curley Baggett; two children. 4. *James Giboney*, unm.
    v. ELIZABETH, m. JAMES BEASLEY.

31. JOHN[6] POLK (*Charles,*[5] *Capt. John,*[4] *William,*[3] *William,*[2] *Robert*[1]), farmer, born, probably in Mecklenburg Co., N. C., about 1782, died in Nacogdoches Co., Tex., in 1866, "aged 84 years." He married ELIZABETH ALLEN of Kentucky, who died "aged 70 years."

He moved first to Tennessee, and lived near Bolivar; and all of his children were born in that State and most of them married there. About 1840 he moved to Texas.

Children:

69. i. CHARLES GRANDISON,[7] b. in Maury Co., Tenn., 12 Mar. 1811.
    ii. WILLIAM ALLEN, b. in Maury Co., Tenn., in 1813; m. MARTHA BARRETT. He remained in Tennessee when his parents moved to Texas. Children: 1. *Elizabeth Allen.*[8] 2. *Henrietta B.* 3. *James Knox.* 4. *John R.* 5. *Henry C.* 6. *Amanda*, m. Ben A. Shepherd. 7. *William Charles.*
    iii. MARGARET BENIGNA, b. in Tennessee 4 May 1819; d. at San Augustine, Tex., 22 Dec. 1899; m. in Tennessee, 27 Dec. 1837, DR. WILLIAM S. MASSEY, who d. at San Augustine in 1889, brother of Mary Ann Massey, who married Charles Grandison Polk (69), brother of Margaret Benigna Polk. Dr. and Mrs. Massey moved to Texas in 1839, buying land and settling in Walker Co., near Waverly, where they resided twelve years. Then they moved to Nacogdoches Co., and lived there until 1864, when they moved to San Augustine Co., and spent the rest of their days there. Dr. Massey gave up the practice of medicine and became a planter. He was a slaveholder, and bred and raised fine stock. Children (surname *Massey*): 1. *John H.*, b. in Linn Flat, Tex., 6 Aug. 1839; unm.; killed in the Battle of the Wilderness, 1864; he was a student at the University of Lebanon at the outbreak of the Civil War, returned home and enlisted in the First Texas Regiment, Hood's brigade, Confederate Army, and served until his death in battle. 2. *Joel Vincent*, b. 8 Dec. 1841; d. at Albany, Tex., in Feb. 1885; m. in 1869 Bettie Tucker; he served in the Confederate Army, lost his left foot in battle at Suffolk, Va., and was honorably discharged; he was a member of the Texas Legislature for several terms; in 1883 he moved to Albany, Tex., where he was a merchant and engaged also in cattle and sheep raising; five children. 3. *Emily*, b. 15 Feb. 1844; d. 23 May 1920; m. in 1864 Professor Peyton Irving; they had issue. 4. *Charles Polk*, b. 27 Jan. 1846; m. in 1868 Eliza Jones of Rusk, Tex.; in 1864 he joined the Fourth Texas Cavalry, Confederate Army, and served until the end of the War; six children. 5. *Cynthia Benigna*, b. 25 Aug. 1853; m. 25 Nov. 1886 George E. Gattling, a lawyer of San Augustine, Tex.; they have issue.
    iv. AMANDA M., b. in Tennessee in Apr. 1821; d. at Kemp, Tex., in June 1912; m. at San Augustine, Tex., 12 Mar. 1840, REV. RICHARD OVERTON WATKINS, b. near Clarksville, Tenn., 31 Mar. 1816,

d. at Kemp 27 May 1897, s. of Capt. Jesse, who was killed by Indians in Texas in Nov. 1838. He attended school in Sharon, Miss., went to Texas with his father in 1833 and settled in Clarksville in that State, and later moved to Nacogdoches Co. He was the first Presbyterian minister ordained in the Republic of Texas, the presbytery meeting on that occasion at old Fort Sam Houston. He was a soldier in the early Indian wars and in the Mexican War. He spent his adult years continuously in the ministry, and was much interested in the higher educational problems of his church in Texas. Children (surname *Watkins*): 1. *John Polk*, b. 22 Dec. 1840; d. 30 Jan. 1908; m. Lorena McCallum; he was a soldier in the Confederate Army; five children. 2. *Jesse Allen*, b. 1 May 1843; d. 21 Dec. 1911; m. Eudora Harr; four children. 3. *Richard Overton*, b. 6 Aug. 1846; d. unm. 20 Apr. 1919. 4. *Dr. William Archibald*, b. 4 June 1849; d. 16 June 1920; m. Jennie Noble; six children. 5. *Robert Smith*, b. 31 Jan. 1852; m. Morphia Collins; no issue. 6. *Mary Elizabeth*, b. 31 Oct. 1854; d. unm. 14 Jan. 1870. 7. *Judge Alfred Bacon*, of Athens, Tex., b. 14 Aug. 1857; m. Laura Murchison; he was graduated at Trinity University, Waxahachie, Tex., in 1877, studied law in Kauffman, Tex., was admitted to the bar in 1879, and is a lawyer of high standing; he served in 1892 and later as judge of the Third Judicial District of Texas, comprising Houston, Anderson, and Henderson Counties, and has held high office in the Masonic fraternity; one son.

v.   EMILY B., b. in Tennessee 25 Feb. 1827; d. 3 Jan. 1875; m. in San Augustine Co., Tex., 25 Feb. 1846, JOSIAH TAYLOR CHILDERS, b. in Giles Co., Tenn., 21 June 1817, d. in San Augustine Co. 10 Dec. 1879. He came to Texas in very early years, fought with the settlers against the Indians in Anderson Co., and served as captain in the Confederate Army. Children (surname *Childers*): 1. *Mary Elizabeth*, b. 3 Feb. 1847; m. 3 Oct. 1868 L. F. Branch; they had issue. 2. *John Polk*, b. 8 Feb. 1849; m. 27 Dec. 1874 Jennie Gilbert; he served his county as a land commissioner and for one term as a member of the State Legislature; residence, Shiro, Tex.; eight children. 3. *Charles Vaulton*, b. 23 Aug. 1851; d. in Oct. 1912; m. 2 Dec. 1879 Julia Ann Matthews; four children. 4. *Joseph William*, b. 17 Dec. 1853. 5. *James Micajah*, b. 22 Aug. 1856; m. 29 Aug. 1880 Margaret M. Kirksey, dau. of Dr. W. S. A. Kirksey of Palestine, Tex.; eight children. 6. *Richard Jackson*, b. 8 Apr. 1859; d. 14 Sept. 1860. 7. *Margaret Benigna*, b. 9 Aug. 1861; m. Frank Powell of Shelbyville, Tex. 8. *Emily Blanche*, b. 21 June 1864; m. at San Augustine, Tex., in Jan. 1881, J. William Gilbert. 9. *Alfred Lee*, b. 13 Aug. 1867; d. at San Augustine, Tex., 10 Oct. 1872. 10. *Ophelia Amanda*, b. 19 June 1873; d. 24 June 1894; m. Henry McKinney.

vi.   NANCY, m. in 1850 NORMAN P. BRANCH. Children (surname *Branch*): 1. *Elbert*, d. at San Antonio, Tex.; m. Jessett Beeson; he was a prominent lawyer of Nacogdoches, Tex., where he resided until his health failed, when he moved to San Antonio; no issue. 2. *Hood*, m. Della Kay of Starville, Tex. 3. *Kline Polk*, m. Flossie Smith; residence, Nacogdoches, Tex. 4. *Ella May*.

vii. VICTORIA, m. 28 Jan. 1856 WILLIAM BIRDWELL. They lived in Nacogdoches Co., and both died when their children were respectively seven and three years old. The children were brought up by their aunt, Mrs. Nancy (Polk) Branch (31, vi). Children (surname *Birdwell*): 1. *Charles Grandison*, m. Mary Gorman of Big Sandy, Tex.; both are now dead; he attended school in Nashville, Tenn., and on returning to Texas he and his sister moved to Smith Co. and lived at Winona; three children. 2. *Willie Allen*, m. 1 Jan. 1885 J. S. Kay; residence, Mission, Tex.

32. WILLIAM KNOX[6] POLK (*Charles,*[5] *Capt. John,*[4] *William,*[3] *William,*[2] *Robert*[1]), born probably in Mecklenburg Co., N. C., died near Holly Springs, Miss. He married NANCY PETTY.

They emigrated first to Tennessee and then, in later years, to Mississippi, where he was a cotton planter.

Children:

    i.   ISABELLA,[7] b. 7 Oct. 1815; d. in 1896; m. in 1834 DR. C. S. BOWEN. Children (surname *Bowen*): 1. *Emily,* b. in 1835; d. in 1865; m. in 1853 Dr. S. P. Lester of Batesville, Miss.; four children. 2. *Eliza,* b. 13 Sept. 1837; d. 11 Oct. 1909; m. 21 Apr. 1861 Dr. Wilbur F. Hyer; six children. 3. *David,* b. in 1839; d. in 1895; m. in 1870 Emma Kay; five children. 4. *Amanda,* b. in 1841; m. in 1865, as his third wife, Van H. Potts (*vide infra,* 32, ii, 1 and 2); five children. 5. *William Polk,* b. in 1844; m. in 1866 Alice Bost; he resides in Texas; three children. 6. *Mattie,* b. in 1846; m. in 1869 James S. Taylor; five children. 7. *Robert,* b. in 1848; unm. 8. *Christopher Strong,* b. in 1850; d. in 1885; m. in 1879 Georgia Mims; three children. 9. *Charles,* b. in 1852; d. in 1858. 10. *Alice,* b. in 1856; unm. 11. *Edward Reece,* b. in 1862; m. in 1891 Rose Eddins; one child.

    ii.   EMELINE, b. about 1817; m. PETER B. JONES. Children (surname *Jones*): 1. *Laura,* m. as his first wife, Van H. Potts, who m. (2) her sister Kate Jones (*vide infra*), and m. (3), in 1865, their first cousin, Amanda Bowen (32, i, 4), b. in 1841, dau. of Dr. C. S. and Isabella (Polk). 2. *Kate,* m. as his second wife, Van H. Potts, whose first wife was her sister, Laura Jones (*vide supra*); one daughter. 3. *Marshall Branch,* m. Ellen Nesbit, living as his widow at Memphis, Tenn.; six children. 4. *Lucius Polk,* m. Virginia Spencer, living as his widow in the West; four children. 5. *Mollie,* d. in 1897; m. W. W. Perkins; six children. 6. *Kate* [*sic*], m. Marshall Bouldin; one son. 7. *Lily,* now deceased; m. W. D. Porter of Oxford, Miss.; one son. 8. *Sue,* unm.

    iii. JANE, b. in 1819; d. in 1865; m. DR. R. S. LUCAS. Children (surname *Lucas*): 1. *Mollie J.* 2. *Baza,* d. unm.

    iv. LAURENTINE S., b. about 1821; d. unm., aged 27.

    v.   AMANDA, b. about 1823; d. young.

    vi. WILLIAM I., b. about 1825; m. (1) MAGGIE COOPWOOD; m. (2) MATTIE E. MOORE. Children by first wife: 1. *William C.*[8] 2. *Jessie Lee Forest.* 3. *Frank.* 4. *Alice L.*

33. JUDGE ALFRED[6] POLK (*Charles,*[5] *Capt. John,*[4] *William,*[3] *William,*[2] *Robert*[1]), born in Stewart Co., Tenn., 15 Dec. 1808, died in San Augustine Co., Tex., 22 Jan. 1891. He married in Tipton Co., 27 Dec. 1831, NANCY McIVOR, born in Chatham Co., N. C., 11 Feb. 1800.

He removed from Tipton Co., Tenn., to San Augustine Co., Tex., arriving there about 1 Feb. 1837. He was chief justice during the existence of the Republic of Texas, and, after Texas entered the Union, he remained in office for nine years. After eighteen years of public life he retired to his farm in San Augustine Co., and spent the rest of his days there.

Children:

    i.   CHARLES ISAAC[7] (twin), merchant, farmer, and real-estate dealer, b. in Tipton Co., Tenn., 9 Sept. 1832; d. in Texas 22 Mar. 1889, m. 21 Mar. 1860 VICTORIA THOMAS, b. in San Augustine Co., Tex;. 30 Jan. 1841, living (1923) at Beaumont, Tex., dau. of Iredell D. and Penelope (Edwards). He went to Texas with his parents in 1839, and grew up, lived, and died there. He served in the

Confederate Army. Children: 1. *Judge Harry K.*,[8] merchant,
farmer, and real-estate dealer, b. at San Augustine, Tex., 12 Feb.
1861; d. there 16 July 1915; m. there, 27 Dec. 1887, Ella Word
Burleson, dau. of James Marcus and his second wife, Mollie
(Alexander); he was a judge at San Augustine County at the
time of his death; seven children. 2. *Iredell D.*, b. at San Augustine,
Tex., 21 Mar. 1863; d. at Beaumont, Tex., 30 Aug. 1913; m. at
San Augustine, 28 Mar. 1889, Mamie Sims, dau. of T. William
and Bettie C.; he was a real-estate dealer and was interested
in the oil business; he moved to Beaumont in 1892, promoted
development projects in that city, and built the street railway
and the waterworks there; two children. 3. *James V.*, of Beaumont, Tex., real-estate dealer, unm.

ii. JOHN KENNETH (twin), farmer, b. in Tipton Co., Tenn., 9 Sept.
1832; d. in Texas 2 Oct. 1905; m. 24 Nov. 1881 MARY THOMAS,
who d. in 1909, dau. of a clergyman and cousin of Victoria Thomas,
wife of his twin brother, Charles Isaac Polk (*vide supra*). He
served in the Confederate Army. Children: 1. *Ludie Gertrude*,[8]
b. in 1882; m. in 1905 Murray B. Thomas; one child. 2. *Charles
[sic] Wesley*, b. in 1886; m. (1) in 1907 Charles Francis Sossman,
who d. 22 Feb. 1913; m. (2) W. B. Sherman; two children by first
husband and one daughter by second husband. 3. *John D.*, b. in
1892; d. in 1901.

iii. ANN ELIZABETH, b. in Tipton Co., Tenn., 24 Feb. 1834; m. at San
Augustine, Tex., 29 Apr. 1858, BENJAMIN E. SMITH, who d. 9 Feb.
1908. She resides at Coleman, Tex. Children (surname *Smith*):
1. *James Silas*, b. 4 Feb. 1859; d. 11 Apr. 1861. 2. *Alfred Polk*,
b. 28 Oct. 1860; d. 31 July 1905; m. 22 Dec. 1904 Ina Barfield;
one son, who d. in infancy. 3. *Eva Tyus*, b. 4 Nov. 1862; d. 31 Jan.
1885; m. in Feb. 1884 B. Hardeman. 4. *Benjamin E.*, of Coleman,
real-estate dealer, b. 28 Oct. 1865; m. 26 May 1896 Bettie Lowrie.
5. *L. Holman*, of Dallas, Tex., real-estate dealer, b. 18 Sept. 1867;
m. 17 Jan. 1893 Anne Swor. 6. *Nannie M.*, b. 3 Feb. 1870.
7. *Stonewall Jackson*, b. 27 Feb. 1872; m. 4 Mar. 1903 Emma
Margaret Lewis. 8. *Marlin Rocelius*, b. 8 Mar. 1874; m. 22 Aug.
1898 Mary E. Beard. 9. *Bland*, b. 28 May 1877; m. 24 May 1900
Jimmie Kate Dunn.

iv. SILAS GELASPY, a soldier in the Confederate Army, b. in Tipton Co.,
Tenn., 18 Feb. 1835; d. *s.p.* at San Augustine, Tex., in 1905; m.
ALTHEA McKNIGHT.

v.   DREW SMITH, a soldier in the Confederate Army, b. in Tipton Co.,
Tenn., in 1836; killed in action at Thompson's Station, Tenn.;
bur. in the Polk family burying ground near Columbia, Tenn.

vi. MARGARET CATHERINE, b. in San Augustine Co., Tex., 20 Dec.
1839; m. at San Augustine, Tex., in 1860, ROBERT WILLIAM
BROWNING, b. at Spartanburg, S. C., d. at San Augustine in 1865.
She resides at Orange, Tex. Her husband was a planter and
slaveholder, and rendered service to the Confederate forces in
the Civil War, superintending the construction of breastworks
at Sabine Pass and furnishing supplies to the Army. His slaves
remained loyal to the family, and assisted in this work. Children
(surname *Browning*): 1. *Annie Robert*, b. at San Augustine 21
Oct. 1862; m. in San Augustine Co., 10 Oct. 1888, Joseph H.
Porcher, farmer, b. in the Beaufort District, S. C., 26 Jan. 1844;
he served in the Confederate Army, first in Hampton's legion,
and after the reorganization in Company B, Second South Carolina
Cavalry. 2. *Katherine Priscilla*, b. 25 Feb. 1865; m. at San
Augustine, 19 Dec. 1883, John Albert Slaughter, b. 2 Apr. 1861,
s. of Thaddeus (who was killed in battle in the Confederate Army,
near Yazoo City, Miss.) and Ollie (Teel) (dau. of George and
Rebecca); three children.

vii. MARY CYNTHIA (twin), b. in San Augustine Co., Tex., 21 Nov.
1841; d. 8 Aug. 1918; m. in San Augustine Co., 21 June 1867,

LUDWELL RECTOR DAVIS, b. five miles from San Augustine, Tex., on the King's Highway, 10 Aug. 1828, d. 28 Aug. 1915. He was a very young child, when, on General Santa Anna's advance into Texas, his mother and other women, with their families and servants, retreated across the Sabine River. He went to California in 1852 and resided at San Francisco until 1859, when he returned to Texas. He served in the Confederate Army throughout the Civil War, and after the War made his home in Texas. Children (surname *Davis*): 1. *Drew Smith*, physician, b. 4 May 1868; d. 20 Oct. 1918; m. in Apr. 1901 Effie May Greer; five children. 2. *William Thomas*, lawyer and former district judge, b. 1 Mar. 1870; m. 1 Oct. 1892 Fanny B. Price; six children. 3. *Elias Kincheloe*, b. 17 May 1872; d. *s.p.* 21 Oct. 1914; m. 2 Mar. 1908 Anna Hill. 4. *Margaret Isabella*, b. 18 Mar. 1874. 5. *Anna Browning*, b. 26 Apr. 1876; m. 23 Oct. 1912 A. W. Nicholson. 6. *Mary Johnnie*, b. 13 June 1878. 7. *Alfred Polk*, b. 1 Nov. 1880; unm. 8. *Ludwell Rector*, b. 16 Dec. 1882; m. 16 Dec. 1905 Hattie Anderson. 9. *Kate Winifred*, b. 5 July 1888; d. 19 Mar. 1890.

viii. WILLIAM ALFRED (twin), b. in San Augustine Co., Tex., 21 Nov. 1841; d. unm. at the old homestead near San Augustine, Tex., 19 July 1922. In the Civil War he served in Whitfield's legion in the Confederate Army, in the First Cavalry Company, commanded by Capt. John H. Broocks (*vide infra*, 36, iii), then, after Captain Broocks was promoted to a colonelcy, by his brother, Capt. James A. Broocks, until the latter was killed at the Battle of Thompson's Station, Tenn., and after that by Capt. James Ingram. He was taken prisoner, but escaped, and served to the end of the War. After the death of his father he owned and lived on the family homestead. He was an elder of McRea Church.

70. ix. ANDREW TYLER, b. in Texas 21 Mar. 1846.

x. SARAH ISABELLA, b. at San Augustine, Tex., 21 Mar. 1848; d. at Shelbyville, Tex., 25 July 1916; m. 7 Feb. 1867 GEORGE MALONE SMITH, merchant, brother of Benjamin E. Smith, the husband of her sister, Ann Elizabeth (33, iii). Children (surname *Smith*): 1. *Charles Polk*, b. 31 Dec. 1867; m. Benigna Massey. 2. *Margaret Isabella*, b. 30 Nov. 1869; m. John W. Porcher. 3. *Janie Elizabeth*, b. 7 June 1872; deceased. 4. *George Malone*, physician, b. 13 Mar. 1874; m. Lousetta Sharp. 5. *Gussie Evaline*, b. 6 May 1876; deceased. 6. *Robert Benjamin*, b. 5 Mar. 1878. 7. *Byron John*, b. 7 Apr. 1880. 8. *Thomas Huntington*, b. 17 Jan. 1882. 9. *Tolbert Tyus*, b. 28 Jan. 1885. 10. *Annie May*, b. 16 Dec. 1887.

34. BENJAMIN D. A.[6] POLK (*John*,[5] *Capt. John*,[4] *William*,[3] *William*,[2] *Robert*[1]), born, probably in the Greenbrier District of western Virginia, 1 Jan. 1790, died at San Augustine, Tex., 2 June 1840. He married in Tennessee, 26 Sept. 1816, MARGARET R. MOORE, born 10 Oct. 1797, living in 1842, daughter of James and Katherine.

He moved from Tennessee to Texas in 1839, and settled in San Augustine Co.

There is on file in Maury Co., Tenn., the power of attorney of his widow, as guardian of her minor children, issued by the Probate Court of San Augustine Co., Tex., to collect money due her children under the will of their grandfather, John Polk of Carter's Creek, near Columbia, Tenn. The probate records of San Augustine County show that on 28 Sept. 1840 Henry Brooks, husband of the oldest daughter of Benjamin D. A. Polk, was appointed administrator of the estate of his father-in-law, and that on 10 Nov. 1842 the petition of Henry

Brooks for the partition of the estate between himself, Margaret R. Polk, the widow, and the five minor children was granted. The minors named in the partition were Lucius, Franklin, Margaret Jane, Robert Green, and Sarah R.

Children:

i.   ELIZABETH ANN,[7] b. in Maury Co., Tenn., 19 Oct. 1817; d. in San Augustine Co., Tex., 14 Oct. 1844; m. in Tennessee, 25 Feb. 1836, HENRY BROOKS, b. in Tennessee 27 Dec. 1810, d. on his farm, six miles west of San Augustine, Tex., 8 Oct. 1858, s. of Joseph, who migrated to Texas in very early days. He m. (2) 28 Aug. 1845 Mary Jane Ellison; and m. (3) 3 Jan. 1856 Nancy Hollis. Children (surname *Brooks*): 1. *Joseph*, b. 6 Dec. 1836; m. in 1865 Eliza Randal. 2. *Sidney*, b. 30 Oct. 1838. 3. *Sarah Viola*, b. 10 Apr. 1840; m. in San Augustine Co., Tex., 18 Apr. 1860, John Burleson, who d. 10 Mar. 1885, s. of Joseph; two children. 4. *William*, b. 1 Nov. 1842.

ii.   JAMES MOORE, b. 19 Mar. 1820; d. unm. 24 Mar. 1840.

iii. JOHN, b. 12 May 1822; d. 1 June 1822.

iv.   LUCIUS B., b. 2 June 1823; d. in Feb. 1910; m. MAGGIE MILLER. Children: 1. *Benjamin F.*,[8] b. in San Augustine Co. 3 Mar. 1862; d. in San Augustine Co. 9 Nov. 1904; m. in San Augustine Co., 11 Dec. 1900, Mary Runnels, dau. of Jason W. and Mary Elizabeth (Heusherling), who m. (2) J. W. Bryan; he was a stockman, owning and operating several farms; two children. 2. *Matthew*, m. Mary Border. 3. *Mollie*, m. B. F. Sharp, s. of Dr. James. 4. *Jane Margaret*, b. 4 Aug. 1874; m. 12 Oct. 1893 William W. Johnson, b. at Decatur, Miss., 18 Nov. 1862. 5. *Kate*, m. Brune Wall. 6. *Edna*, m. Randolph Nobles.

v.   VIOLA CATHERINE, b. 4 Sept. 1825; d. unm. 7 July 1840.

vi.   FRANKLIN ARMSTEAD, b. 1 Dec. 1827; d. unm. 24 June 1843.

vii. MARY OPHELIA, b. 13 Oct. 1829; d. 28 July 1836.

viii. JOHN THADDEUS, b. 17 Mar. 1832; d. 16 Oct. 1832.

ix.   MARGARET JANE, b. 1 Nov. 1833; m. WYATT F. TEEL, one of Austin's Texas colonists. They lived in Tenaha, Tex., and had issue.

x.   ROBERT GREEN, b. 13 Apr. 1836; d. 5 Aug. 1852.

xi.   SARAH ROBINA, b. 19 Apr. 1838; m. (1) JOSEPH BURLESON; m. (2) JOHN C. PRITCHETT.

35. EVAN SHELBY[6] POLK (*John,[5] Capt. John,[4] William,[3] William,[2] Robert[1]*), born, probably in the Greenbrier District of western Virginia, 16 Dec. 1791, died at Huntsville, Ark., 23 Oct. 1878. He married, 18 July 1818, JANE MILLER of Carter's Creek, Maury Co., Tenn., born 17 Apr. 1804, died 29 Mar. 1872. Both are buried at Huntsville.

He migrated to Tennessee with his father's family, and moved thence to Arkansas in 1836. He served in the War of 1812 as corporal in the Tennessee Militia, from 10 Dec. 1812 to 30 Apr. 1813 in Capt. Henry Newland's company and from 18 Dec. 1813 to 15 Feb. 1814 in Capt. James McMahon's company.

Children:

i.   THOMAS CALVIN,[7] b. 27 Apr. 1820; d. in infancy.

71. ii.   WILLIAM VINCENT, b. 9 Mar. 1822.

iii.   MARY ELIZABETH, b. 5 Nov. 1824; d. 22 Nov. 1867; bur. at Huntsville, Ark.; m. (1) ——— SANDERS; m. (2) DR. ISAAC B. McREYNOLDS. Child by first husband (surname *Sanders*): 1. *Drusilla*, d. in childhood. Child by second husband (surname *McReynolds*): 2. *Evan Shelby Polk*, b. 31 Mar. 1855; living near Hollister, Okla.; m. (1) 25 July 1877 Laura S. Vandersickle, who

d. 5 Apr. 1893; m. (2) 3 Sept. 1894 Mary Elizabeth Coffee; four children by first wife and two daughters by second wife.

72. iv. JOHN SHELBY, b. 9 Nov. 1827.
   v. LONZY FRANCES, b. 14 Sept. 1830; d. in childhood.
73. vi. BENJAMIN RUFUS, b. in Maury Co., Tenn., 3 June 1833.
  vii. ROBERT BRUCE, b. 23 Feb. 1836; d. unm. 12 May 1876.
 viii. VIOLA TRANQUILLA, b. at Huntsville, Ark., 22 June 1838; d. at Fayetteville, Ark., 1 Oct. 1911; m. 11 Mar. 1853 CHARLES BURTON SANDERS, b. at Huntsville 14 Feb. 1836, d. there 18 Sept. 1898. Children (surname *Sanders*): 1. *Isabel Malvin*, b. at Huntsville 15 Nov. 1855; d. at Portales, N. Mex., 7 Mar. 1909; m. 6 Mar. 1872 Albert A. Brodie, b. in 1848, d. in Aug. 1911; four children. 2. *Bruce*, b. 18 Oct. 1857; d. in 1859. 3. *Cener Boon*, b. 21 Feb. 1859; m. 23 Feb. 1902 Judge Jefferson Taylor Hight, b. at Rover, Ark., 25 Aug. 1848, d. at Riverside, Calif., 24 Apr. 1917; no issue. 4. *Mediline*, b. in 1861; d. in 1866. 5. *Collister*, b. in 1863; d. in 1866. 6. *Nathaniel Lee*, b. 16 Mar. 1865; m. at Huntsville, Ark., 25 Dec. 1884, Lutie Berry; five children. 7. *Albert Bruce*, b. 9 Aug. 1867; m. 25 Nov. 1886 Mary Skaggs; five children.
  ix. MARTHA JANE, b. in 1840; d. in 1859; m. YOUNG BEARD. One child, who d. in infancy.
   x. CHARLES KING, b. in 1843; d. in 1917; m. DRUSILLA WILLIAMS. Child: 1. *Elmer E.*,[8] b. in 1875; m. Ollie Massie; one son, who d. in infancy.
   x. JAMES KNOX, b. in 1849; d. in infancy.

Horace Moore Polk, Jr., son of Horace Moore & Ophelia (Bills) Polk. *From Alice M. Fitts, Okla. City.*

Mary Louise (Campbell) Polk, wife of Horace Moore Polk, Jr. *From Alice Mitchum Fitts, Oklahoma City.*

L. to R. Mary Lizinka, Alice Ophelia, Allen Campbell, & Horace Moore Polk III, children of Horace Moore Polk, Jr. *From Alice Mitchum Fitts.*

36. JOHN[6] POLK (*John,*[5] *Capt. John,*[4] *William,*[3] *William,*[2] *Robert*[1]), born, probably in the Greenbrier District of western Virginia, 25 Oct. 1798, died in Madison Co., Tex., 14 Feb. 1864. He married first, probably in Tipton Co., Tenn., 28 Oct. 1825, his first cousin, CYNTHIA SPRINGS[6] POLK (13, v), born, probably in western Tennessee, 25 Feb. 1801, died in Leon Co., Tex., 28 Aug. 1855, daughter of Charles and Margaret (Baxter); secondly, 30 July 1856, MRS. MARY (FLOYD) McILHENNY, who died 22 June 1859; and thirdly, at Leona, Leon Co., Tex., 10 Dec. 1861, NANCY NEWSOME, born in Georgia 2 Nov. 1842, died at Madisonville, Tex., 14 July 1865, daughter of Nathaniel and Susan (Jones) of Georgia, who had migrated to Texas.

On 16 Aug. 1828 his father, in a deed recorded in the register's office of Maury Co., Tenn. (Book iv, page 163), "for the love and affection he bore him," conveyed to him land; and this conveyance probably accounts for the absence of his name from his father's will, as it was, no doubt, considered his share in the family fortune. He transferred this land on the same day to his brother, Evan Shelby Polk (35).

He moved to Texas with the family of his uncle, Charles Polk (13), in 1839, and lived successively in San Augustine, Leon, and Madison Counties. He was a planter and stockman, and was grand master of Rising Star Chapter No. 9, a Masonic lodge at San Augustine, Tex.

Children by first wife:

i.   ISAAC CARLO,[7] b., probably in Tipton Co., Tenn., 15 Oct. 1826; d. unm. in Texas 18 Mar. 1852. He served in the Texas Legislature.

ii. MARGARET OLIVIA, b. in Tipton Co., Tenn., 22 Apr. 1829; m. at San Augustine, Tex., 3 Sept. 1846, Rev. E. F. Foster, minister of the Gospel, officiating, COL. JAMES MARCUS[4] BURLESON, b. in Missouri in 1823, d. in San Augustine Co., Tex., 9 Oct. 1895, eldest s. of Joseph.* Colonel Burleson, who was a very prominent planter and stockman of San Augustine County, m. (2) Mollie Alexander, and by her had two daughters, Florence, who m. Capt. A. Phillips, and Ella Wood, who m. Judge Harry K.[8] Polk (33, i, 1), *q.v.* Children (surname *Burleson*): 1. *Priscilla*, d. young. 2. *Jerome*, d. young. 3. *Joseph*, a planter and stockman of San Augustine Co., b. 21 Jan. 1852; now deceased; m. Kate King. 4. *Edward Carlo*, d. young. 5. *James Marcus*, a prominent rancher and stockman, living in San Augustine Co. in 1923; m. Elizabeth Border; four children.

iii. ELIZABETH JEROME, b. in Tipton Co., Tenn., 31 Jan. 1831; d. at San Augustine, Tex., 3 Sept. 1900; m. in Leon Co., Tex., in July 1854, COL. JOHN H. BROOCKS, b. near Columbia, Tenn., 12 Oct. 1829, d. in San Augustine Co., Tex., 16 Apr. 1901, s. of Gen. Travis Green and Elizabeth Ann (Morris).† John H. Broocks served in the Mexican War in 1846, under General Taylor, in Capt. O. M. Wheeler's company; and throughout the Civil War he served in the Confederate Army, first as captain of a company which he had raised in San Augustine in 1861 and afterwards as major and colonel. His service was principally in Ross's brigade. His brother, James A. Broocks, who succeeded on his promotion to the command of the company, led it and was killed in the battle of Thompson's Station, Tenn. John H. Broocks was a planter in San Augustine. Children (surname *Broocks*): 1. *A daughter*, b. and d. in 1855. 2. *Travis Green*, b. in 1856; d. in 1859. 3. *Cynthia*

*This Burleson family was of Welsh origin, and was descended from Aaron[1] Burleson, who came to North Carolina in 1726 and reared seven sons and six daughters. All his sons served in the Revolution, three falling in battle and the youngest, Capt. Edward Burleson, being captured by the British and shot, when on his way to be married. At the end of the Revolutionary War one of the sons, Aaron,[2] set out for Kentucky, but was killed by the Indians at Clinch River, in Tennessee. His son Aaron[3] was killed at Campbell's Station, Tenn., but the other sons, James,[3] Joseph,[3] and John,[3] pressed on to Kentucky, and thence moved to Tennessee. In 1816 Joseph[3] moved on to Missouri, but returned to Tennessee, and then moved to Texas in 1829. He was the father of Col. James Marcus Burleson, the husband of Margaret Olivia Polk (36, ii). Soon after the Civil War the Burlesons moved to Navarro Co., Tex., with the exception of Col. James Marcus Burleson, who remained in San Augustine Co. In 1889 Rev. Rufus Burleson, D.D., president of Baylor College, Tex., published a pamphlet on the Burleson family, in which some of the prominent members of the family are mentioned. The family played an important part in the early history of Texas.

†Gen. Travis Green Broocks moved from the neighborhood of Columbia, Tenn., to San Augustine Co., Tex., in 1838, with his wife and sons, John H., Moses A., and James A. He was a contractor and a merchant before settling down on his plantation, and he owned nearly one hundred slaves. He fought in the early Texan wars, and died in San Augustine Co. in 1865, "aged 56 years."

Elizabeth, d. young. 4. *Margaret Eugenia*, b. at San Augustine
22 Apr. 1860; living in 1923 at Dallas, Tex.; m. 2 Sept. 1884
Hon. George Clapp Greer, S.B. (Vanderbilt University, 1883*),
b. in San Augustine Co., Tex., 24 Apr. 1862, d. at the Johns
Hopkins Hospital, Baltimore, Md., 7 May 1920, s. of Dr. Lewis
Vance and Maria Blakely (McLauren); he was a lawyer of high
repute, was a member of the Texas Senate from San Augustine Co.
for one term, and was a trustee of Vanderbilt University; he was
a partner in business with his brother, John A. Greer; in 1896 he
removed from San Augustine to Beaumont, Tex., and lived there
until 1914, when he moved to Dallas, where he was general attorney for the Magnolia Petroleum Company; three sons.† 5.
John Henry, of Beaumont, Tex., lawyer, planter, and real-estate
dealer, b. at San Augustine 15 Mar. 1862; m. 26 Aug. 1906 Mrs.
Laura Sims (Allen) Broocks, b. at Frankfort, Ky., 4 Feb. 1874,
dau. of William H. and Ara Julian (Sims) Allen and widow of his
brother, Benjamin Carlo Broocks (36, iii, 7); one daughter. 6.
Hon. Moses Lycurgus, LL.B. (University of Texas, 1891), b. in
San Augustine Co. 1 Nov. 1864; d. unm. at San Augustine 27
May 1908; he was educated in the common schools of San Augus-
tine Co., studied law at the University of Texas, served in the
Texas Legislature in 1892, moved to Beaumont, Jefferson Co.,
Tex., was elected district attorney of the First Judicial District of
Texas in 1896, represented the San Augustine district in the
United States House of Representatives in the Fifty-ninth Con-
gress (1905–1907), and then resumed the practice of his profession
at San Augustine. 7. *Benjamin Carlo*, b. in San Augustine Co.
19 Apr. 1866; killed at San Augustine 2 June 1900; m. at Rich
Hill, Bates Co., Mo., 4 Sept. 1894, Laura Sims Allen, who m. (2)
her first husband's brother, John Henry Broocks (36, iii, 5), *q.v.*;
three children. 8. *Ella Jerome*, b. in 1869; d. in infancy.
  iv. EUGENIA, b. in Tipton Co., Tenn., 27 July 1834; d. in Texas 24
Jan. 1864; m. in Leon Co., Tex., 13 Oct. 1855, DR. THOMAS
BISER DAVENPORT‡ of Nashville, Tenn., b. 7 Feb. 1831, d. in
Leon Co. 11 Dec. 1863. He was a physician, and as a young man
served as secretary to his uncle, who was United States minister
to Peru.   Children (surname *Davenport*): 1. *Mary Cynthia*, b.
in Leon Co. 18 July 1856; living in 1923; m. at Pittsburg, Tex.,
24 July 1876, Matthew Cartwright, Jr., b. 11 Aug. 1855, living in
1923, s. of Matthew and Amanda (Holman), who came in 1834
to San Augustine, Tex., from the old Cartwright home at Lebanon,
Tenn.; his grandfather, John Cartwright, was one of the early

*He received the Founder's Medal there for attaining the highest general average in his studies.
†The three sons of Hon. George Clapp and Margaret Eugenia (Broocks) Greer are: 1. Lewis
Vance, LL.B., of Dallas, Tex., b. at San Augustine 13 June 1885; m. at Denver, Colo., 27 Jan.
1910, Muriel Jarvis Millar, dau. of Stocks and Margaret (Richards). He was graduated at the
United States Military Academy at West Point in 1907, remained in the Army five years as a
lieutenant and then resigned his commission, studied law at the University of Texas and received
his degree in law, and began the practice of his profession. He volunteered for service in the
World War, and was commissioned captain and promoted to be major and colonel before the war
ended. He served with the Ninetieth Division Ammunition Trains, American Expeditionary
Forces, and was in the Army of Occupation six months after the Armistice. He is assistant attorney for the Magnolia Petroleum Company. 2. John Broocks, B.A. (University of the South,
1908), b. at San Augustine 5 Feb. 1887; m. at Shreveport, La., 26 Nov. 1912, Nita Whited,
dau. of Frank Thayer and Emma (Bowman) (Gordon). He is in the oil business in Louisiana and
Oklahoma. 3. George Jerome, of Shreveport, La., b. at Beaumont, Tex., 16 Feb. 1898. He was
graduated at the Lawrenceville (N. J.) School, and was a student at Vanderbilt University when
the United States entered the World War. He volunteered for service, and served as a private,
corporal, and sergeant, going overseas with the One Hundred and Thirty-third Field Artillery,
Thirty-sixth Division. In a competitive examination for assignment to the Saumur School of
Artillery and Equestration in France he was ranked first, and was commissioned second lieutenant.
After the war he studied at Princeton University, and now resides at Shreveport, La., where he
is manager of the Caddo Steel Products Company.
  ‡Dr. Davenport was a grandson of James and Mary (Rutherford) Davenport of Goochland
Co., Va. See record of their marriage in the *William and Mary College Quarterly Historical
Magazine*, vol. 8, p. 94.

settlers of Texas, represented the United States Government in taking possession of Texas, in order to strengthen its claims to the Rio Grande instead of the Sabine River as the western boundary line of the Louisiana Purchase, built the first cotton gin in Texas, and was one of the founders of the Methodist Episcopal Church, South, in Texas; for twenty years Matthew Cartwright, Jr., was president of the First National Bank of Terrell, Tex., besides being engaged in live-stock and agricultural interests; he was mayor of Terrell for two terms; his wife has served as chairman of the Associated Charities, president of the Pioneer Club, district president of the State Federation of Women's Clubs, and district chairman of the Red Cross in the World War; residence, Terrell; ten children. 2. *John de Kalb*, b. 7 July 1858; d. 27 Oct. 1859. 3. *Eugene Beauregard*, b. 15 Apr. 1861; d. 30 Oct. 1863. 4. *Elizabeth de Kalb*, b. in Leona, Leon Co., Tex., 11 May 1863; m. at Pittsburg, Camp Co., Tex., 3 Oct. 1881, Dr. Samuel Miller Gladney of Terrell, Tex., physician, b. at Harmony Hall, Henderson Co., Tex., 20 July 1854, d. at Terrell; four children.

v.   JOHN DE KALB, b. at San Augustine, Tex., 10 Nov. 1839; m. in Leon Co., Tex., 10 Nov. 1857, ELIZABETH BILLS. He served throughout the Civil War in the Confederate Army as captain of Company D, Gould's battalion of Texas Cavalry, Walker's division, in the Trans-Mississippi Department. Children: 1. *James H.*,[8] b. in Leon Co. 8 Sept. 1858; d. in Louisiana in 1906. 2. *William*, b. in Leon Co. in 1862; d. at Eagle Pass, Tex., in 1886. 3. *Benjamin Carlo*, b. in Leon Co. in 1865; killed in a train wreck at or near Austin, Tex., in 1898; d. unm. 4. *Fessonia*, b. in Titus Co., Tex., 27 Oct. 1869; m. 27 Oct. 1886 David A. Blake; residence, Lometa, Tex.; five children.

vi.   BENJAMIN CARLO, b. in San Augustine, Tex., 20 Feb. 1843; d. unm. in western Texas after the Civil War. He served in the Confederate Army as a bugler in Terry's Rangers. Among the historical objects in the old Land Office Museum at Austin, Tex., is the bugle which he used in the war.

Children by second wife:

vii.   BETTY GEORGIANA (twin), b. 18 July 1857; m. about 1881 FRANK HUDGEONS. They moved to Parker Co., Tex., and then to Marthaville, La.

viii.   ERASMUS (twin), b. 18 July 1857; d. in infancy.

Child by third wife:

ix.   ALMONTE LEE, b. at Madisonville, Tex., 12 Sept. 1863; m. at Houston, Tex., 27 Nov. 1894, FRANK L. WILDER of San Antonio, Tex., b. in Illinois. She now lives at San Antonio. Child (surname *Wilder*): 1. *Greeta*, b. at San Augustine, Tex., 6 Nov. 1897; m. at San Antonio, 15 June 1914, Nelson Cory, b. at Norfolk, Va., 2 July 1885, s. of William Henry Harrison and Martha Eley (Blanchard); one son, Nelson, b. 31 Aug. 1915.

37. FRANKLIN ARMSTEAD[6] POLK (*John*,[5] *Capt. John*,[4] *William*,[3] *William*,[2] *Robert*[1]), born, probably in the Greenbrier District of western Virginia, 10 Apr. 1804, died in Maury Co., Tenn., 2 June 1887. He married first, in 1824, MARY ELIZA STEVENS, who died 2 Aug. 1862; and secondly, in June 1870, EMELINE WINIFRED (LANE) HANCOCK.

He was executor of his father's will, being named in the will as "my son F. A. Polk."

Children by first wife:

OPHELIA ELIZABETH HINES,[7] b. in Maury Co. 18 Apr. 1829; d. 10 Nov. 1894; m. 9 Sept. 1847 DAVID MITCHELL KENNARD. Chil-

54   *The Polks of North Carolina and Tennessee*

dren (surname *Kennard*): 1. *Eliza Adeline*, b. 4 Feb. 1849; d. 19 Feb. 1902; m. 17 Nov. 1867 Felix Polk McGaughey; three children. 2. *Michael*, b. 12 May 1851; d. in infancy. 3. *Mary Elizabeth*, b. 5 July 1852; d. in childhood. 4. *Sallie Foster*, b. 26 Jan. 1855; d. 18 July 1871. 5. *James Knox Polk*, b. 22 Apr. 1857; d. 30 June 1873. 6. *Anna Laura*, b. 3 Nov. 1859; d. 10 Mar. 1875. 7. *David Della Morgan*, b. in Maury Co. 28 Feb. 1862; m. 11 Aug. 1886 William Hardy Blackburn, b. 10 Oct. 1859; five children. 8. *Rebecca Novaline*, b. in Maury Co. 15 Dec. 1869; m. 24 Nov. 1895 Isaac Langsdon; six children.

 ii. REBECCA NOVALINE, b. in Maury Co. 25 Jan. 1831; m. (1) 6 Oct. 1849 WILLIAM JAMES MILLER; m. (2) FRANKLIN ELIEZER AKIN. Children by first husband (surname *Miller*): 1. *Franklin A.* 2. *Cameron.* Children by second husband (surname *Akin*): 3. *William Polk.* 4. *Myrtle.* 5. *Emma Winifred.*

 iii. MARY ELIZA, b. 2 July 1834; d. unm. 2 Sept. 1854.

 iv. SALLIE ANN, b. in Maury Co. 29 Oct. 1836; d. *s.p.* 10 Mar. 1867; m. COL. WILLIAM ADDISON FOSTER of Tennessee, who served in the Confederate Army.

74. v. JAMES KNOX, b. in Maury Co. 23 May 1839.

38. TAYLOR[6] POLK (*Taylor,*[5] *Capt. John,*[4] *William,*[3] *William,*[2] *Robert*[1]), planter, born near Nashville, Davidson Co., Tenn., in 1800, died in Texas 2 June 1886. He married first, near Hot Springs, Ark., PRUDENCE ANDERSON, daughter of James;* secondly MRS. EVELYN (JAMES) CARLEY, widow of Hiram Carley (both were born in the old Wilkes Co., N. C., and migrated to Arkansas); and thirdly ―――― BURKE.

He was taken with his father's family to Arkansas in 1808, and grew up in the Valley of the Ouachita. When his sons were grown, before the Civil War, they moved to Texas.

Children by first wife:

 i. ELEANOR (ELLEN),[7] b. in the Valley of the Ouachita, in Arkansas, 27 Oct. 1823; m. DANIEL McKINLEY HUDDLESTON, b. 27 Apr. 1817. Children (surname *Huddleston*): 1. *Prudence*, m. Joseph Story of Centre Point, Ark., farmer; seven children. 2. *Daniel*, m. Asa Stimsen; six children. 3. *Jane*, m. Moses Williams. 4. *Rachel*, m. Jefferson Cunningham. 5. *Thomas*, m. Jane Polk. 6. *Katherine*, m. James Stevens.

75. ii. ANDERSON, b. in the Valley of the Ouachita, in Arkansas, 14 Sept. 1824.

76. iii. CUMBERLAND, b. 4 Nov. 1830.

77. iv. HENRY CLAY, b. near Mount Ida, Montgomery Co., Ark., 28 Jan. 1833.

78. v. SYLVESTER WALKER, b. in Montgomery Co., Ark., 29 Jan. 1835.

 vi. MITCHELL ANDERSON, b. 3 June 1836; d. aged 16 years.

 vii. SARAH DELANEY, b. in Montgomery Co., Ark., 22 Dec. 1837; m. CAPT. GEORGE T. EPPERSON, brother of Eliza Epperson, who m. Sarah Delaney Polk's brother, Anderson Polk (75). Captain Epperson served in the Confederate Army, and was a wealthy property owner in Arkansas. Children (surname *Epperson*): 1. *Mary*, m. Blount Bullock; two children. 2. *Peyton*, m. Emma Rose; six children. 3. *Taylor*, m. Sarah Bush; five children. 4. *Isabella*, m. George Jacobs; six children.

 viii. TAYLOR, b. in Montgomery Co., Ark., 22 Nov. 1839; m. 20 Aug. 1858 MARY ANN PETTY, b. 10 Dec. 1840. Both are living in Oklahoma. He joined the Confederate Army, at Little Rock,

*James Anderson migrated from North Carolina to Missouri and thence moved to Arkansas. His children were: 1. Henry. 2. Mitchell, m. Jency Polk. 3. Sarah. 4. Prudence, m. Taylor Polk (38).

Ark., as a private in the Cavalry, was made a sergeant, and for a time during the fighting at Corinth, Miss., commanded his company. He was disabled by wounds and discharged, but in one year had so far recovered that he enlisted in a Cavalry company, went to the frontier of Texas, and served until the end of the war. Children: 1. *Laura*,[8] b. 20 May 1859. 2. *Augusta*, b. 25 Nov. 1860. 3. *Mary Bell*, b. 15 Oct. 1863. 4. *James K.*, b. 10 Dec. 1866. 5. *Lee* (twin), b. in 1868. 6. *Lala* (twin), b. in 1868. 7. *William*, b. 15 Apr. 1870. 8. *Henry*, b. 10 Apr. 1872. 9. *Leonidas*, b. 20 Nov. 1874. 10. *Myrtle*, b. 10 June 1876. 11. *Beverly Porter*, b. 18 Mar. 1878.

 ix. PRUDENCE, b. in Pike Co., Ark., 7 Apr. 1842; d. at Denton, Tex., 4 Jan. 1922; m. BEVERLY RANDOLPH DICKSON, farmer. Children (surname *Dickson*), the eldest b. in Pike Co., Ark., the others at Black Jack Grove (now Cumby), Tex.: 1. *Charles Mitchell*, b. 7 July 1863; d. *s.p.* in Mar. 1892; m. in 1884 Carrie Young. 2. *Minnie E.*, b. 12 Jan. 1869; m. 21 June 1885 Oscar M. Smith, M.D.; she is prominent in women's circles, and has been at the head of the State organizations of the Eastern Star and Daughters of Rebecca in Texas; three children. 3. *William Beverly*, of Mineola, Tex., cotton buyer, b. 10 July 1870; m. (1) Georgiana Epperson, who d. in Arkansas in 1909; m. (2) in 1913 Mrs. Ada Harris; two children by first wife. 4. *Larissa Lee* (*Pearl*), b. 18 Jan. 1874; m. in 1890 Russell J. Williams; two children. 5. *Ethel Prudence*, b. 18 Apr. 1877; m. 29 Sept. 1896 George W. Holland, b. at Petersburg, Tenn., 18 Mar. 1869; twelve children.

 x. ALFRED SAPINGTON, farmer and cattleman, b. in 1845; d. at his home, a farm three miles from La Junta, Colo., 30 July 1890; m. SARAH WILSON. Children: 1. *Sylvester*.[8] 2. *Burt*. 3. *Mabel*. 4. *James*. Probably others, including a son named *Alfred*.

39. JAMES[6] POLK (*Taylor*,[5] *Capt. John*,[4] *William*,[3] *William*,[2] *Robert*[1]), born near Nashville, Davidson Co., Tenn., in 1801, died in Arkansas 28 Feb. 1836. He married first NANCY TRAMMELL; and secondly SARAH (SALLY) COX, daughter of Joel and Frances (Bartlett), who migrated from Kentucky to Arkansas in 1816, and sister of Nancy Cox, who married Cumberland Polk (40), brother of James Polk.

He went to Arkansas when a child (1808), with his parents.
Children by first wife:

 i. JENCY,[7] m. FIELDING TWEEDLE. Child (surname *Tweedle*): 1. *William*, d. aged 19 years.

 ii. ELIZABETH, b. in Arkansas 7 May 1828; d. in Texas 7 Sept. 1904; m. in Montgomery Co., Ark., in 1847, MARTIN NEWMAN. With her family she removed to Texas. Children (surname *Newman*): 1. *James Franklin*, b. 20 Dec. 1849; m. in Navarro Co., Tex., in Sept. 1873, Josephine Rushing; three children. 2. *Mary Jane*, b. in Navarro Co., Tex., 16 Nov. 1855; d. 24 Feb. 1906; m. in Navarro Co., 4 Jan. 1872, Thomas Trammell; three children.

79. iii. BENJAMIN FRANKLIN, b. in Arkansas 29 Jan. 1829.

   Children by second wife:

 iv. JAMES, m. LIZZIE ROBERTS. Child: 1. *Robert*.[8] Perhaps others.

80. v. CUMBERLAND, b. in the Valley of the Ouachita, Ark., 1 Apr. 1836.

40. CUMBERLAND[6] POLK (*Taylor*,[5] *Capt. John*,[4] *William*,[3] *William*,[2] *Robert*[1]), born near Nashville, Davidson Co., Tenn., 7 Aug. 1803, died at "Red Top," Grimes Co., Tex., 16 June 1857. He married, in the Valley of the Ouachita, Ark., 10 Nov. 1826, NANCY COX, born in Kentucky 5 Jan. 1811, died near

Mount Calm, then in Limestone Co., Tex., 18 May 1867, daughter of Joel and Frances (Bartlett) Cox,* who migrated from Kentucky to the Valley of the Ouachita in 1816. She was a sister of Sarah Cox, who married Cumberland Polk's brother James (39).

Cumberland Polk was but five years of age when his parents moved to Arkansas. Soon after his marriage he returned to Tennessee, having inherited property there; and he lived for a time in Hardeman County, near the present town of Bolivar, near the family of his great-uncle, Col. Ezekiel Polk (8), and there his two eldest children were born. He then returned to his old home in Arkansas, where his other children were born, except the youngest, who was born in Texas. Cumberland Polk moved to Texas in 1848, and was a planter in Grimes County.

Children:

i.   LUCINDA,[7] b. near Bolivar, Hardeman Co., Tenn., 16 Sept. 1827; d. in infancy.

ii.   LUCRETIA, b. near Bolivar, Hardeman Co., Tenn., 16 July 1829; d. at San Jose, Calif., at the home of her daughter Louise Elizabeth (Mrs. George Babcock), 28 May 1895; m. near Hot Springs, Ark., 3 Aug. 1845, EDMUND CEARLEY, b. near Taylorsville (then in Wilkes Co.), N. C., 27 Sept. 1806, d. at Vallejo's Mills (now Niles), Calif., 21 Apr. 1881, s. of Larkin and Mary (Barnes).† Edmund

*Both the Cox and the Bartlett families were of Colonial and Revolutionary ancestry. The children of Joel and Frances (Bartlett) Cox were: 1. Nancy, m. Cumberland Polk (40). 2. Joel. 3. Betsy. 4. Louis. 5. James. 6. Sarah (Sally), m. James Polk (39). 7. Polly. 8. Jesse. 9. Isaac.

†The name Cearley is variously spelled in the Colonial records of Massachusetts and Connecticut, and later in Virginia, where Edmund Cearley's great-grandfather, William, Sr., held a land patent in Lunenburg County, issued to him in the name of King George II on 5 July 1751, and also in North Carolina, whither the family removed after the Revolution, the forms that have been found including Carley, Carly, Carlye, Cearley, Cerly, Kearley, Kerley, and Kerly.

Land was surveyed in Virginia for William Kerly, Sr., in 1743 and for William, Jr., in 1748 (Stith's Virginia Surveys). The patent of 1751 is on file at Richmond, Va. (Patent Book 30, p. 470), and shows that King George II, through "our trusty and well-beloved Lewis Burwell," issued to William Kerly, 5 July 1751, "in the twenty-fifth year of our Reign," a patent of land "in our County of Lunenburg," touching Byrd's line, "with all woods, swamps, marshes and low grounds, meadows, feedings, and his due share of all veins, mines, and quarries, as well discovered as not discovered, within the grounds aforesaid, . . . and the rivers, waters, and water courses therein contained, together with the privilege of hunting, hawking, fishing, fowling, and all other profits, commodities, and hereditaments whatsoever to the same or any part thereof belonging or in any wise appertaining. To have and to hold, possess, and enjoy the said Parcel of land and all other the afore-mentioned Premises, and every part thereof, with their lands and every of their appurtenances, to the said William Kerly, his heirs and assigns forever, to be held of us, our Heirs and Successors, as of our Manor of East Greenwich in the County of Kent, in free and common soccage, and not in Capite or Knight's service. Yielding and paying unto us, our Heirs and Successors, for every fifty acres of land, and so proportionally a greater or lesser quantity than fifty acres, the Fee Rent of one Shilling yearly, to be paid on the Feast of St. Michael the Archangel, and also cultivating and improving three acres of every fifty of the Tract above mentioned within three years after the date of these Presents. . . . In witness whereof we have caused these letters Patent to be made. Witness our trusty and well-beloved Lewis Burwell, Esqr., President of our Council and Commander-in-Chief of our said Colony and Dominion at Williamsburg."

William Kerly, the grantee under this patent of 1751, sold the land in 1756, but, as William Carley (also spelled *Cereley* and *Careley*), received another grant in 1760, which is on file in the land office at Richmond, Va. (Land Grants, vol. 2, p. 563, where it is indexed under William Carly), and which reads as follows:

"George the Second [etc.]. Whereas by one patent under the seal of this our Colony and Dominion of Virginia, bearing date xxv day of June, one thousand seven hundred and forty-seven, there was granted unto William Buttrom One certain Tract or Parcel of Land Containing One hundred and seventy acres, lying and being then in the County of Brunswick, now Halifax, on the South Side of Banister River, and bounded as followeth, to wit; Beginning at a Hiccory on the said River, thence South Eighty-one degrees, West sixty-two poles to a Red Oak, Thence South Fifty-two degrees, West Sixty poles, to a pine, thence North thirty-two Degrees, West one hun-

Cearley was a planter in Arkansas, and early in 1859, with his family and a party of friends, who had assembled for the journey at St. Joseph, Mo., he started to cross the plains and mountains to California. They took with them mules as a speculation. They were delayed on the plains by their cattle being stampeded and their mules stolen by Indians, and they reached western Nevada too late to finish the crossing that year, being deterred by tales of the unfortunate and tragic fate of the Donner party. They remained in Washoe Co., Nev., until the spring of 1860. On reaching California, they remained for a very short time at Stockton, and then moved to Vallejo's Mills, where Edmund Cearley bought land and spent the rest of his life. He was a farmer and an express owner. There were other Southern people in this community, and among them he became a prominent Democrat. Both he and his wife are buried in Odd Fellows' Cemetery, Irvington, Calif.

dred and seventy-eight poles, to a Poplar, in a Branch, thence North thirty-seven degrees, East one hundred and forty poles, to a beech on aforesaid [river]. Thence down the said River, as it meanders, to the Beginning. Which said Tract or Parcel of land was granted on condition of paying our Quit Rents and cultivating and Improving as in the said patent is expressed. And Whereas William Buttron failed to pay such Quit rents and to make cultivation and Improvements, and William Carley hath made humble Suit to our Lieutenant Governor and Commander-in-Chief of our said Colony and Dominion and hath obtained a grant for the same. Therefore know ye that for divers good causes and considerations, but more especially in consideration of Twenty Shillings of good and lawful money for Our use, paid to our Receiver General in this our Said Colony and Dominion, we have given, granted, and confirmed, and by these presents for our own heirs and successors do give, grant, and confirm unto the said William Cereley, and to his heirs and successors, Do Give, Grant, and Confirm unto the said William Careley, and to his heirs and assigns forever, all the said tract or Parcel of Land and every part and Parcel thereof, with all [etc.]. Witness our trusty and well-beloved Francis Fauquier, Esquire, our lieutenant governor and commander-in-chief of our said Colony and Dominion at Williamsburg, under the seal of our said Colony, the fifteenth day of July, One thousand seven hundred and sixty, In the thirty fourth year of our reign. Fran: Fauquier."

In 1760 there were granted to James Careley, brother of the above-named William, 400 acres of land in Halifax County.

In 1783 the land granted to William Carley in 1760 was sold, but in the deed William and his wife Martha wrote their surname *Kerley.*

William Kerly (or Carley), Sr., married Martha Carter; and in his will, proved at Wilkesboro, Wilkes Co., N. C., in the March term of 1796, he names his sons William, Joseph, John, and Larkin, and his daughters Lucy, Martha, Sarah, and Wilmoth. The eldest son, William, Jr., married Rachel Neale, and they removed to North Carolina about 1794. Their children were: 1. Larkin. 2. Clemond. 3. Absalom, who married Elizabeth Teague. 4. Elijah. 5. Elizabeth. 6. Sarah. 7. Chloe. Larkin, the eldest son of William, Jr., was born in Halifax Co., Va., 10 Jan. 1776, and died in North Carolina 1 Oct. 1841, the inscription on his tombstone in the churchyard of Three Fork Church, Alexander Co., near Taylorsville, N. C., reading: "Sacred to the memory of Larkin Cearley born on 10 January 1776, and departed this life the 1st of October 1841 aged 65 years 8¾ months." He married, 6 Feb. 1800, Mary Barnes, born 20 Dec. 1781, died near Taylorsville, N. C., 12 Nov. 1864, daughter of Solomon and Elizabeth (Murphy). In his will, proved at Wilkesboro, Wilkes Co., N. C., in the November session of 1841, Larkin Cearley gave "all my lands stock and household furniture to my wife Mary," and named each of his children. Larkin and Mary (Barnes) Cearley had fourteen children, as follows: 1. George, b. 15 Jan. 1802; m. Polly Lowdermilk. 2. Nancy, b. 1 May 1803; m. Joshua Greer. 3. Ruth, b. 25 Apr. 1805; m. William Anderson. 4. Edmund, b. 27 Sept. 1806; m. Lucretia Polk (*vide supra*, 40, ii). 5. Elizabeth, b. 28 May 1808; m. Edwin Greer. 6. Hiram, b. 6 Mar. 1810; m. Evelyn James. 7. Solomon, b. 29 Sept. 1811; m. Polly Laws. 8. Sarah, b. 21 June 1813; m. William Brown. 9. Anna, b. 16 Jan. 1815; m. James Brown. 10. Clemond, b. 12 Oct. 1816; m. Elizabeth Laws, sister of Polly Laws, who m. his brother Solomon. 11. Rachel, b. 25 Feb. 1818; m. Frank Morris. 12. Charles, b. 31 Mar. 1820; m. Rebecca Harrington. 13. Chloe, b. 17 May 1822; m. her second cousin, Edward Carley. 14. Henry, b. 25 June 1825; d. unm. in Arkansas, aged 23.

Solomon Barnes, father of the wife of Larkin Cearley, was of New England ancestry, the family having migrated via Virginia to North Carolina, where they settled in the old Wilkes County (now Alexander County). He was well-to-do, brought with him to North Carolina cattle, sheep, and slaves, and built a stone house, part of which was standing in 1880. In his will, proved in the February term of 1807 and on file in Wilkes Co., N. C., he calls himself "planter," gives to his wife Elizabeth "the plantation on which I now live," with all his personal estate and slaves, names his children, and leaves to those of his children "who have not yet had their portion" an aggregate of 640 acres of land and other property. His children were: 1. Reuben, m. Isabell Teague. 2. Charles. 3. George. 4. Solomon, m. Sallie Swaim. 5. John, m. Polly Swaim. 6. Peter, m. Martha Bryant. 7. Lydia, m. William Isbell. 8. Betty, killed by lightning; d. unm. 9. Sallie, m. her cousin, Bartel Barnes. 10. Mary, m. Larkin Cearley. 11. Ruth, m. William Chapman. 12. Rachel.

Children (surname *Cearley*), all except the last two b. near Hot Springs, Ark.: 1. *Samuel Reyburn*, b. 7 July 1846; d. unm. 3 Mar. 1877. 2. *Newton Fleming*, b. 15 Dec. 1847; living unm. 3. *Mary Jane*, b. 17 July 1849; d. 28 July 1852. 4. *Cumberland Polk*, b. 14 July 1851; d. 29 Aug. 1852. 5. *Louise Elizabeth*, b. 10 May 1853; d. at Fresno, Calif., 23 June 1917; m. at Centerville, Alameda Co., Calif., in St. John's Church (Protestant Episcopal), the rector, Rev. John H. Babcock, father of the bridegroom, officiating, George Babcock, b. at Ballston Spa, N. Y., 9 Jan. 1854, d. at Fresno, Calif., 25 Jan. 1917, s. of Rev. John H. and Margaret Pierce (Bull), a merchant of Fresno, in business with his brother-in-law, Charles Talant Cearley (40, ii, 9).* 6. *Cyrus Granville*, b. 6 Oct. 1855; d. unm. 26 July 1879. 7. *John Brackville*, b. 4 Mar. 1858; living unm. 8. *Emma Cornelia*, b. near Washoe City, Washoe Co., Nev., 29 Feb. 1860, while her parents were *en route* to California; m. at the home of her sister, Mrs. George Babcock, at Irvington, Calif., 27 Dec. 1884, Rev. Henry Bruce Norton of San Jose and Skyland, Calif., officiating, Frank Marion Angellotti of San Rafael, Calif., LL.B. (Hastings College of the Law, University of California, 1882), b. at San Rafael 4 Sept. 1861, s. of Giuseppe and Lois Frances (Osgood), who were m. in Marin Co., Calif., 18 Nov. 1860;† he was educated in private schools, at the

---

*Rev. John H. Babcock, father of George Babcock, was a descendant of James[1] Babcock, who was admitted as an inhabitant of Portsmouth, R. I., 25 Feb. 1642, was prominent at Westerly, R. I., took part in the "Swamp Fight" in King Philip's War, and was a deputy to the Colonial Legislature in 1682 and 1684, through John,[2] Job,[3] Job,[4] Josiah,[5] and Rev. Deodatus,[6] D.D., his father, who was for many years rector of Christ Church, Ballston Spa, N. Y., where a beautiful window has been placed in his memory by relatives and friends. (Cf. the Babcock Genealogy.) George Babcock's mother, Margaret Pierce (Bull), was daughter of Judge Bull of Ballston Spa.

†Giuseppe Angellotti was born in Italy, and participated in the revolutionary uprisings there in 1848-9. He was in Rome at the time of the fighting in defence of the Roman Republic, his sister Geltruda being then a nun in that city. He fought with the Volunteers for a few weeks preceding the fall of Rome, and joined in the retreat of the Four Thousand, under Garibaldi, as far as San Marino. When this force was disbanded, he escaped, secured passage a little later on a sailing vessel, and went to Montevideo. Thence, when the news of the discovery of gold in California had reached him, he sailed around the Horn to San Francisco. Not caring for the work in the mines, he settled in Marin County, where his first deed of land, recorded in Deed Book 1, is dated 5 Oct. 1852. His name appears frequently thereafter in deeds, sometimes in the Spanish form, José, and later in the English form, Joseph. He was a landowner, merchant, and hotel owner, and resided in Marin County until 1883, when he went on a business trip to Mexico, contracted yellow fever, and died at Guaymas, in the State of Sonora, 22 Sept. 1883. He was buried at Guaymas. Besides their son, Frank Marion Angellotti, Giuseppe and Lois Frances (Osgood) Angellotti had a daughter, Emma Teresa, b. 11 Dec. 1865, d. at St. Helena, Calif., 15 Jan. 1899, bur. in Mount Tamalpais Cemetery, San Rafael, Calif., who married (1) at Calvary Presbyterian Church, San Francisco, 16 Sept. 1885, the pastor, Rev. John Hemphill, officiating, Prescott[8] Loring, b. in Boston 12 May 1859, eldest son of David Webster[7] (Caleb Gould,[6] Caleb,[5] Samuel,[4] Samuel,[3] Benjamin,[2] Dea. Thomas[1]) and Susan Sophia (Leach), and married (2) at San Francisco Albert Woodburn Scott, Jr., A.B. (University of California, 1891), merchant, lawyer, b. at San Francisco 6 Nov. 1869, son of Albert Woodburn and Georgiana (Smith) of San Francisco. By her first husband, Prescott Loring, Emma Teresa (Angellotti) had two children: 1. William Stowell Loring, of Dallas, Tex., b. at San Francisco 16 June 1886; m. at Sherman, Tex., 4 Mar. 1911, Mabel Velma Reynolds, dau. of John William; children, b. at Dallas: (1) Marjorie Angellotti, b. 15 Sept. 1912, (2) William Stowell, b. 1 Mar. 1914, and (3) Frank Edward, b. 10 Apr. 1916. 2. Harold Angellotti Loring, b. 20 Oct. 1889; d. 26 Sept. 1890. Dea. Thomas[1] Loring, the immigrant ancestor of Prescott[8] Loring, was of Axminster, co. Devon, Eng., whence he emigrated to New England with his wife, Jane (Newton), 23 Dec. 1634, and, after a short stay at Dorchester, Mass., settled at Hingham, Mass., in 1635, and moved thence to Hull, Mass., where he died 4 Apr. 1661. His descendant David Webster[7] Loring, son of Caleb Gould[6] and Harriet (Tuttle), was born in Boston 16 Sept. 1836, and died 30 Nov. 1904. He married in Boston, 5 Aug. 1856, Susan Sophia Leach, born at East Bridgewater, Mass., in 1836. He was a dealer in hardware and saddlery in Boston, and later removed to San Francisco, where he engaged in business. He was an accomplished musician and a musical organizer and leader of great ability, and he founded at San Francisco the Loring Club, a musical organization for male voices, which in 1922 was in its forty-seventh season. (Cf. the Loring Genealogy, by Charles Henry Pope, 1917.)

Lois Frances Osgood, wife of Giuseppe Angellotti, was born at Blue Hill, Me., 17 Sept. 1836, died at San Francisco 3 Sept. 1913, and is buried in Mount Tamalpais Cemetery at San Rafael, Calif. She was the eighth and youngest child of Isaac Smith[6] and Lois Hibbert (Stover) Osgood of Blue Hill. Her father, a farmer of Blue Hill, was born there 18 Dec. 1794 and died there 3 June 1877. For twenty-five years he was a selectman of Blue Hill, and for ten years, from 1866 on, he

Lowell High School, San Francisco, and at the Hastings College of the Law, University of California, practised law at San Rafael, was elected and served as district attorney of Marin Co., Calif., for three terms, 1885–1891, was judge of the Superior Court of Marin County, 1891–1903, associate justice of the Supreme Court of California, 1903–1915, and was elected chief justice of California for a twelve-year term, beginning in Jan. 1915, but resigned this position 14 Nov. 1921, in order to resume the practice of his profession; he is chief counsel for the Western Pacific Railroad Company and a member of the Society of Colonial Wars, and was grand master of the Ancient Free and Accepted Masons of the State of California, 1898–99; Mrs. Angellotti served in the War with Spain as a member and vice president of the California Red Cross, and in the World War she organized and superintended, until 1 Jan. 1919, the cutting and assembling department of the Pacific Division of the Red Cross; she contributed to vol. 74 of the REGISTER (1920) a genealogy entitled "John Devereux of Marblehead, Mass., and Some of His Descendants," and she is the compiler of this article on the Polk family; she was elected a resident member of the New England Historic Genealogical Society 6 Feb. 1923; children (surname *Angellotti*), b. at San Rafael: (1) Frances Louise, b. 5 Dec. 1885, d. 25 Jan. 1887, and (2) Marion Polk, b. 12 Nov. 1887, who was educated at private schools, is the author of "Sir John Hawkwood," "The Burgundian," "Harlette," "The Firefly of France," "Three Black Bags," and many magazine stories, spent the year 1915–16 in Italy and France, observing war conditions, and served as a volunteer in Red Cross canteen work in France in 1918–19, at San Germain des Fossés, Châlons-sur-Marne, and Chaligny (with Evacuation Hospital No. 13, during the St. Mihiel offensive), and with the Army of Occupation in Germany at advance general headquarters at Trèves (Trier).

9. *Charles Talant*, of Fresno, Calif., merchant, b. at Vallejo's Mills (now Niles), Calif., 21 Nov. 1865; m. at Los Angeles, Calif., 2 Nov. 1891, Rhoda Jeannette Mangrum, b. at Paola, Kans., 28 Apr. 1871, dau. of Charles William and Jane (Tueuler); he was a member of the Fresno Exemption Board in the World War, was a director of the fourth and fifth Liberty Loan drives, and is a Knight Templar; child: (1) Mila Mangrum, A.B. (University of California, 1915), A.M. (Columbia University, 1917), b. at Fresno 2 Aug. 1892, m. there, 3 May 1919, Earl Thomas Parrish of Berkeley, Calif., A.B. (University of California, 1915), b. at San Francisco 2 Apr. 1893, s. of Edwin and Julia (Reynolds), trained in the first Reserve Officers' Training Camp, at the Presidio, San Francisco, for three months, commissioned second lieutenant 1 Jan.

---

was deputy collector of customs at Castine, Me. The immigrant ancestor of this Osgood family was Christopher[1] Osgood of Ipswich, Mass., who died in 1650. His son Christopher[2] removed to Andover, Mass., where he was lieutenant and captain of the troop and represented the town in the General Court in 1690, 1693, 1696, and 1705–1708. Ezekiel[4] Osgood, son of Ezekiel[3] and grandson of Christopher,[2] moved, with his eight sons and four daughters, in 1768, from Andover to Blue Hill, where he had bought land from Nicholas Holt, the deed being dated 24 Apr. 1764. His son Phineas[5] Osgood, a farmer and shipowner at Blue Hill, was born at Andover 19 May 1753 and died 31 Oct. 1836. In 1774–5 he was living, with his brother Christopher, in the family of Mrs. Elizabeth (Wardwell) Osgood, his aunt by marriage, at Andover; and on 19 Apr. 1775 the two brothers, both minutemen, responded to the alarm and served in Capt. Benjamin Ames's company, Colonel Frye's regiment. Phineas also served eight months during the siege of Boston, and after his return to Blue Hill was a sergeant in Capt. Nathan Parker's company of the local militia. He married (1) 1 June 1779 Mary Smith of Sedgwick, Me., born 2 July 1762, died 30 Sept. 1821, daughter of Lemuel and Mary (Joyce), who was the mother of all his children, and (2) 17 Jan. 1824 Mrs. Desire Freeman of Castine, Me., who died 3 Aug. 1844. Phineas was the father of Isaac Smith[6] Osgood and the grandfather of Lois Frances (Osgood) Angellotti. (Cf. A Genealogy of the Descendants of John, Christopher and William Osgood, edited by Eben Putnam, Salem, 1894, pp. 255–307.)

Lois Hibbert Stover, first wife of Isaac Smith Osgood, to whom she was married at Blue Hill, 10 Sept. 1821, was born at Blue Hill 20 Apr. 1794 and died there 19 June 1837, daughter of Jeremiah and Abigail (Devereux) Stover and a descendant of John[1] Devereux of Marblehead, Mass. (Cf. REGISTER, vol. 74, pp. 204–205, 301–302, 306–309.)

1918, promoted to first lieutenant, served at Camp Lewis, assigned to Co. F, Second Battalion, Three Hundred and Sixty-third Regiment, Ninety-first Division, First Army Corps, American Expeditionary Forces, took part in the St. Mihiel and Meuse-Argonne offensives, severely wounded at Montfaucon, 26 Sept. 1918, now a bond salesman, residing at Berkeley, with one child, Patricia Jane, b. at Fresno 5 Aug. 1920.

iii. MARSHALL ALEXANDER, b. 11 May 1831; d. young.

iv. ELIAS RECTOR, b. 10 Dec. 1833; served in the Civil War in Kennard's regiment, Confederate Army; d. unm. after the war from the effects of exposure in the war.

v. WILLIAM JACKSON, b. 19 Apr. 1836; now deceased; m. at Cypress City, Tex., ESTHER WOODWARD. He served in the Confederate Army. Children: 1. *Thomas.*[8] 2. *Julia.*

vi. LOUISA JANE, b. in the Valley of the Ouachita, near Hot Springs, Ark., 2 May 1839; d. at Billington, Tex., 7 Dec. 1898; m. in Limestone Co., Tex., 24 Feb. 1875, REV. EZEKIEL JACKSON BILLINGTON, b. in Tennessee 1 Jan. 1826, d. at Billington 5 Aug. 1896, s. of Penniuel (b. 24 Dec. 1791, d. in Limestone Co., Tex., 22 Apr. 1857) and Nancy (Wadsworth) (b. 29 Dec. 1795, d. 8 Sept. 1868, m. 5 Dec. 1815). Ezekiel Jackson Billington went with his parents in 1830 from Tennessee to Ballard Co., Ky., and in 1854 they removed to Texas. He was a Baptist missionary and minister and a farmer. The town of Billington was named for him. Children (surname *Billington*), b. at Billington: 1. *Mary Lucretia,* b. 9 Dec. 1875; m. 8 Feb. 1897 Zephina Jackson Moore, b. in Stewart Co., Ga., 27 June 1875, s. and fourth child of Rev. Absalom Jackson Moore, Baptist missionary and minister and a farmer (b. in Randolph Co., Ala., 5 Jan. 1849), and his wife Martha (b. in Stewart Co., Ga., in 1847); seven children. 2. *Birtie Jackson,* farmer, b. 28 Feb. 1877; m. in Nov. 1897 Daisy Blanche Starnader, b. 28 Nov. 1882, d. 9 Jan. 1919, dau. of E. Riley and Belle (Davis) of Billington; six children. 3. *Julia Angeline,* b. at Billington 25 Nov. 1878; m. there, 12 July 1897, Robert William Warwick of Billington and Stamford, Tex., farmer, b. at Axtell, Tex., 11 Jan. 1873, s. of Samuel (b. in Louisiana in 1848, whose father was b. in Yorkshire, Eng.) and Hallie (White) (b. in Nacogdoches Co., Tex., in 1846); five children.

vii. JENCY ALEXANDER, b. in the Valley of the Ouachita, near Hot Springs, Ark., 9 July 1841; d. 3 Nov. 1880; m. 17 Dec. 1868 WILLIAM McGEE O'NEAL, farmer, b. in Benton Co., Ala., 4 Dec. 1844. He served in the Confederate Cavalry, in Bagley's regiment, Green's brigade. Children (surname *O'Neal*): 1. *Nancy Lucinda,* b. in Montgomery Co., Tex., 17 Oct. 1870; m. 18 Jan. 1888 Robert Ross, b. at Corsicana, Tex., 20 Oct. 1866, d. at Ada, Okla., 11 Mar. 1913; eleven children. 2. *Martha Augusta,* b. at Mexia, Tex., 12 July 1872; m. 2 May 1888 Elisha C. Ross, b. 2 Feb. 1868, d. at Ada, Okla., 3 Jan. 1896; one daughter. 3. *Robert James,* b. at Mexia, Tex., 22 Aug. 1874; d. at Mexia in July 1883. 4. *Mary Prudence,* b. at Mexia, Tex., 10 Mar. 1876; d. at Ada, Okla., 6 Mar. 1897; m. 8 Mar. 1893 Benjamin Franklin Ross, b. 8 Feb. 1871. 5. *John Franklin,* b. at Mexia, Tex., 10 Feb. 1878.

viii. LOUIS TAYLOR, b. 9 Sept. 1843; served in the Confederate Army, in Nelson's regiment; killed at Arkansas Post, Ark., in Jan. 1863, when General Sherman's forces attacked the Confederate position; d. unm.

ix. PRUDENCE, b. near Little Rock, Ark., 19 May 1846; d. 22 Mar. 1889; m. at Huntsville, Tex., 17 Dec. 1868, FREDERICK P. JONES, farmer, b. at Brownsville, Tenn., 31 Oct. 1846, living in 1921. He served in the Civil War in the Confederate Army, from Oct. 1863 to June 1865, under General Forrest, in the Thirty-first Tennessee Regiment. He moved to Texas in 1867. Children (surname *Jones*): 1. *Jane Emily,* b. in Madison Co., Tex., 15 Sept. 1871;

m. 16 Feb. 1890 William Frederick White, s. of Harvey and Lydia (West); six children. 2. *William*, b. in Limestone Co., Tex., 5 Feb. 1874; living unm. in 1921.

x. MARY ANN, b. 17 July 1848; living in 1921; m. in 1877 CHARLES JACKSON, farmer. No children.

xi. MARTHA ROBINSON, b. 23 Feb. 1850; living in 1921; m. 29 Jan. 1874 WILLIAM HARDY WALKER, farmer. Children (surname *Walker*): 1. *Jency*, b. 7 Feb. 1876; m. 24 Jan. 1898 Meady Jones, b. in Hunt Co., Tex., 16 Feb. 1879; three children. 2. *James Knox*, b. in Limestone Co., Tex., 1 Aug. 1877; m. 28 June 1901 Okie Kesmire, b. 11 Apr. 1885; six children. 3. *Ella Martha*, b. 2 Sept. 1881; m. in 1902 Claud M. Hunt; five children, all b. near Harmony, Tex.

xii. JAMES KNOX, farmer and stockman, b. in Limestone Co., Tex., 24 Nov. 1850; lived in Texas and Oklahoma; unm.

41. ALFRED[6] POLK (*Taylor*,[5] *Capt. John*,[4] *William*,[3] *William*,[2] *Robert*[1]), born at "The Wilds," Montgomery Co., Ark., 3 Sept. 1814, died on his farm near Belton, Bell Co., Tex., 12 Nov. 1897. He married first, in Pike Co., Ark., in 1840, SARAH IRENE CHANDLER, born in Tennessee, died on the farm near Belton in 1859, daughter of Josiah and Mary, who came from England and settled in Tennessee; and secondly, in 1865, MRS. ELIZABETH (BLACKBURN) RICKETTS, born near Columbia, Maury Co., Tenn., 24 Feb. 1828, died on the farm near Belton 31 Oct. 1906, youngest child of Capt. John Porter and Nancy (Churchill) Blackburn* and widow of E. J. Ricketts, who was killed in Arkansas while serving in the Confederate Army.†

Alfred Polk moved to Texas in 1851 and bought a farm of 100 acres in Nolan's Valley, five miles from Belton, on which he lived and to which he made additions until he owned more than 300 acres. He served in early years as justice of the peace in Nolan's Valley, was in the militia for two years in the Civil War, when older men were called out, was on detached service with the Commissary Department and issued provisions to widows and orphans of those who had died in the service, and in the first part of the war relieved his oldest son for a short time at the front. He was a prominent and influential man in his community.

Children by first wife:

81. i. JAMES ANDERSON,[7] b. in Polk Co., Ark., 4 July 1841.

*Capt. John Porter Blackburn, a soldier of the War of 1812, was a native of South Carolina, and moved in 1853 to Belton, Tex., where he died. On 4 June 1923 a monument to his memory was unveiled at the Blackburn Cemetery, near Killeen, Tex., the regent of the Daughters of the American Revolution of Belton, the Daughters of 1812 (represented by Mrs. Harry Hyman, a great-granddaughter of Captain Blackburn), Captain Blackburn's son, Merriweather Whitley Blackburn, and several of his grandchildren, including Robert Lee Polk and Richard Tyler Polk, sons of Alfred Polk (41), taking part in the ceremony. Captain Blackburn's children were: 1. Francis. 2. Rosana. 3. Valera. 4. Elias H. 5. E. J. 6. Ella. 7. John. 8. William H. 9. Merriweather Whitley. 10. Richard. 11. Elizabeth.

Capt. John Porter Blackburn's father was Capt. Ambrose Blackburn, who was born in Ireland about 1750, emigrated to America, served throughout the Revolution, and after its close settled in South Carolina. He married Frances Elizabeth Jones of Greenville, S. C., and died in 1820, aged about 70.

†Elizabeth (Blackburn) Ricketts had three children by her first husband; 1. Mary, who married William Hall of Bell Co., Tex., farmer. 2. James Knox, of Bell Co., farmer. 3. Belle A., who married James Parker.

ii.   JOSIAH L., m. ———. Children: 1. *Samuel.*[8] 2. *Fannie.* 3. *Rosa.*
      4. *Janie.* Possibly others.
iii. MARY JANE, b. in Polk Co., Ark., 26 Jan. 1844; m. in 1866 WILLIAM
      WASHINGTON GARNER, farmer, b. in Tennessee 8 Oct. 1845. Resi-
      dence, Killeen, Tex. Children (surname *Garner*): 1. *Sarah Irene,*
      b. in Bell Co., Tex., 17 Oct. 1867; m. in 1888 William James
      Willess, farmer, b. in Parker Co., Tex., 22 Mar. 1866; ten children.
      2. *Samuel Leander,* of Bell Co., Tex., farmer. 3. *William Alfred,*
      farmer, living near Killeen, Tex. 4. *Mary Alice,* b. in Bell Co.,
      Tex., 1 May 1871; m. there, 1 Jan. 1896, Charles Monroe Elms
      of Killeen, Tex., farmer, b. in Coryell Co., Tex., 29 May 1874, s.
      of Thomas (b. at Independence, Ark., 25 Feb. 1849, d. 14 Apr. 1913)
      and Margaretta Irene (Clements) (b. in Cass Co., Tex., 12 Apr.
      1850, m. 17 Nov. 1870); twelve children. 5. *James Newton,* of
      Killeen, Tex., farmer. 6. *Katie Bell,* m. Newton Elms of Valera,
      Tex. 7. *Louisa Ellen,* m. Robert Wiggin of Killeen, Tex. 8. *Dolly
      Tennessee.* 9. *Harriet Elizabeth,* b. 22 Feb. 1882; m. 12 Oct. 1902
      John Medart, farmer, b. 11 Nov. 1881, d. 27 Jan. 1913; five chil-
      dren. 10. *Lucy Josephine,* m. Rufus Young of Wichita Falls, Tex.
82. iv. MITCHELL ALFRED, b. 24 Apr. 1845.
    v.   CAROLINE, m. L. DENNIS of Callahan Co., Tex., farmer.
    vi. BENJAMIN, of the Panhandle District in Texas, stockman.
    vii. SAMUEL T., of Bell Co., Tex., farmer, d. in Oct. 1894; m. ———.
         Children: 1. *James D.,*[8] farmer. 2. *Charles N.* 3. *Clyde.* 4.
         Grace, m. Albert Bishop of Killeen, Tex.
    viii. ALMEDA, b. 23 Jan. 1853; d. 17 June 1918; m. 18 May 1877 JOHN
         N. STANSILL of Killeen, Tex., farmer, b. in Alabama. Children
         (surname *Stansill*): 1. *Mary Irene.* 2. *Bennett Jay.* 3. *Alfred
         Newton.* 4. *Dora Beatrice.* 5. *Thomas Jefferson.* 6. *Arthur
         Baylor.* 7. *Ada Bell.* 8. *Robert Lewis.*
    ix. YOUNG C., d., aged 12 years.

Children by second wife, born near Belton, Tex.:

    x.   ROBERT LEE, of Killeen, Tex., b. 11 Nov. 1865; m. at Killeen, 10
         Apr. 1892, CURRIE YOUNG, b. in Warren Co., Ark., 16 Jan. 1874.
         He was educated in the schools of Palo Alto, Tex., and at the
         Thomas Arnold School, Salado, Tex., has been an officer of the
         peace at Temple, Bell Co., Tex., and is a commercial traveller and
         salesman, going to the West Indies, Mexico, etc. Children: 1.
         Nora,[8] b. at Killeen 12 Jan. 1893; m. 6 Aug. 1914 Frank J. Rear-
         don; residence, Savannah, Ga.; two children. 2. *Margaret,* b.
         at Belton, Tex., 20 June 1895; m. 12 Mar. 1917 Henry D. Young;
         residence, Fort Worth, Tex. 3. *Currie Young,* b. at Belton, Tex.,
         27 Feb. 1897; m. 30 Apr. 1915 C. K. Sadler; residence, Killeen;
         one son. 4. *Mary,* b. at Killeen 4 Dec. 1900. 5. *Robert Lee,* b. at
         Temple 4 Dec. 1901.
    xi. WILLIAM PORT, box maker and contractor, b. near Belton, Tex., 12
         Dec. 1867; m. at Killeen, Tex., 3 Jan. 1896, LILA M. KEYLICH, b.
         at Giddings, Tex., 29 Mar. 1872, dau. of Feodor and Anna. Chil-
         dren: 1. *Wilport Alfred,*[8] of Los Angeles, Calif., bank teller, b. at
         Killeen 1 May 1898. 2. *James K.,* of Los Angeles, Calif., railroad
         accountant, b. at Killeen 10 Sept. 1899; he enlisted in the United
         States Navy, at Los Angeles, 12 Aug. 1918, was ordered to the
         naval station at San Diego, Calif., 14 Aug. 1918, and served as a
         seaman until 14 Mar. 1919, when he was honorably discharged.
    xii. RICHARD TYLER, of Killeen, Tex., stockman and manager of a hard-
         ware company, b. near Belton, Tex., 16 Oct. 1869; m. at Killeen,
         18 Oct. 1891, TILLIE WALLING, b. near Streator, La Salle Co., Ill.,
         5 Nov. 1869, dau. of J. H. A. and Elisabeth, who moved to Texas
         in 1882. Richard Tyler Polk was postmaster at Killeen from 1898
         to 1914. Child: 1. *Winnie Elisabeth,*[8] b. at Killeen 29 July 1894;
         m. there, 4 Mar. 1920, Ira Abraham Swope of San Angelo, Tex.,
         bank treasurer, b. at Kempner, Lampasas Co., Tex., 16 May
         1885, s. of Abraham Lee and Mary Allie; in the World War he

served in France, in the Ninetieth Division, American Expeditionary Forces, from June 1918 to June 1919, and took part in the St. Mihiel and Argonne offensives; his wife was educated at the Killeen High School, studied music at Baylor College, Belton, and during the World War was a director of women's work for the Red Cross at Killeen and chairman of surgical dressings and of the executive committee of the Red Cross; one son, b. in 1920, d. in infancy.

42. JAMES IRVIN⁶ POLK (*Thomas,*⁵ *Col. Ezekiel,*⁴ *William,*³ *William,*² *Robert*¹), born, probably in Robertson Co., Tenn., 29 Oct. 1799, died there in 1856 or 1857. He married in Cheatham Co., Tenn., about 1825, ELIZABETH KINCHIN WILSON.

Children:

i.   MARY ABIGAIL,⁷ b. in Robertson Co. 23 Apr. 1826; d. at Springfield, Tenn., 12 Oct. 1872; m. in Robertson Co., 3 Oct. 1841, DAVID DANIEL HOLMAN, s. of Daniel. Children (surname *Holman*): 1. *James Irvin*, b. at Springfield 29 Aug. 1842; d. there 20 Sept. 1912; m. there, 21 May 1867, Leota Fisher, dau. of Pleasant H. and Elizabeth (Boren); eight children, b. at Springfield. 2. *Adeline Davy*, b. in Robertson Co. 8 Feb. 1846; d. there 31 Oct. 1882; m. there, 9 July 1875, Henry Sanford Taylor, s. of Jesse Baggett and Amanda Jackson (Thompson); three children. 3. *Edward Thomas*, b. in Robertson Co. 6 May 1848; d. in Montgomery Co., Tenn., 4 Mar. 1896; m. 27 Aug. 1867 Sada Victoria Northington, dau. of Samuel and Sarah Willis (Walton); five children. 4. *Mary Elizabeth*, b. at Springfield 26 Feb. 1850; d. there 29 Aug. 1881; m. there, 19 Nov. 1874, Miles Henry Davis, s. of Jesse and Elizabeth (Featherstone); three children, b. at Springfield. 5. *Davy Johnson*, b. 2 Aug. 1853; d. 6 Dec. 1870. 6. *Sarah Frances*, b. 16 Feb. 1855; d. at Sadlersville, Tenn., 3 Sept. 1884; m. at Springfield, 9 July 1874, Clarke Talley, s. of Jesse and Eliza (Clarke); one daughter. 7. *William John*, b. at Springfield 11 July 1859; m. at Nashville, Tenn., 11 Apr. 1889, Eula Rossie Hager, dau. of Andrew Jackson and Martha Ann (Satterfield); two children. 8. *Mattie Douglas*, b. at Springfield 4 Sept. 1866; d. there 29 Nov. 1908; m. there, 29 Apr. 1885, Burton Ferrell Draper, s. of John Cook and Theresa (Cowan); six children.

83. ii.   THOMAS BENJAMIN, b. in Robertson Co. 6 July 1827.

iii. LOUISE ADELINE, b. in Robertson Co. 17 Jan. 1829; d. at Port Royal, Tenn., 10 July 1865; m. at Port Royal, 21 Apr. 1851, RICHARD ARCHER DAVIS, s. of Jesse and Susan (Kirby). Children (surname *Davis*), b. at Springfield, Tenn.: 1. *Thomas Kirby*, b. 21 Apr. 1852; d. at Springfield 12 July 1883; m. there, 20 Oct. 1874, Emma Frances Patton, dau. of Robert Francis and Ann Eliza (Kirkpatrick); four children, b. at Springfield. 2. *Boyd*, b. 19 July 1853; d. 14 Aug. 1854. 3. *Richard Archer*, b. 1 May 1854; d. 18 June 1865. 4. *Susan Elizabeth*, b. 6 Nov. 1855; d. 24 Jan. 1858.

84. iv. JAMES KNOX, b. at Adams, Tenn., 2 Aug. 1830.

v.   SARAH ELIZABETH, b. in Robertson Co. 1 May 1832; d. there 30 July 1877; m. there, 4 Feb. 1849, JACOB HOLLAND DARDEN, s. of Hezekiah and Mahala (Fizer). Children (surname *Darden*): 1. *Irvin*, b. in Cass Co., Tex., 6 Oct. 1851; d. at Adams, Tenn., 18 June 1854. 2. *Allie Louisa*, b. 17 May 1857; m. at Adams, Tenn., 13 Dec. 1876, Presley Ewing Gilbert, s. of Preston Ozwell and Martha Jane (Townsend); they reside near Franklin, Ky.; five children. 3. *John Jacob*, b. at Adams, Tenn., 11 June 1865; d. at Nebo, Ky., 31 Mar. 1908; m. at Nebo, 20 Dec. 1898, Sallie Rutherford; no children.

vi. MARTHA ANN, b. in Robertson Co. 31 Mar. 1834; d. at Adams, Tenn., 22 Mar. 1906; m. at Adams, 17 May 1854, LEVI SMITH, s. of George and Elizabeth (Marshall). Children (surname *Smith*), b. at Adams:

1. *George Boyd*, b. 8 Oct. 1856; m. at Adams, 15 Oct. 1879, Eugenia Morris Johnston, dau. of John Henry and Martha Emaline (Reed); seven children. 2. *Jack Marshall*, of Adams, b. 12 Nov. 1859; unm. 3. *Irvin Polk*, b. 26 Sept. 1860; d. 3 Oct. 1860. 4. *William Polk*, of Louisville, Ky., b. 13 Aug. 1863; m. at Horse Cave, Ky., 6 May 1890, Verda Ray Moseley, dau. of Robert Warner and Virginia (Hare); no children. 5. *Adeline Elizabeth*, b. 4 Apr. 1866; m. at Adams, 12 Jan. 1896, Joseph Willis Atkins, s. of James Thomas and Virginia (Carr); no children. 6. *Fannie Douglas*, of Adams, b. 6 Oct. 1875; unm.

vii. HENRY ATLAS, b. in Robertson Co. 17 Apr. 1836; d. in Waxahachie, Tex., 6 Jan. 1888; m. at Springfield, Tenn., 1 Mar. 1870, NANCY KATHERINE RYBURN, dau. of Hiram. Children: 1. *Eugene*,[3] of Beaumont, Tex., b. at Springfield 20 Nov. 1870; unm. 2. *George R.*, b. 18 Jan. 1874; d. 20 Aug. 1875. 3. *Atlas Erving*, of Sierra Blanca, Tex., b. at Adams Station, Tenn., 4 Jan. 1876; m. at Del Rio, Tex., 26 Apr. 1905, Lottie Isabel Pafford, dau. of Marion and Theresa; two children.

viii. JOHN WILSON, b. in Robertson Co. about 1838; d. unm. at Mc-Minnville, Tenn., while serving in the Confederate Army, as a member of Dorth's company, Morgan's Cavalry.

ix.   WILLIAM EZEKIEL, b. in 1840; died unm. in Apr. 1866.

x.   LECIE AMELIA, b. in Robertson Co. 25 Sept. 1842; m. at Port Royal, Tenn., 5 Nov. 1865, CAPT. THOMAS EBB MALLORY, s. of Benjamin and Mary (Williams). He was in the Confederate service. Residence, Adams, Tenn. Children (surname *Mallory*): 1. *Benjamin Irvin*, b. 21 Feb. 1869; d. unm. 7 July 1889. 2. *Thomas Lyles*, b. at Adams 16 Apr. 1878; unm.

xi.   JAMES IRVIN, d. in infancy.

xii. LUCIUS LEONARD, b. at Adams Station, Tenn., 28 May 1847; m. at Springfield, Tenn., 3 Nov. 1868, MATTIE CATHERINE PIKE, who d. 13 Dec. 1879, dau. of Alfred and Mariah (Mantlo). He resides near Clarksville, Tenn. Children: 1. *Alfred Irvin*,[3] b. 19 Aug. 1869; d. 8 June 1871. 2. *Birdie Douglas*, b. at Springfield 10 July 1871; d. 22 Nov. 1879. 3. *Robert Hicks*, of Clarksville, b. at Springfield 22 Jan. 1874; m. at Saint Bethlehem, Tenn., 6 Sept. 1904, Irene Florence Rollow, dau. of Jesse Curtis and Mary Elizabeth (Metcalf); no children. 4. *Richard Watson*, b. 22 Oct. 1876; d. 18 Nov. 1879.

xiii. FANNIE DOUGLAS, b. at Adams, Tenn., 24 July 1850; m. there, 8 Feb. 1870, FINIS EWING, who d. 1 May 1906, s. of Thompson and Piety (Fort). Mrs. Ewing resides near Clarksville, Tenn. Children (surname *Ewing*): 1. *Lieut. Charles Bowman*, b. at Clarksville 7 July 1871; d. unm. at Nashville, Tenn., 8 Jan. 1916; he served in the United States Army in the Phillippines, and attained the rank of lieutenant. 2. *Finis*, of Thompson's Station, Tenn., b. in Montgomery Co., Tenn., 28 Apr. 1874; m. there, 31 Aug. 1902, Nellie Curtis Rollow, dau. of Jesse Curtis and Mary Elizabeth (Metcalf); one daughter. 3. *Bessie May*, b. 6 Sept. 1876; d. 10 Sept. 1882. 4. *Maude Douglas*, b. in Montgomery Co., Tenn., 5 Aug. 1879; m. there, 23 May 1906, Lesley Garnett Smith, s. of Albert Payne and Alice (Parham); they reside at Clarksville; no children. 5. *Thomas Polk*, b. at Clarksville 19 Apr. 1883; m. at Jackson, Tenn., 8 Nov. 1911, Helen Dodds, dau. of Joseph Sexton and Laura Elizabeth (Newsome); one son. 6. *Robert Lee*, of Memphis, Tenn., b. in Montgomery Co., Tenn., 4 June 1885; m. at Memphis, 16 Aug. 1907, Lillie Bestie, dau. of William and Josephine (Cahill); one son. 7. *Mary Douglas*, b. in Montgomery Co., Tenn., 25 June 1890; m. there, 20 Apr. 1910, Bradley Anthony Martin, Jr., s. of Bradley Anthony and Etha Lee (Jones); they reside near Palmyra, Tenn.; one son.

xiv. RICHARD EDWARD, b. at Adams Station, Tenn., 4 Apr. 1853; m. at Springfield, Tenn., 15 Oct. 1874, CORA ANNA MURPHY, dau. of Robert Hanley and Ann Elizabeth (Braden). They reside near

Clarksville, Tenn. Child: 1. *Minnie Murphy,*[8] b. at Springfield 28 July 1875; d. at Sadlersville, Tenn., 11 Aug. 1904; m. at Springfield, 17 Aug. 1891, Robert Logan Mitchell, s. of Samuel Finley and Mary Elizabeth (Limebaugh); two sons, b. in Robertson Co., Tenn.

43. THOMAS JEFFERSON[6] POLK *(Thomas,[5] Col. Ezekiel,[4] William,[3] William,[2] Robert[1]),* born in Robertson Co., Tenn., 22 Apr. 1805, died there 14 Apr. 1858. He married there MARY HURT GOSSETT, daughter of Elisha Hurt and Sally (Hutchinson). Children:

  i.   SALLY ABIGAIL,[7] b. in 1834; d. in 1913; m. DANIEL JAMES FRASER. Children (surname *Fraser*): 1. *Mary Ida.* 2. *Samuel Polk.* 3. *Leonidas Polk.* 4. *Walter.* 5. *Laura.* 6. *Ruth.* 7. *William Ebbert.* 8. *Blanche.*
  ii. MARY LOUISE, b. at Springfield, Tenn., 20 Apr. 1838; m. in Ballard Co., Ky., 17 May 1864, JOHN THOMAS ROSS. They reside near Paducah, Ky. Children (surname *Ross*): 1. *Clarence Eclipse,* of Oak Park, Ill., b. at Daysville, Ky., 7 Apr. 1869; m. at St. Louis, Mo., in 1896, Cora King; five children. 2. *Polk,* b. 7 Jan. 1872; m. (1) at Huntingdon, Tenn., in 1896, Nora Walters; m. (2) at Huntsville, Ala., in 1907, ———; four children by first wife and one son by second wife.
  iii. SUSAN, d. in childhood.
  iv. LEONIDAS TENNESSEE, b. in 1841; m. in 1870 ELIZABETH BONDS. Children: 1. *Minnie.*[8] 2. *Irvin.* 3. *Will.* 4. *John.* 5. *James.* 6. *Marvin.* 7. *Effie.* 8. *Samuel.* 9. *Marjorie.* 10. *Mary.*
  v.   VIRGINIA ADELINE, d. in 1882; m. W. W. GARDNER. Children (surname *Gardner*): 1. *Elizabeth.* 2. *Robert.* 3. *Thomas.* 4. *Emma Lou.*
  vi. ELIZABETH, d. in childhood.
  vii. EMMA THOMAS, b. at Turnersville, Tenn., in 1851; m. at Paducah, Ky., JOHN MELVILLE BYRD. Children (surname *Byrd*): 1. *Elizabeth Adeline.* 2. *Tennessee.* 3. *Jessie Abigail.* 4. *John Melville.* 5. *Polk.* 6. *Mary Agnes.*
  viii. LUCY BLOUNT, d. in childhood.

44. MARSHALL TATE[6] POLK *(Samuel,[5] Col. Ezekiel,[4] William,[3] William,[2] Robert[1]),* A.B. (University of North Carolina, 1825), planter, a younger brother of President Polk, born in Mecklenburg Co., N. C., 17 Jan. 1805, died at Charlotte, N. C., 12 Apr. 1831. He married at Charlotte, 25 Oct. 1827, LAURA T. WILSON, daughter of Judge Joseph and Mary (Wood). Children:

  i. ROXANA (EUNICE OPHELIA*),[7] b. in 1828; d. in 1842.
85. ii. MARSHALL TATE, b. at Charlotte 15 May 1831.

45. HON. WILLIAM HAWKINS[6] POLK *(Samuel,[5] Col. Ezekiel,[4] William,[3] William,[2] Robert[1]),* A.B. (University of Tennessee), a younger brother of President Polk, born in Maury Co., Tenn., 24 May 1815, died at Nashville, Tenn., 16 Dec. 1862. He married first BELINDA G. DICKINSON, who died *s.p.*; secondly, in New York City, 29 May 1847, MARY L. CORSE; and thirdly, at Montmorenci, N. C., 14 July 1854, LUCY EUGENIA WILLIAMS of Warren Co., N. C., daughter of Joseph John and Mary (Davis).

*She was probably christened Roxana, but was always called Eunice Ophelia, probably for an aunt.

He was a student at the University of North Carolina, 1832–33, continued his academic studies at the University of Tennessee, where he was graduated, studied law, and was admitted to the bar and began the practice of his profession at Columbia, Tenn., in 1839. He served as a representative in the Tennessee Legislature, 1842–1845, and was appointed by President Tyler in 1844 United States chargé d'affaires in the Kingdom of the Two Sicilies. This post he held from the early part of 1845 to 31 Aug. 1847, when he resigned to take part in the Mexican War, in which he saw active service as major in the Third Tennessee Dragoons, an organization which was disbanded 20 July 1848. He was a delegate to the Nashville Convention of 1850, and was elected as a Democratic Representative from Tennessee to the Thirty-second Congress, 1851–1853. He opposed the secession movement in Tennessee in 1861, and supported the cause of the Union.

Child by second wife:

i.   JAMES KNOX,[7] b. at Columbia, Tenn., 7 Nov. 1849; d. *s.p.* at Hartford, Conn., 5 Nov. 1912; m. at Saugatuck, Conn., in 1885, LOUISE VON ISBERG.

Children by third wife, born at Columbia, Tenn.:

ii. WILLIAM HAWKINS, b. 14 Aug. 1855; d. *s.p.* at Birmingham, Ala., 17 Oct. 1886; m. at Birmingham, 18 Nov. 1885, ADELAIDE MARABEL.

iii. TASKER, of Warrenton, N. C., b. 24 Mar. 1861; m. at Warrenton, 24 Jan. 1895, ELIZA TANNAHILL JONES, dau. of Charles J. and Alice (Tannahill). He was admitted to the bar in 1885, was first lieutenant in the Third North Carolina Infantry, solicitor of Warren County, three times mayor of Warrenton, and a State senator, 1907–08 and 1915–16. Children, b. at Warrenton: 1. *William Tannahill,*[8] b. 12 Mar. 1896. 2. *Mary Tasker,* b. 15 Dec. 1898. 3. *Lucy Fairfax,* b. 3 Dec. 1901. 4. *James Knox,* b. 4 May 1904.

46. JOHN JACKSON[6] POLK (*William Wilson,*[5] *Col. Ezekiel,*[4] *William,*[3] *William,*[2] *Robert*[1]), born in Maury Co., Tenn., 5 Sept. 1813, died at Hickory Valley, Hardeman Co., Tenn., 3 Sept. 1871. He married in Hardeman Co., 24 Feb. 1835, THRESSIA BOWLES.

Children, born in Hardeman Co.:

i.   WILLIAM EPPS,[7] b. 16 Mar. 1836; d. 30 Dec. 1855.

ii. JAMES KNOX, b. 26 Jan. 1838; d. 26 Aug. 1846.

iii. ANNA ELIZABETH, b. 21 Dec. 1840; d. at Jackson, Tenn., 7 Nov. 1905; m. at Hickory Valley, 15 June 1860, JOHN CHARLES MC-NEILL, s. of Alexander and Martha Anne (Phillips). Children (surname *McNeill*): 1. *Theresa,* b. in Hardeman Co. 1 June 1861; m. at La Grange, Tenn., 25 Nov. 1881, Kenneth Garrett Turner, s. of Midicus Joel and Henrietta (Garrett); one son. 2. *Martha Ann,* b. in Hardeman Co. 14 June 1862; d. at Birmingham, Ala., 17 Jan. 1906; m. at La Grange, Tenn., 11 Jan. 1880, George Grigg Adams, s. of Jerry and Emmie (Gilchrist); three children. 3. *Julia,* b. 2 Aug. 1863; d. 13 Oct. 1863. 4. *Annie Polk,* b. in Hardeman Co. 7 Dec. 1864; m. at La Grange, Tenn., 8 Nov. 1888, Marion Edward Withington, s. of William A. and Julia (Milligan); four children, b. at Birmingham, Ala. 5. *Tymoxena,* b. at La Grange, Tenn., 10 Jan. 1871; d. there *s.p.* 28 Dec. 1897; m. there, in July 1889, Joel L. Pulliam. 6. *Virginia,* b. at La Grange, Tenn., 21 Nov. 1871; m. there, 26 Nov. 1895, Saunders Thornley Schoolar, s. of Thornley and Laura (Saunders); two children. 7. *Jack,* of

Memphis, Tenn., b. in Fayette Co., Tenn., 1 Jan. 1874; m. there, 22 Nov. 1899, Mamie Frances Garnett, dau. of John and Frances (Rutledge); two children. 8. *Katherine Elnora*, b. at La Grange, Tenn., 6 Mar. 1875; m. at Jackson, Tenn., 5 Jan. 1903, Francis Montgomery Swift, s. of John Julian and Susie (Lanier); residence, Holly Springs, Miss.; three children. 9. *John Charles*, b. 10 May 1877; d. unm. 20 Mar. 1901. 10. *Willie Polk*, b. 6 July 1880; d. at Holly Springs, Miss., 13 June 1913; m. at Holly Springs, 26 Jan. 1909, James Tort Daniel, s. of Chesley and Frances (Tort); one child, b. 13 June 1913.

iv. MARY CAROLINE, b. 3 Dec. 1842; d. 23 Sept. 1843.
v. WILLIAM D., b. 4 Aug. 1844; d. 27 Feb. 1845.
vi. VIRGINIA GREEN, b. 14 Jan. 1846; d. at Somerville, Tenn., 16 Sept. 1878; m. at Memphis, Tenn., 15 Mar. 1864, PATRICK HENRY BOWERS, s. of George and Mary. Children (surname *Bowers*): 1. *Patrick Henry*, b. at Somerville 25 Sept. 1865; unm. 2. *Jennie*, b. 1 Aug. 1867; m. at Hickory Valley, 8 Oct. 1884, A. W. Schevenell; residence, Memphis; three children. 3. *Albert Sidney*, b. at Somerville 2 Dec. 1868; m. (1) at Memphis, 6 Feb. 1898, Anna Kate Ramey, dau. of William Nathaniel and Anna (Key); m. (2) at Memphis, 12 June 1907, Margarett Waters Stark, dau. of Thomas Augustus and Martha (Robinson); three daughters. 4. *Anna Polk*, b. 15 Feb. 1870; d. 17 Sept. 1878. 5. *Mary J.*, b. at Somerville 20 Mar. 1871; m. at Marion, Ark., 3 Mar. 1888, Alvin B. Irwin; residence, Memphis; four children. 6. *Jack Polk*, b. at Somerville 16 Nov. 1873; m. in Fayette Co., Tenn., 16 Dec. 1893, Elizabeth Griggs Atkeison, dau. of Richard Drewry and Agnes (Griggs); six children. 7. *Oscar Polk*, b. 31 Mar. 1875; d. 10 Apr. 1875. 8. *Olivia*, b. 23 July 1876; d. 2 Mar. 1879.
vii. OSCAR BOWLES, b. 1 Mar. 1849; m. at Memphis, Tenn., 21 Nov. 1879, MRS. ADA CLARISSA (BOYLE) LOWE, dau. of Thomas and Margaret Boyle. He was a planter at Hickory Valley until 1889, when he moved to Memphis. He was first vice president of the first trust company organized in Memphis, and since 1908 has been president of the Security Bank and Trust Company. He is owner of the old William Wilson Polk homestead near Hickory Valley. Children: 1. *Oscar Bowles*,[8] of Hickory Valley, b. at Hickory Valley 6 Feb. 1881; living there unm. 2. *Ada Thressia*, b. at Hickory Valley 25 Jan. 1883; m. at Memphis, 16 Oct. 1907, Nathaniel Riddick Prichard; no children. 3. *Pearl Margaret*, b. at Hickory Valley 4 Sept. 1887; m. at Memphis, 8 June 1911, Charles Emory Chapleau; one son. 4. *Elizabeth Parmelia*, b. 26 Oct. 1889; unm.
viii. JOHN JACKSON, b. 14 Nov. 1850; d. unm. 16 Sept. 1878.
ix. THOMAS MARLBOROUGH, of Jackson, Tenn., b. at Hickory Valley 27 Nov. 1852; m. (1) in Hardeman Co., 15 July 1874, WILLIE RODGERS; m. (2) 16 June 1909 LAURA LEE SHARP. He is president of the Second National Bank of Jackson and mayor of Jackson. Children, b. in Hardeman Co.: 1. *John Jackson*,[8] b. 27 Apr. 1875; d. in July 1893. 2. *Florence*, b. 17 May 1877; m. in Nov. 1898 John Chester Botts; residence, New York City; two sons. 3. *Theresa*, b. 20 Aug. 1879; m. at Jackson, in Oct. 1904, Bond Anderson; residence, Anderson, S. C.; one son. 4. *Iola*, b. 27 Nov. 1881; unm. 5. *Wilma*, b. at Jackson 16 Oct. 1893; unm.
x. JOHN McGOWAN, b. 26 June 1855; d. *s.p.* 13 July 1894; m. ANNIE GOODWIN.

47. THOMAS MARLBOROUGH[6] POLK (*William Wilson*,[5] *Col. Ezekiel*,[4] *William*,[3] *William*,[2] *Robert*[1]), born near Columbia, Maury Co., Tenn., 11 Sept. 1815, died in Navarro Co., Tex., 18 Dec. 1872. He married first, in Greene Co., Mo., 8 Nov. 1837, LUCINDA YOUNGER, born 15 Apr. 1823, died in Phillips Co., Ark., 24 Mar. 1861, daughter of Alexander and Jane (Hancock);

and secondly, in Phillips Co., Ark., 11 Mar. 1862, FANNIE
TABITHA FOSTER, born in Tennessee 27 Sept. 1838, died in
Navarro Co., Tex., 3 June 1873, sister of Rev. William R.
Foster of Arkansas.

He migrated about 1835 to Greene Co., Mo., and settled
about five miles east of Springfield. In 1840 he moved to
Lawrence Co., Mo., and settled near the head of Honey Creek,
about twelve miles south of Mount Vernon. Upon the death
of his father in 1848 he inherited land at Walnut Bend, Phillips
Co., Ark., and moved thither in 1849. In 1859 and 1860 he
made prospecting trips to Texas, and in 1861 bought timber
land and erected a sawmill in Navarro Co. in that State. In
1866 he moved his family from Arkansas, and settled perma-
nently near Dresden, Tex.

Children by first wife:

86. i. JAMES MONROE,[7] b. in Greene Co., Mo., 7 Oct. 1838.
    ii. ELIZABETH JANE, b. in Lawrence Co., Mo., 24 Jan. 1841; d. at Kerens,
        Tex., 15 Sept. 1882; m. in Phillips Co., Ark., in 1859, DR. W. FORD
        COATES. Child (surname *Coates*): 1. *Leslie Melville*, b. at Harnes-
        ville, Miss., 19 July 1860; d. at Corsicana, Tex., 25 May 1912; m.
        at Corsicana, 14 Feb. 1883, Mattie Barnett Bennett, dau. of Elijah
        and Mattie Belle (Grant); two daughters.
87. iii. WILLIAM ALEXANDER, b. in Lawrence Co., Mo., 14 Feb. 1844.
    iv. SARAH, b. 29 Jan. 1846; d. 14 Oct. 1846.
    v. A SON, b. 29 Aug. 1847; d. 5 Sept. 1847.
    vi. JOHN, b. 8 Aug. 1848; d. 18 May 1850.
    vii. OLIVIA, b. in Phillips Co., Ark., 11 Sept. 1850; d. at Hillsboro, Tex.,
        5 May 1884; m. in Navarro Co., Tex., 20 Feb. 1872, ETHAN BEDEN
        STROUD, s. of Mandred and Narcissus (Oliver). Children (surname
        Stroud): 1. *Thomas Mandred*, b. in Parker Co., Tex., 2 Feb. 1873;
        m. at Hillsboro Della Walker; residence, Wichita Falls, Tex.;
        no children. 2. *Ora*, b. 7 Dec. 1879; m. at Hillsboro, 3 Sept.
        1899, Thomas William Slack, b. at Mexico, Mo., 7 Nov. 1866, s.
        of Thomas and Eliza (Reiley); residence, Fort Worth, Tex. 3.
        Roderick, d. in infancy. 4. *Napoleon*, d. in infancy. Two other
        infants, d. unnamed.
    viii. A SON, b. and d. 23 Dec. 1854.
    ix. ELLIE (twin), b. 10 Jan. 1856; d. 18 Sept. 1856.
    x. A SON (twin), b. and d. 10 Jan. 1856.
    xi. MATTA, b. 3 Dec. 1858; d. 9 Feb. 1859.

Children by second wife:

    xii. JULIA ANNE, b. in Phillips Co., Ark., 12 Oct. 1862; d. in Navarro
        Co., Tex., 24 June 1877.
    xiii. LULA ELLA, b. at Walnut Bend, Phillips Co., Ark., 28 Nov. 1864;
        m. at Forrest City, Ark., 21 Apr. 1882, REV. LEONIDAS GIDEON
        ROGERS, b. in White Co., Ill., 27 Jan. 1848, d. at Strawn, Palo
        Pinto Co., Tex., 21 Sept. 1915, s. of Mark Washington and Sarah
        Tabitha (Mitchell) Rogers and grandson of Charles Thomas and
        Elizabeth (Hutton) Rogers.* The childhood of Leonidas Gideon

*Charles Thomas Rogers was born, probably in Wake Co., N. C., about 1795, and died at South
Harpeth, Williamson Co., Tenn., 26 Sept. 1824. He married at Fall Creek, Rutherford Co., Tenn.,
9 Apr. 1817, Elizabeth Hutton, daughter of John M. While still in his teens he ran away from
home, because of a boyish misunderstanding, and went to Tennessee. In the War of 1812 he enlisted at Franklin, Williamson Co., 20 Dec. 1813, in Capt. Matthew Johnston's company, Col.
Nicholas T. Perkins's regiment, First Tennessee Mounted Volunteers. In the fight at Enotochapco
Creek, 24 Jan. 1814, he was wounded in the right arm, was discharged from the service 8 Feb.
1814, and returned to Franklin. At his death, which was caused indirectly by his wound, after
several years of poor health, he left his family in straitened circumstances; for, although his children were entitled to a considerable inheritance from their grandfather's estate in North Carolina,

Rogers was passed on the plantation of his maternal grandfather, in Weakley Co., Tenn. He was educated at home, at "subscription schools" in the neighborhood, at private schools at Fulton, Ky., and at McKenzie College. During the Civil War his maternal grandfather died, and all of this grandfather's lands, except the widow's dower in the home and 200 acres besides, were sold to pay security debts which he had incurred in helping his neighbors weather the storm of war. In young manhood Leonidas Gideon Rogers entered the ministry of the Methodist Episcopal Church, South, serving first in the West Tennessee Conference and in Dec. 1882 in the Northwestern Conference. For a short time he was in the White River (Ark.) Conference. Residence, Dallas, Tex. Children (surname *Rogers*): 1. *Leonidas Winfield*, of Austin, Tex., A.B. (Southwestern University, Georgetown, Tex., 1909), b. at Groesbeck, Limestone Co., Tex., 15 May 1883; m. at Mineola, Tex., 23 Dec. 1914, Marcia Butts, dau. of John Henry and Lelia (Lawrence); he was on the staff of the *Galveston News*, 1911, principal of the high school, Mineola, Tex., 1911–1914, teacher of history in the high school at Dallas, 1915–1917, superintendent of schools, Huntsville, Tex., 1918, and special State supervisor of rural schools, 1919–1922; no children. 2. *Ethel Olivia*, of Dallas, A.B. (Southwestern University, 1908), b. at Burnett, Tex., 18 Feb. 1885; unm. 3. *Fannie Tabitha*, A.B. (Southwestern University, 1909), b. at Wheatland, Dallas Co., Tex., 19 Mar. 1887; m. at Dallas, 16 June 1920, Dr. William Saunders Baldwin, s. of Dr. Benjamin Joseph and Willie Catherine (Saundors); residence, Mineral Springs, Tex.; no children. 4. *Wilmot Polk*, of Berkeley, Calif., b. at Rice, Navarro Co., Tex., 16 Jan. 1889; m. at Gate, Beaver Co., Okla., 1 June 1910, Edna Sarah Beardsley, b. at Ottawa, Kans., 3 Oct. 1888, dau. of William Lincoln and Maggie Oliver (Miller) Beardsley and granddaughter of Col. Ezra Marvin and Sarah (Lemmon) Beardsley of Rock Island, Ill.; he was educated at Weatherford College and Southwestern University; he enlisted at Weatherford, 4 June 1907, in Co. G, Fourth Infantry, Texas National Guard, and was discharged 4 June 1910; soon after

they were ignorant of their rights, since their father had never communicated with his father's family after running away from home. The children of Charles Thomas and Elizabeth (Hutton) Rogers were: 1. John Henry, b. in Mar. 1818. 2. Zane Mira, m. —— Allen. 3. Mark Washington, b. in Maury Co., Tenn., 19 Oct. 1822. 4. James William.

As these children grew up, John Henry was apprenticed to a printer and Mark Washington to a saddler. In the late fifties John Henry Rogers, who was then on the staff of the *St. Louis Republican*, in looking through some old files of that newspaper, came across an advertisement for his father or his heirs, which had been inserted in the paper in the early thirties by the executors of the estate of Charles Thomas Rogers's father. He immediately took steps to establish the right of his father's family to share in the inheritance, and about 1860 went to North Carolina and entered suit to have his father's share in the estate distributed to the latter's heirs. Before the case came to trial the Civil War broke out, John Henry Rogers died in 1863, the estate became impoverished by the emancipation of the slaves, and the heirs of Charles Thomas Rogers did not prosecute their claims further.

Mark Washington Rogers married in Weakley Co., Tenn., 11 Sept. 1844, Sarah Tabitha Mitchell, daughter of Rev. Matthew Freeman Mitchell. Soon afterwards he migrated, with his wife, to White Co., Ill., where John Henry Rogers and others of the family settled. On 10 Feb. 1853, while on a journey to Evansville, Ind., by an Ohio River steamboat, to purchase stock, Mark Washington Rogers fell overboard and was drowned, his body being recovered and buried at Caseyville, Ky. His widow, with her young children, returned to her father's home, a plantation in Weakley Co., Tenn. The children of Mark Washington and Sarah Tabitha (Mitchell) Rogers, born in White Co., Ill., were: 1. John Matthew Freeman, b. 20 Mar. 1846; d. in Weakley Co., Tenn., 7 Sept. 1862. 2. Leonidas Gideon, b. 27 Jan. 1848 (see above, under 47, xiii). 3. Charles Thomas, b. 22 July 1849; d. 13 Aug. 1849. 4. Wesley Newton, b. 1 Oct. 1850 (see below). 5. Theodore Pressley, b. 30 Oct. 1852; d. unm. in Weakley Co., Tenn., 14 Sept. 1902.

Wesley Newton Rogers married at Fulton, Ky., 1 Nov. 1880, Fannie Bates Reams, daughter of David Crockett and Louise (Moss) Reams, and resides in Weakley Co., Tenn. Children: 1. Arthur Graham, b. in Weakley Co. 7 July 1881; unm. 2. Effie Eleana, b. 3 Nov. 1882; d. in Weakley Co. 1 Apr. 1905. 3. Lula, b. in Weakley Co. 1 Apr. 1885; d. 3 Apr. 1885. 4. Ernest Crockett, b. 19 Jan. 1888; d. at Fulton, Ky., 3 Mar. 1890. 5. Herman Titus, b. at Fulton, Ky., 5 June 1891; m. at Martin, Tenn., 7 Sept. 1913, Eunie Edwards, dau. of Duke and Mattie (Green) Edwards; they have issue.

the entrance of the United States into the World War he enlisted, 19 May 1917, in the Fifteenth Provisional Regiment, Reserve Officers' Training Corps, at Leon Springs, Tex., and was discharged 14 Aug. 1917; he was then commissioned, 15 Aug. 1917, as captain of Infantry and was assigned to the Ninetieth Division, at Camp Travis, Tex., was transferred, 29 Aug. 1917, to the Fortieth Division, at Camp Kearney, Calif., and was attached to the Second California Infantry, stationed at Fort Mason, San Francisco; he was transferred, 19 Dec. 1917, to the Ninety-first Division, at Camp Lewis, Wash., and was attached to the Three Hundred and Sixty-third Infantry; he was transferred, 23 Mar. 1918, to the Eighth Division of the Regular Army, at Camp Fremont, Calif., was assigned to the Eighth Train Headquarters and Military Police, and was appointed adjutant; he was transferred with the division to Camp Mills, Long Island, 24 Oct. 1918, *en route* to France, but the overseas orders were cancelled and the division was transferred, 26 Nov. 1918, to Camp Lee, Va.; he was detailed as acting division adjutant 31 Jan. 1919, for the demobilization of the division, was transferred and assigned to the Sixty-second Infantry, 21 Feb. 1919, and was placed in command of Co. H; was transferred 15 Oct. 1919 to the Presidio, at San Francisco, and was discharged 30 Oct. 1919; one daughter, Edna Beardsley, b. at the home of her maternal grandparents, about three miles west of Gate, Beaver Co., Okla., 27 July 1911. 5. *William Matthew*, b. about eight miles southeast of Vernon, Tex., 17 July 1891; d. *s.p.* at Fort Worth, Tex., 9 Sept. 1920; m. at McKinney, Tex., 9 Nov. 1913, Cleora May Harris, dau. of Zachariah Asbury Coleman and Mary Jane (Cusenberry); he enlisted at Weatherford, Tex., 29 Jan. 1908, in Co. G, Fourth Infantry, Texas National Guard, and was discharged 6 May 1911; soon after the entrance of the United States into the World War he enlisted, 9 May 1917, in the Fifteenth Provisional Regiment, Reserve Officers' Training Corps, at Leon Springs, Tex., and was discharged 14 Aug. 1917; he was then commissioned second lieutenant, Quartermaster's Corps, 15 Aug. 1917, and was assigned to the Three Hundred and Fourth Motor Repair Unit, Camp Travis, Tex., 11 Dec. 1917; he was transferred to El Paso, Tex., in June 1918, and assigned to the Three Hundred and Ninth Motor Repair Unit; he joined, with his unit, 15 Sept. 1918, the American Expeditionary Forces in France, was promoted to first lieutenant 12 May 1919, returned to the United States, and was discharged at Newport News, Va., 13 Aug. 1919. 6. *Lulu May*, b. at Vernon, Tex., 26 Sept. 1893; d. at Throckmorton, Tex., 10 Oct. 1897. 7. *Lewis Galloway*, of Dallas, Tex., b. at Farmer, Young Co., Tex., 7 Apr. 1899; m. at Dallas, 4 Sept. 1920, Vivian Bell, dau. of Marshall and Nellie (Watts); he enlisted at Dallas, 7 July 1917, in Co. C, Sixth Texas Infantry, which on 14 Oct. 1917 became Co. B, One Hundred and Forty-fourth Infantry, at Camp Bowie, Tex.; he was transferred, 8 Apr. 1918, as part of a replacement detachment, and sailed from New York 3 May 1918, landing in Liverpool, Eng., 14 May, and at Calais, France, 15 May; he was sent about forty kilometers south to Lombres, and was attached to the Twenty-eighth Division, then serving with the British Army in Flanders as a part of its reserve; about a month later he was sent to the classification camp at St. Aignan, and on 4 July 1918 was assigned to the Thirtieth Infantry, Third Division, then occupying a sector between Chateau Thierry and Donnons; he participated in the Champagne-Marne defensive, in the Aisne-Marne, St. Mihiel, and Meuse-Argonne offensives, and in minor engagements and skirmishes; he returned to the United States, and was discharged at San Antonio, Tex., 11 Mar. 1919.

[To be continued]

48. WILLIAM[7] POLK (*Brig. Gen. Thomas Gilchrist,[6] Lieut. Col. William,[5] Brig. Gen. Thomas,[4] William,[3] William,[2] Robert[1]*), born at Salisbury, N. C., 17 Nov. 1821, died at New Orleans, La., 24 Jan. 1898, and was buried at Alexandria, La. He married, 20 Jan. 1857, REBECCA EVALINE LAMAR of Georgia, who died in 1912 and was buried beside her husband, a niece of Gen. Mirabeau Buonaparte Lamar, one of the Presidents of the Republic of Texas, and a cousin of the late Lucius Quintus Cincinnatus Lamar, Associate Justice of the United States Supreme Court.

He was a student at the University of North Carolina, 1837–38, and became a prominent sugar planter of Rapides Parish, La. His home, Ashton Plantation, near Alexandria, was widely known as a social centre. He was a member of the North Carolina Chapter of the Society of the Cincinnati, the membership having descended to him from his grandfather, Lieut. Col. William Polk (9). He was an authority on the culture of the sugar cane.

Children:

i. ALICE,[8] b. at Holly Springs, Miss., 11 Mar. 1858; m. at Asheville, N. C., 4 Aug. 1890, WILLIAM POLK FLOWER. Residence, New Orleans. Child (surname *Flower*): 1. *William Polk*, b. 26 May 1891.

ii. WILLIAM, b. at Ashton Plantation, Rapides Parish, La., 6 Feb. 1862; m. 8 Aug. 1893 ELLA BAILLIO HAYES. He resides near Alexandria, La., and is a member of the North Carolina Chapter of the Society of the Cincinnati. Children: 1. *Lamar,[9]* b. 4 May 1894; served in the World War as a first-class sergeant in the Artillery, in Battery C, One Hundred and Forty-first Regiment, Seventeenth Division. 2. *Ella*, b. 5 June 1904.

iii. MARY ELOISE, b. in Texas 4 Sept. 1864; m. 20 Jan. 1885 DAVID S. FERRIS of Westchester Co., N. Y. Child (surname *Ferris*): 1. *Livingston Polk*, b. at Grove Farm, Westchester Co., N. Y., 30 Aug. 1886.

49. MAJ. ALLEN JONES[7] POLK (*William Julius,[6] Lieut. Col. William,[5] Brig. Gen. Thomas,[4] William,[3] William,[2] Robert[1]*), of Helena, Ark., cotton planter, born at Farmville, N. C., 5 Mar. 1824, died at Helena 17 Mar. 1897. He married first, in 1846,

MARY CLENDENNIN; and secondly, 16 June 1859, ANNA
CLARK FITZHUGH, who died 3 Dec. 1902, daughter of Judge
Dennis Fitzhugh of Louisville, Ky., and a grandniece of Brig.
Gen. George Rogers Clark, the famous soldier who in the
Revolution wrested the territory beyond the Ohio from the
British and the Indians.

He was enrolled at the University of North Carolina, 1840–
1843, and studied law with Judge Russell Houston at Columbia,
Tenn. At the age of twenty-one he moved to Helena, Ark.,
where he was a successful cotton planter. During the Civil
War he held a commission as major in General Hindman's
Arkansas Legion, but did not see active service. At the close
of the War he moved to Louisville, Ky., and remained there
for several years, until the end of "Carpetbag" rule in the
South. Then he returned to his plantation at Helena.

Children by first wife:

i.   WILLIAM,[8] d. in infancy.
ii. MARY, b. at Columbia, Tenn., 18 Oct. 1852; m. 18 Dec. 1877 FRANK
     B. HEMPHILL. Residence, Louisville, Ky. Children (surname
     Hemphill): 1. *Mary Polk*, d. in childhood. 2. *Frankie Polk*, b. 15
     Aug. 1890. 3. *Allen Polk*, b. 26 Oct. 1893; served in the World
     War as first lieutenant, Company L, Three Hundred and Twenty-
     third Infantry. 4. *Polk*, b. 4 May 1896; served in the World
     War with the United States Ambulance Corps.

Children by second wife:

iii. ALLEN JONES, b. 22 Mar. 1860; d. 13 Feb. 1875.
iv. CLARK FITZHUGH, b. 10 May 1861; d. 6 May 1885.
v.   SUSAN HUNTINGTON, b. at Terre Haute, Ind., 1 Jan. 1864; m. 13
     Jan. 1887 T. W. KESEE. Children (surname *Kesee*): 1. *Zelda
     Polk*, b. at Helena, Ark., 31 Jan. 1889; m. 15 June 1912 William
     J. O'Brien; residence, Helena. 2. *Thomas Woodfin*, b. at Helena,
     Ark., 13 July 1891; m. 7 Aug. 1913 Sarah Gladys Key. 3. *Allen
     Polk*, b. 1 Oct. 1896.
vi. ANNA LEE, b. at Louisville, Ky., 28 Nov. 1866; m. 17 Feb. 1887
     SAMUEL A. PEPPER. Residence, Memphis, Tenn. Children (sur-
     name *Pepper*): 1. *Allen Polk*, b. at Memphis 5 Dec. 1887; m. 19
     May 1909 Hugh Barrett Speed of Memphis. 2. *Zelda Fontain*,
     b. 27 Mar. 1889; m. John J. Gill. 3. *Anna Fitzhugh*, b. 7 Feb.
     1895. 4. *Samuel Alexander*, b. 28 Sept. 1897; served in the World
     War as corporal, Company E, One Hundred and Fifteenth Field
     Artillery, American Expeditionary Forces, and was in the Army
     of Occupation.
vii. GRISELDA HOUSTON, b. at Louisville, Ky., 8 Nov. 1868; m. 12 Nov.
     1890 D. T. HARGRAVES. Residence, Helena, Ark. Children
     (surname *Hargraves*): 1. *David Thomson*, b. 3 July 1900; served
     in the World War as a private, Infantry Officers' School, Replace-
     ment Camp, Camp Pike. 2. *Griselda Polk*, b. 29 May 1904. 3.
     Anna Fitzhugh, b. 27 Oct. 1907. 4. *James Fitzhugh*, b. 11 Sept.
     1909.

50. CAPT. THOMAS GILCHRIST[7] POLK (*William Julius*,[6] *Lieut. Col.
    William*,[5] *Brig. Gen. Thomas*,[4] *William*,[3] *William*,[2] *Robert*[1]),
    M.D. (Jefferson Medical College, Philadelphia), born in
    Mecklenburg Co., N. C., 25 Dec. 1825, died at Decatur, Ala.,
    14 June 1877, and was buried in St. John's Churchyard, Maury
    Co., Tenn. He married, 15 May 1851, LAVINIA C. WOOD,
    who died at Decatur in 1887, daughter of Jonas Wood of

Charleston, S. C., and a descendant of George Mason, who came from Staffordshire, England, to Stafford Co., Va., and was the progenitor of the well-known Mason family of Virginia.

He was enrolled at the University of North Carolina, 1840–41, was graduated at the Jefferson Medical College, Philadelphia, and was an assistant surgeon in the Mexican War. He was a captain in the Confederate Army, took part in the defence of Vicksburg, served as a volunteer aide on the staff of Gen. J. C. Tappan in the operations against Banks's Red River expedition, and was also present at the Battle of Pleasant Hill.

Children:

i. MARY REBECCA,[8] b. in St. Mary's Parish, La., 12 Mar. 1852; m. 10 Apr. 1872 W. W. LITTLEJOHN of Decatur, Ala., who d. there 8 Feb. 1907. Residence, Decatur. Children (surname *Littlejohn*): 1. *Thomas*, b. at Memphis, Tenn., 22 Mar. 1873; m. in 1895 Margaret Wallace of Decatur. 2. *Margaret*, b. at Memphis, Tenn., 14 Apr. 1875; d. at Decatur 29 May 1897; m. 8 Sept. 1896 William R. Spright. 3. *William Whitson*, d. in infancy. 4. *Lavinia Polk*, b. at Decatur 28 June 1888; m. in Dec. 1914 Richard Norfleet Harris.

ii. CAROLINE, b. at Millikin's Bend, La., 7 Sept. 1853; m. 6 May 1873 HAMILTON SEYMOUR HORNOR. Residence, Helena, Ark. Children (surname *Hornor*): 1. *John Sidney*, of Helena, banker, b. at Helena 14 Dec. 1873; m. 3 Jan. 1900 Frances May Moore. 2. *Mabel*, d. in childhood. 3. *Mimi Polk*, b. at Helena 1 Feb. 1879; m. (1) 17 Dec. 1900 William B. Pillow, who d. 23 May 1904; m. (2) 18 Apr. 1912 Walter B. Wright of Granville, Ohio.

iii. GRISELDA, b. near Greenville, Miss., 8 Dec. 1855; d. at Helena, Ark., 25 Oct. 1906; m. 5 July 1877 HENRY R. STERLING. Child (surname *Sterling*): 1. *Mary Ruffin*, b. near Barton, Ark., 10 Feb. 1879; m. 17 Oct. 1914 Alexander Hogan Ames; residence, Starkville, Ala.

iv. WILLIAM JULIUS, b. in Washington Co., Miss., 14 June 1862; d. at Decatur, Ala., 12 Apr. 1902; m. 2 Jan. 1893 EUOLA GREENLEAF. Child: 1. *Madeleine Tasker*,[9] b. in 1894; m. 27 Dec. 1915 James Allen Fuller of Huntsville, Ala.

51. BRIG. GEN. LUCIUS EUGENE[7] POLK (*William Julius,[6] Lieut. Col. William,[5] Brig. Gen. Thomas,[4] William,[3] William,[2] Robert[1]*), of "Westbrook," Maury Co., Tenn., planter, lawyer, born at Salisbury, N. C., 10 July 1833, died at "Westbrook" 1 Dec. 1893, and was buried in St. John's Churchyard. He married at the Forks of the Cypress, near Florence, Ala., 19 Aug. 1863, his first cousin, SALLY MOORE[7] POLK (9, ix, 1), born there 1 Sept. 1841, daughter of Rufus King[6] and Sarah Moore (Jackson).

He was a student at the University of Virginia in 1850–51, and settled near Helena, Ark., where he engaged in cotton planting. At the outbreak of the Civil War he enlisted in the Confederate Army as a private in Capt. Patrick R. Cleburne's company, known as the "Yell Rifles," which afterwards formed a part of the First Arkansas Regiment. He was soon commissioned as first lieutenant, and at the Battle of Shiloh, 6 Apr. 1862, where the regiment was cut to pieces, took command of his company and led it during the two days' fighting. He was promoted to be colonel of the regiment, and was commended for gallantry in General Hardee's official report. In the Kentucky Campaign he served under Gen. Kirby Smith, and was wounded at Richmond, Ky., and Perryville, Tenn. In Dec. 1862 he was made a brigadier general, and commanded the First Brigade (formerly commanded by Cleburne), Second Division (Cleburne's), Hardee's corps, in the Battle of Stone River (Murfreesboro), Tenn., 31 Dec. 1862. He participated in the fighting in Tennessee and Georgia in 1863 and 1864, including the battles at Chickamauga, Chattanooga, Ringgold Gap (27 Nov. 1863), where he captured three Union flags, and New Hope Church (25 May 1864), where he was wounded and crippled for life. He returned to his plantation, "Westbrook," in Maury Co., Tenn., and made his home there for the rest of his days. He was a delegate to the Democratic National Convention in Chicago in 1884, and a member of the Tennessee Senate in 1887.

Children:

i. HON. RUFUS KING,[8] of Danville, Pa., B.S. (Lehigh University, 1887), M.E. (*ib.*, 1888), b. at Columbia, Maury Co., Tenn., 23 Aug. 1866; d. in Philadelphia, Pa., 5 Mar. 1902; m. 27 Oct. 1892 ISABEL GRIER, dau. of Isaac K. and Emma (Porter) of Danville. He attended Webb's Academy, Culleoka, Tenn., and Lehigh University, South Bethlehem, Pa., where he studied to be a mining engineer and metallurgist. He settled at Danville, held several positions in the iron and steel industry of that region, and became general manager of the North Branch Steel Company of Danville. In 1896 he took part in establishing the firm of Howe & Polk, manufacturers of iron and steel. In the War with Spain he served as first lieutenant in Company F of the Twelfth Regiment, Pennsylvania Volunteer Infantry. After the War he was elected to the Fifty-sixth Congress from the Seventeenth District of Pennsylvania, as a Democrat, and was reëlected to the Fifty-seventh Congress, his service as a member of the House of Representatives extending from 4 Mar. 1899 until his death in the midst of his second term. He had been a delegate at large to the Democratic National Convention in 1900, and had declined to be a candidate for election to the Fifty-eighth Congress. He was a member of the North Carolina Chapter of the Society of the Cincinnati. Children: 1. *Emma Grier*,[9] b. 12 Nov. 1893. 2. *Porter Grier*, b. 24 Feb. 1895; served in the World War in France as first lieutenant in Company D, One Hundred and Ninth Infantry, Twenty-eighth Division, American Expeditionary Forces, and was in the Army of Occupation. 3. *Isabel Grier*, b. at Danville 22 Sept. 1897; m. there, 21 June 1917, Dr. Harold Leighton Foss; one daughter. 4. *Sarah Moore* (twin), b. 15 May 1900; d. in infancy. 5. *Mary Rebecca* (twin), b. 15 May 1900.

ii. MARY REBECCA, b. at "Westbrook," Maury Co., Tenn., 20 May 1868; m. 4 Feb. 1890 SCOTT P. HARLAN. Residence, near Nashville, Tenn. Children (surname *Harlan*): 1. *Sarah Polk*, b. 20 Dec. 1891. 2. *Benjamin Joseph*, b. 9 Aug. 1893; served in the World War as corporal in Company D, Forty-second Engineers, in camp at Washington, D. C. 3. *Lucius Polk*, b. 24 June 1895; served in the World War as sergeant in the One Hundred and Fifty-first Field Hospital, Camp Shelby, Hattiesburg, Miss. 4. *Katherine Scott*, b. 14 Jan. 1898.

iii. LUCIUS EUGENE, civil engineer, b. at "Westbrook," Maury Co., Tenn., 22 Mar. 1870; d. 18 May 1904; bur. in St. John's Churchyard; m. 30 Aug. 1898 BLANCHE CLEMENTS. In the War with

Spain he served as first lieutenant in the Fourth Regiment, Tennessee Volunteer Infantry, and later as captain in the Forty-third Regiment, United States Volunteer Infantry. Child: 1. *Lucius Eugene,*[9] b. 14 Feb. 1900.

iv. WILLIAM JULIUS, b. at "Westbrook," Maury Co., Tenn., 13 June 1875; m. 21 June 1899 WILLIE MAY GLASS. He resides near Franklin, Tenn. He was graduated from the Battleground Academy, Franklin, and entered Lafayette College, Easton, Pa., in Sept. 1896. Later he attended the Medical Department of Vanderbilt University, Nashville, Tenn. He volunteered for service in the War with Spain as assistant surgeon in the First Tennessee Regiment, Volunteer Infantry, and served until the regiment was disbanded at San Francisco. He took a special course in hospital work at Tulane Hospital, New Orleans, La. Children: 1. *Mary Rebecca,*[9] b. 16 July 1901. 2. *Sarah Glass,* b. 1 July 1904.

v. JAMES KNOX, b. at "Westbrook," Maury Co., Tenn., 14 Jan. 1882; d. *s.p.* at Paris, Tex., 13 Feb. 1912; m. 10 Mar. 1907 LOTTIE SCHWARTZ.

52. COL. CADWALLADER LONG[7] POLK (*William Julius,*[6] *Lieut. Col. William,*[5] *Brig. Gen. Thomas,*[4] *William,*[3] *William,*[2] *Robert*[1]), of Helena, Ark., cotton planter, A.B. (University of North Carolina, 1857), was born at Columbia, Maury Co., Tenn., 16 Oct. 1837. He married, 29 Mar. 1864, CAROLINE LOWRY.

At the outbreak of the Civil War he enlisted in the First Tennessee Infantry, Confederate Army, and was made second lieutenant of his company. He served with his regiment in the Army of Virginia, and then returned West in time to take part in the Battle of Shiloh. After his term of enlistment expired he joined Hindman's Legion, was appointed major in one of the new regiments, and was afterwards promoted to a lieutenant colonelcy. At the Battle of Prairie Grove, Ark., 7 Dec. 1862, he was severely wounded and was taken prisoner. After being exchanged he was made colonel of his regiment, and served in this capacity to the end of the War.

Children:

i. WILLIAM JULIUS,[8] of Helena, Ark., commission merchant, b. at Camden, Ark., 17 Jan. 1865; m. LULU DONNELL. Children: 1. *George Donnell,*[9] b. 27 Jan. 1893; served in the World War as sergeant, Machine Gun Company, One Hundred and Fifty-fourth Infantry, Thirty-ninth Division. 2. *Carry May,* b. 19 Nov. 1899. 3. *Ellis Rivere,* d. in childhood.

ii. ANNIE T., b. 8 Dec. 1867; m. 19 Nov. 1890 CHRISTOPHER AGEE. Residence, Helena, Ark. Child (surname *Agee*): 1. *Polk Watkins.*

iii. RUFUS WALTER, of Little Rock, Ark., real-estate dealer, b. 27 Jan. 1869; m. in 1898 SUE LOUISE POWELL. Children: 1. *Edward Winfield,*[9] who in the World War was at the Artillery Officers' Training School, Camp Taylor. 2. *Rufus Walter.* 3. *Caroline.*

iv. CADWALLADER LONG, of Helena, Ark., merchant, b. at Helena 12 May 1870; m. in 1897 LUCILLE QUARLES. Children: 1. *Greenfield Quarles,*[9] d. in childhood. 2. *Cadwallader Long.* 3. *Lucille Quarles,* d. in infancy.

v. CORNELIA LOWRY, b. at Helena, Ark., 19 Mar. 1874; m. in 1903 WILLIAM A. COOLIDGE. Children (surname *Coolidge*): 1. *William A.,* who in the World War was a corporal in the Artillery Officers' Training School, Remount Station 317, Eighty-seventh Division. 2. *Elizabeth.* 3. *Annie Agee.*

vi. EDWIN MOORE, b. 31 Mar. 1880.

vii. CLEORA LAWRENCE, d. in childhood.

53. CAPT. RUFUS JULIUS[7] POLK (*William Julius,*[6] *Lieut. Col. William,*[5] *Brig. Gen. Thomas,*[4] *William,*[3] *William,*[2] *Robert*[1]), of Little Rock, Ark., planter, born in Maury Co., Tenn., 30 July 1843, died at Little Rock in 1912. He married, 2 Dec. 1867, CYNTHIA MARTIN, daughter of George W. and Narcissa (Pillow) of Columbia, Tenn.

He was a student at the University of North Carolina in 1860–61, and at the outbreak of the Civil War he returned to his home in Columbia, Tenn., enlisted in the Confederate Army, and was made second lieutenant of Artillery. Later he was appointed lieutenant on the staff of his uncle, Gen. Leonidas Polk, was captured at Island No. 10, and was sent to the Federal prison at Camp Chase, Ohio, and then to Johnson's Island, on Lake Erie, but after five months was exchanged. He then served as captain and aide-de-camp on his brother's staff and later on those of Generals Roddy and Frank Armstrong.

Children:

i.   LUCIUS EUGENE,[8] b. at Columbia, Tenn., 20 Nov. 1868; m. 18 Dec. 1912 BESSIE STITT of Hot Springs, Ark. No children.

ii.   RUFUS EUGENE, b. 4 Apr. 1873; unm.

iii. WILLIAM JULIUS, b. in Phillips Co., Ark., 12 Mar. 1874; m. 15 Jan. 1910 SARAH E. CHAMBERS of St. Louis, Mo. Children: 1. *William Julius,*[9] b. in St. Louis 11 Oct. 1911. 2. *Mary Delphine,* b. in St. Louis 19 June 1913.

iv.   CHARLES MARTIN, of St. Louis, Mo., lawyer, b. at Helena, Ark., 28 June 1878; m. 6 Nov. 1906 NANNIE LEE of St. Louis. Children: 1. *William Lee,*[9] b. in St. Louis 11 Sept. 1907. 2. *Cynthia Martin,* b. in St. Louis 6 Feb. 1910.

54. GEORGE WASHINGTON[7] POLK (*Hon. Lucius Junius,*[6] *Lieut. Col. William,*[5] *Brig. Gen. Thomas,*[4] *William,*[3] *William,*[2] *Robert*[1]), of San Antonio, Tex., civil engineer, was born at Hamilton Place, Maury Co., Tenn., 7 July 1847. He married, 29 Oct. 1885, JANE JACKSON of Florence, Ala., daughter of George Moore and Sarah Cabell (Perkins) Jackson.

He studied engineering at the University of Virginia, 1867–68, and then followed the profession of civil engineer. Early in 1869 he was rodman in the construction of the Missouri Pacific Railway from Leavenworth to Atchison, Kans., and later worked on the branch from Sedalia to Lexington, Mo. He was division engineer on the Kansas Pacific Railroad (now the Union Pacific) in Colorado, was employed in the fall of 1870 in the location and construction of the Lexington, Lake & Gulf Railroad, and in the following year took part in the survey and construction of various short lines in Kansas. In May 1872 he went to Texas, and was engaged in the location and survey of railway land grants on the frontier. In 1873 he was appointed assistant engineer of the Galveston, Harrisburg & San Antonio Railway, in charge of location and construction in Texas. Later he was chief engineer of the Louisiana Western Railroad in Louisiana and assistant chief engineer of the Galveston, Harrisburg & San Antonio Railway and the Mexican International Railway in Mexico. In the fall of 1885 he was appointed assistant land commissioner of the Southern Pacific

Railroad lands in Texas. He is a member of the North Carolina Chapter of the Society of the Cincinnati.
Children:

i. KATE JACKSON,[8] b. 13 Jan. 1887; d. 23 Aug. 1888; bur. in St. John's Churchyard, Maury Co., Tenn.

ii. GEORGE WASHINGTON, civil engineer, b. at Houston, Tex., 13 May 1889; m. 18 June 1923 BLANCHE LINTON of Dayton, Ohio. In the World War he enlisted in the Air Service and served throughout the War as second lieutenant. In 1921 he was commissioned first lieutenant in the Regular Army, and is now stationed at Dayton, Ohio.

iii. JANE JACKSON, b. at Houston, Tex., 20 Jan. 1893; m. in St. Mark's Church (Protestant Episcopal), San Antonio, 14 Sept. 1918, LIEUT. (now CAPT.) GEORGE GILL BALL, of the Fourteenth United States Cavalry, A.B. (Harvard, 1908), s. of George Homer and Florence (Gill) Ball of Boston, Mass. Children (surname *Ball*): 1. *George Gill*, b. at Fort Sam Houston, San Antonio, Tex., 22 July 1919. 2. *Jane Polk*, b. at Manila, P. I., 16 Apr. 1923.

iv. HARRISON JACKSON, b. at Houston, Tex., 16 May 1896. In the World War he enlisted, 27 Oct. 1917, in the Twenty-third Engineers, being enrolled as a private in Company B and serving in the American Expeditionary Forces in France. He was honorably discharged 28 June 1919.

55. LUCIUS JUNIUS[7] POLK (*Hon. Lucius Junius,[6] Lieut. Col. William,[5] Brig. Gen. Thomas,[4] William,[3] William,[2] Robert[1]*), of Sherman, Tex., born at Hamilton Place, Maury Co., Tenn., 14 Aug. 1854, died at Temple, Tex., 30 Sept. 1923, and is buried in St. John's Churchyard, Maury Co. He married, 28 Nov. 1878, DAISY CANTRELL, daughter of Dr. William and Ellen Maria (Harrell) Cantrell of Little Rock, Ark.

After studying at the Virginia Military Institute, Lexington, Va., he entered the service of the Atlantic & Great Western Railroad as clerk in the general freight office at Cincinnati, Ohio. In Jan. 1876 he went to Texas, serving in the engineer corps of the Galveston, Harrisburg & San Antonio Railway until the completion of the road in 1877. In the fall of that year he went to Mississippi, and was engaged in managing a cotton plantation in Washington County. Returning to Texas, he entered the service of the Texas & New Orleans Railroad, in the general freight department, and when this road was consolidated with the Galveston, Harrisburg & San Antonio Railway, under the management of the Southern Pacific Company, he served as claim clerk, rate clerk, and, finally, chief clerk. He was then appointed general freight agent of the San Antonio & Aransas Pass Railway, general freight agent of the Gulf, Colorado & Santa Fe Railway, at Galveston, and then acting general manager of the last-named road. In 1910 he was made general agent of all departments of the Gulf, Colorado & Santa Fe Railway, and held this position until his death. He was a member of the North Carolina Chapter of the Society of the Cincinnati.
Children:

i. ARMOUR CANTRELL,[8] civil engineer, b. at Little Rock, Ark., 12 Sept. 1879; m. 29 Sept. 1907 CHARLOTTE PAYNE of Mobile, Ala. No children.

    ii.   ANNE LEROY, b. at Little Rock, Ark., 16 Dec. 1881; m. 10 Oct.
1903 ALLEN CUCULA of Mobile, Ala. Children (surname *Cucula*):
1. *Allen Polk*, b. 1 Aug. 1904. 2. *Margaret Augustine*, b. 14 June
1907. 3. *Anne Polk*, b. 9 Sept. 1908.

    iii. LUCIUS JUNIUS, of Pharr, Hidalgo Co., Tex., lawyer, b. 19 Mar.
1886; m. 7 Jan. 1914 MARY VIRGINIA NICHOLS of Brownsville,
Tex. Children: 1. *Lucius Junius*[9] (twin), b. at Brownsville 31
Dec. 1914. 2. *A son* (twin), b. at Brownsville 31 Dec. 1914; d.
4 Jan. 1915. 3. *Mary Virginia*, b. at Pharr 26 Nov. 1916. 4.
Daisy Ellen, b. 10 Apr. 1918.

    iv. MARGARET WENDELL, b. at San Antonio, Tex., 13 Jan. 1888; m.
at Sherman, Tex., 28 Apr. 1914, EUGENE ADAMS YATES of New
York City. Children (surname *Yates*): 1. *Margaret Polk*, b. in
New York City 9 Dec. 1915. 2. *Eugene Adams*, b. at Monmouth
Hills, N. J., 5 July 1919.

    v.   DAISY CANTRELL, b. 29 July 1890; unm.

    vi. ELLEN HARRELL, b. 15 Mar. 1893; d. 10 May 1895.

56. ALEXANDER HAMILTON[7] POLK (*Lieut. Gen. Leonidas,*[6] *Lieut.
Col. William,*[5] *Brig. Gen. Thomas,*[4] *William,*[3] *William,*[2] *Robert*[1]),
planter, born at Richmond, Va., 27 Jan. 1831, died at Hartford,
Conn., 2 Oct. 1872, and was buried there. He married, 15
June 1854, EMILY BEACH, who died 9 Mar. 1902 and was
buried beside her husband.

He resided in Mississippi and North Carolina.

Children:

    i.   ALEXANDER HAMILTON,[8] d. in childhood.

    ii. FRANK DEVEREUX, b. at New Orleans, La., 17 Mar. 1858; d. 25
Sept. 1891; bur. in Louden Park, Baltimore, Md.; m. 23 Nov.
1877 MARGARET CALLAWAY, who m. (2) Hamilton R. Polk (56, v),
q.v., brother of her first husband. Children: 1. *Emily Hamilton,*[9]
b. 23 Aug. 1880; unm. 2. *Leonidas Charles*, b. 19 July 1883;
d. 30 Dec. 1887. 3. *Francis Devereux*, of Baltimore, Md., b. at
Asheville, N. C., 6 Nov. 1885; m. 7 Nov. 1912 Margaret A. Rose,
dau. of John and Mary Agnes (Cumberland); no children. 4.
Magdalen Tasker, b. 25 Feb. 1887; d. 19 July 1887. 5. *Alexander
Hamilton*, b. at Asheville, N. C., 20 July 1889; m. 21 July 1914
Margaret Ethel Worthington, dau. of Charles Hammond and
Margaret (Kent); no children.

    iii. GEORGE BEACH, b. 17 Nov. 1861; unm.

    iv. MARIA, d. in childhood.

    v.   HAMILTON R., of Baltimore, Md., b. at Raleigh, N. C., 15 Sept.
1863; d. *s.p.* 9 Nov. 1906; bur. in Louden Park, Baltimore; m.
14 May 1896 MARGARET (CALLAWAY) POLK, widow of his brother,
Frank Devereux Polk (56, ii), *q.v.*

    vi. LEONIDAS, of Baltimore, Md., b. at Hartford, Conn., 27 Nov. 1865;
m. 10 June 1901 CHARLOTTE H. ZIMMERMAN. Children: 1.
Leontine Adele,[9] b. 10 Mar. 1902. 2. *Charlotte Patricia*, b. 3 Jan.
1905.

    vii. NICHOLS BEACH, b. 15 Sept. 1868; unm.

57. CAPT. WILLIAM MECKLENBURG[7] POLK (*Lieut. Gen. Leonidas,*[6]
Lieut. Col. William,[5] *Brig. Gen. Thomas,*[4] *William,*[3] *William,*[2]
Robert[1]), of New York City, M.D. (College of Physicians and
Surgeons, Columbia University, 1869), LL.D. (University of
the South, 1894, Columbia University, 1904, University of
Georgia, 1913), born at Ashwood Hall, Maury Co., Tenn.,
15 Aug. 1844, died at Atlantic City, N. J., 24 June 1918. He
married first, at Demopolis, Ala., 14 Nov. 1866, IDA A. LYON,

who died 7 Nov. 1912; and secondly, 12 May 1914, MARIE H. DEHON of New York.

At the outbreak of the Civil War he was a cadet at the Virginia Military Institute, Lexington, Va., and in April of that year enlisted in the Confederate Army, being one of the one hundred and fifty cadets taken by Professor Thomas Jonathan ("Stonewall") Jackson to Richmond, Va., to drill troops. After serving there for two months, he was transferred to the West, and served in the same capacity under General Zollicoffer. In consideration of his services in the Army the faculty of the Virginia Military Institute later enrolled him among its graduates of the Class of 1861. He enlisted as a private in the Cavalry, later became a second lieutenant of Artillery, in Bankhead's battery, at Columbus, Ky., was promoted to be first lieutenant of Artillery, in Scott's battery, in 1862, and was made assistant chief of Artillery in his father's corps, Army of the Tennessee, in 1863. In Mar. 1865 he held the rank of captain in the Adjutant and Inspector General's Department, Army of the Tennessee. He took part in the fighting at Bowling Green, Columbus, Ky., New Madrid, Mo., Shiloh, Corinth, and Fort Pillow, in the Kentucky Campaign, in the Battles of Perryville, Stone River (Murfreesboro), and Chickamauga, in the Atlanta and Tennessee Campaigns, and in the surrender at Meridian, Miss., in May 1865.

After the War he studied medicine at the University of Louisiana, 1867–68, moved to New York City, and received the degree of Doctor of Medicine at the College of Physicians and Surgeons in 1869. In the same year he entered on the practice of his profession in New York City. He was professor of therapeutics and clinical medicine in the Bellevue Hospital Medical College, 1876–1879, professor of obstetrics and gynæcology in the Medical Department of the University of the City of New York, 1879–1898, and dean and professor of gynæcology in the Cornell University Medical College from 1898 on. He was gynæcologist at the Bellevue Hospital, and consulting gynæcologist for St. Luke's, St. Vincent's, and the New York Lying-in Hospitals and the New York Infirmary for Women and Children. In the World War he held a commission as first lieutenant in the Medical Reserve Corps, United States Army.

He was a member of several important medical societies in this country and abroad and of the North Carolina Chapter of the Society of the Cincinnati, the Tennessee Society, and the Southern Society, and was the author of many contributions to medical journals and of a biography of his father, in two volumes, entitled "Leonidas Polk, Bishop and General," which was published in 1893 and appeared in a new edition in 1915. He was a vestryman of Trinity Church, New York.

Children by first wife:

i. LEONIDAS,[8] b. 24 Feb. 1868; d. 29 Apr. 1877.
ii. HON. FRANK LYON, of New York City, B.A. (Yale, 1894), LL.B. (Columbia, 1897), honorary M.A. (Yale, 1918), lawyer and diplo-

mat, b. in New York City 13 Sept. 1871; m. 28 Feb. 1908 ELIZA-
BETH STURGIS POTTER, dau. of James of Philadelphia, Pa. He
was graduated at the Groton School, Groton, Mass., in 1890, at
Yale University in the Class of 1894, and at the Columbia University Law School in 1897, and entered on the practice of law in
New York City in the last-mentioned year. In the War with
Spain he was enrolled in Troop A, New York National Guard,
and served as captain and assistant quartermaster on the staff of
General Ernst and in Porto Rico. He was a member of the Civil
Service Commission of New York, 1907–1909 (president, 1908–09),
and of the New York Board of Education, 1907–1910, an officer
of the Bureau of Municipal Research in New York City, 1911–
1913, and corporation counsel of New York City, 24 Jan. 1914–16
Sept. 1915. Entering the service of the United States, in the administration of President Wilson, he was called to Washington as
counsellor for the Department of State, succeeding Hon. Robert
Lansing, who had been made Secretary of State after the resigna-
tion of Secretary Bryan, and holding that office from 30 Aug.
1915 to 1 July 1919. He was Acting Secretary of State during the
absence of Secretary Lansing, who was a member of the United
States Peace Commission, 4 Dec. 1918 to 18 July 1919, and was
Under Secretary of State from 1 July 1919 on. On 17 July 1919
he was appointed a commissioner plenipotentiary of the United
States to negotiate peace, and was head of the United States dele-
gation at the Peace Conference in Paris, 28 July — 9 Dec. 1919.
On his retirement from public office at the close of the Wilson
administration he resumed the practice of his profession in New
York City. He is a director of the Erie Railroad Company and
of the Northern Pacific Railroad Company, a member of the New
York Southern Society, of the Society of Sons of the Revolution,
and of several New York and Washington clubs, and of the
Protestant Episcopal Church. Children: 1. *John Metcalfe,*[9] b. 18
Nov. 1908. 2. *Elizabeth Sturgis,* b. 31 July 1910. 3. *Frank Lyon,*
b. 3 Nov. 1911. 4. *James Potter,* b. 24 Nov. 1914. 5. *Alice
Potter,* b. in Washington, D. C., 26 Nov. 1917.

iii. JOHN METCALFE, of New York City, Ph.B. (Yale, 1896), M.D.
(Cornell, 1899), b. 6 May 1875; d. 29 Mar. 1904.

iv. SERENA DEVEREUX, b. 19 Mar. 1877; d. 8 May 1878.

58. CAPT. JAMES HILLIARD[7] POLK (*George Washington,*[6] *Lieut. Col.
William,*[5] *Brig. Gen. Thomas,*[4] *William,*[3] *William,*[2] *Robert*[1]), of
Fort Worth, Tex., planter, was born in Maury Co., Tenn., 8 Jan.
1842. He married, 24 Nov. 1885, MARY DEMOVILLE HARD-
ING of Nashville, Tenn.

He was a student at the University of North Carolina,
1858–1861, became a captain of Cavalry in the Confederate
Army, and served throughout the War. He lived for a while
in Mississippi.

Children:

i. CAPT. HARDING,[8] b. 16 Mar. 1887; m. 29 Dec. 1910 ESTHER FLEMING,
dau. of John J. and Mary (Bracken) of Burlington, Iowa. He was
admitted as a cadet to the United States Military Academy at
West Point 15 June 1906, and was commissioned second lieutenant of Cavalry, United States Army, 15 June 1910, first lieutenant
1 July 1916, and captain 15 May 1917. In the World War he
served in the American Expeditionary Forces. Children: 1.
James Hilliard,[9] b. at Manila, P. I., 13 Dec. 1911. 2. *John
Fleming,* b. at Burlington, Iowa, 11 Aug. 1914. 3. *Mary Gertrude,*
b. at Burlington, Iowa, 29 Jan. 1917.

ii. GEORGE WASHINGTON, of Fort Worth, Tex., lawyer, b. at Fort Worth
18 Nov. 1888; m. there, 28 Dec. 1912, ADELAIDE E. ROE, dau.

of Addison J. and Jennie H. (Scranton). In the World War he served as captain in Battery C, One Hundred and Thirty-second Field Artillery, Thirty-sixth Division, American Expeditionary Forces. Children: 1. *George Washington*,[9] b. 11 Oct. 1913. 2. *Adelaide Elizabeth*, b. 2 Sept. 1915. 3. *Milbry Catherine*, b. 16 Mar. 1919.

59. LIEUT. RUFUS KING[7] POLK (*George Washington*,[6] *Lieut. Col. William*,[5] *Brig. Gen. Thomas*,[4] *William*,[3] *William*,[2] *Robert*[1]), born at "Rattle and Snap," Maury Co., Tenn., 31 Oct. 1843, died at Nashville, Tenn., 27 Aug. 1902, and was buried in St. John's Churchyard, Maury Co. He married, 28 Apr. 1881, MARGARET PHILLIPS of Nashville, who is buried beside her husband.

He was a first lieutenant in the Confederate Army.

Child:

i. MARY ELIZABETH,[8] b. at Nashville 3 July 1883; m. 26 Apr. 1911 JOHN WHITE MOORE, M.D. Residence, Nashville. Children (surname *Moore*): 1. *Margaret Phillips*, b. 27 Dec. 1914. 2. *John Polk*, b. 24 Oct. 1918.

60. ISAAC HILLIARD[7] POLK (*George Washington*,[6] *Lieut. Col. William*,[5] *Brig. Gen. Thomas*,[4] *William*,[3] *William*,[2] *Robert*[1]), born at "Rattle and Snap," Maury Co., Tenn., 8 Aug. 1854, died at Monrovia, Calif., 14 Oct. 1919. He married first, 13 Apr. 1889, ELLA MARTHA COOK; and secondly, 19 Apr. 1897, MINERVA J. BRADBURY of Los Angeles, Calif., who died 26 Oct. 1919.

Child by first wife:

i. SALLIE HILLIARD,[8] b. at Los Angeles 22 Feb. 1891; m. 15 Apr. 1914 HULETT CLINTON MERRITT, JR. Residence, Los Angeles. Child (surname *Merritt*): 1. *Antoinette Polk*, b. at Pasadena, Calif., 26 May 1916.

Children by second wife:

ii. ISAAC HILLIARD, b. at Los Angeles 6 Apr. 1898. He was a cadet in the United States Military Academy at West Point, 14 June to 11 Nov. 1918.

iii. LEWIS BRADBURY, b. at Los Angeles 30 July 1899. In the World War he enlisted as a seaman, 3 Aug. 1918, was stationed at Camp Balboa, San Diego, Calif., and was appointed a cadet in the United States Naval Academy.

iv. MINERVA JOSEPHINE, b. at Monrovia, Calif., 6 Jan. 1911.

61. CHARLES BINGLEY[7] POLK (*Thomas Independence*,[6] *Charles*,[5] *Brig. Gen. Thomas*,[4] *William*,[3] *William*,[2] *Robert*[1]), born in Mecklenburg Co., N. C., 23 Sept. 1809, died 2 Aug. 1886, and is buried in Grayson Co., Tex. He married, 31 Dec. 1834, SARAH JOHN LE NOIR, who died 8 May 1877 and is buried beside her husband.

He resided in Tennessee, Louisiana, and Texas.

Children:

i. JOHN,[8] d. in infancy.

ii. EMMA, b. 3 Feb. 1837; d. unm. 3 Jan. 1872.

iii. EUGENE LE NOIR, b. at La Grange, Tenn., 14 Oct. 1838; d. 5 Feb. 1887; m. (1) MARY ELIZABETH WALTON; m. (2) 10 May 1868 ADA OCTAVIA LITTRELL. He resided at La Grange, Tenn., in

Louisiana, and in Texas. Children by first wife: 1. *Sallie Clymer,*[9]
m. ———— Boiles. 2. *Mary Walton,* b. 23 Sept. 1865; m. 13
Apr. 1887 John M. Gault; residence, Franklin, Tenn.; three
children. Children by second wife: 3. *Marion Deveux,* b. in
Honduras, Central America, 10 May 1869; m. 27 Sept. 1893
Philip Solomon Clarke; residence, Austin, Tex.; two children.
4. *Ada Lee,* b. at Bastrop, La., 11 Mar. 1876; m. 10 Apr. 1913
John Watson Cole of Goliad, Tex.; no children. 5. *Robert Le Noir,*
d. in childhood.

iv.   NEWTON NAPOLEON, d. in childhood.
v.   ELLA, d. young.
vi.   SARAH, d. young.
vii. SARAH ELLA, d. young.
viii. CHARLES BINGLEY, d. young.
ix.   MARY OPHELIA, b. in Jackson Parish, La., 23 Mar. 1851; m. 12
      Nov. 1874 LAFAYETTE BROWN POTTS. Residence, Fort Worth,
      Tex. Children (surname *Potts*): 1. *Pauline,* b. 25 Sept. 1878.
      2. *Cleland,* d. in infancy.
x.   THOMAS POLK, b. in Jackson Parish, La., 23 Dec. 1852; m. at Ham-
      burg, Ashley Co., Ark., ANNIE ALBERTON. No children.
xi.   KATE LILLIAN, b. in Jackson Parish, La., 25 July 1855; m. 16 Jan.
      1883 ROBERT P. DIMMITT. Residence, Austin, Tex. Child (sur-
      name *Dimmitt*): 1. *Le Noir,* b. 10 June 1885.
xii. CHARLES BINGLEY, of Gunter, Tex., b. in Jackson Parish, La., 7
      Nov. 1857; m. 16 Jan. 1879 ALICE ELLIOTT. Children: 1. *Thurs-
      ton,*[9] b. 10 Feb. 1880; d. 12 Sept. 1904. 2. *Kate Lillian,* b. in
      Grayson Co., Tex., 4 Sept. 1885; m. 29 Aug. 1905 James Sutton
      Yowell; residence, Gunter, Tex.; two daughters. 3. *Ralph
      Bingley,* b. 24 Nov. 1886.

62. THOMAS RICHARD[7] POLK (*Thomas Independence,*[6] *Charles,*[5] *Brig.
Gen. Thomas,*[4] *William,*[3] *William,*[2] *Robert*[1]), was born in
Mecklenburg Co., N. C., about 1813. He married first CARO-
LINE LAFAYETTE SMITH; secondly LUCY NICHOLSON COCKE;
and thirdly ELIZABETH HAZYLIN KEAN.
He resided first in South Carolina, and moved thence to
Tennessee and finally to Bastrop, La.
Child by first wife:

i.   LEONIDAS NAPOLEON,[8] of Bastrop, La., b. at La Grange, Tenn., 28
      Apr. 1843; m. at Louisville, Winston Co., Miss., 30 Sept. 1864,
      WYLIE AMANDA MOSELEY, who d. 24 Dec. 1876. Children: 1.
      Caroline James,[9] b. 2 Jan. 1866; d. 4 May 1870. 2. *Leonora
      Maude,* b. at Rayville, La., 10 Apr. 1870; d. at Bastrop, La., 8
      Sept. 1896; m. at Monroe, La., in June 1892, Isaac Arthur Ross;
      two children. 3. *Jessie Irene,* b. 20 Jan. 1872; d. 20 Sept. 1900.
      4. *Mary Lillian,* b. 5 Oct. 1874; d. 10 Dec. 1876.

Children by second wife:

ii.   CLARENCE, d. in childhood.
iii. THOMAS JULIAN (twin), b. at La Grange, Tenn., in July 1851; d. in
      1882.
iv.   JAMES CECIL (twin), b. at La Grange, Tenn., in July 1851; d. at
      Houston, Tex., in Sept. 1900; m. at Houston, in Sept. 1880,
      ANNIE HOLT. Child: 1. *Annie Cecil,*[9] m. at Logansport, La.,
      Ernest E. Price.
v.   IRENE, d. at the age of 16 years.
vi.   WILLIAM ARTHUR, b. 8 Jan. 1857.
vii. LULA GILMER, b. at La Grange, Tenn., 17 Sept. 1858; m. at Sewanee,
      Tenn., 6 Mar. 1877, JAMES SEVERIN GREEN, s. of Right Rev.
      William Mercer Green, Bishop of Mississippi, who d. in June
      1892. Children (surname *Green*): 1. *James Severin,* b. 17 Oct.
      1878. 2. *Clarence Polk,* b. 18 Aug. 1880; m. at Nashville, Tenn.,

21 Dec. 1911, Beulah Beaumont Weber; one son. 3. *Horace Gilmer*, b. 15 Mar. 1882. 4. *William Haiden*, b. 26 July 1884. 5. *Katherine Elizabeth*, b. 30 Apr. 1887; m. at Nashville, Tenn., 19 June 1912, Edgar Jenkins Wells; residence, Louisville, Ky.; one son.

Children by third wife:

viii.   MARY ELIZABETH, b. at Bastrop, La., 25 Jan. 1863; m. at Abilene, Tex., 24 July 1884, EDWARD LAMBRICH WILLIAMS. Residence, Santa Cruz, Calif. Children (surname *Williams*): 1. *Elizabeth Hazel*, b. 3 Aug. 1887; d. 27 Sept. 1898. 2. *Mary Faull*, b. at Amesbury, Mass., 1 June 1890; m. at Santa Cruz, Calif., 19 May 1910, Wedworth Clark Penoyar; two daughters. 3. *Edward Lambrich*, b. in Chicago, Ill., 8 Nov. 1892; served in the World War as captain, Seventy-fourth Air Squadron, Group B, First Provisional Wing, at Mineola, Long Island, N. Y. 4. *Thomas Polk*, b. at Melrose Park, Ill., 27 July 1896; m. at Santa Cruz, Calif., 1 Oct. 1915, Agnes Brown Garrett; in the World War he served in the Medical Corps, with Ambulance Corps No. 32, Eighth Sanitary Train, Eighth Division, at Camps Fremont, Calif., and Mills, Long Island; one son. 5. *Orpha*, b. at Kenosha, Wis., 5 Oct. 1898; m. at Santa Cruz, Calif., 10 Feb. 1918, Charles Harper Massie; residence, Vicksburg, Miss. 6. *Enid Dixie*, b. at Yorkville, York Co., Va., 9 Aug. 1904.

ix.   THOMAS RICHARD, of Abington, La., b. 17 Oct. 1865; unm.

63. HORACE MOORE[7] POLK (*Thomas Independence,*[6] *Charles,*[5] *Brig. Gen. Thomas,*[4] *William,*[3] *William,*[2] *Robert*[1]), A.B. (University of North Carolina, 1841), lawyer, planter, born in Mecklenburg Co., N. C., 11 Oct. 1819, died at Bolivar, Tenn., 14 Sept. 1883. He married at Bolivar, 20 June 1843, his third cousin, OPHELIA JANE BILLS, who died 3 Jan. 1885, daughter of Maj. John Houston and Prudence Tate (McNeal) Bills (8, vi, 3) of Bolivar.

He resided in Louisiana and afterwards at Bolivar, Tenn., and served in the lower branch of the Legislature in both of those States.

Children:

i.   MARY ELIZA,[8] d. in infancy.

ii.   JOHN HORACE, of Nashville, Tenn., b. at Bolivar, Tenn., 16 May 1846; m. at Somerville, Tenn., 13 Apr. 1874, PRISCILLA MCNEAL WARREN, who d. 26 Oct. 1904. Children: 1. *John Houston,*[9] b. 11 Mar. 1875; d. unm. 11 Jan. 1904. 2. *Elise Warren*, b. at Bolivar 24 June 1876; m. 28 Nov. 1908 Percy Hollister Whiting, s. of John Fred and Annie Louise (Hitchcock); residence, Augusta, Me.; two children. 3. *Annie McNeal*, b. 13 Dec. 1878; d. unm. 12 Nov. 1910. 4. *Samuel McNeal*, b. 10 Feb. 1880; unm. 5. *Priscilla*, b. 31 July 1883; unm. 6. *Horace Moore*, b. 12 Aug. 1885; unm.; served in the World War as a private in Co. P, Central Infantry Officers' Training School, Camps Travis and McArthur, San Antonio and Waco, Tex. 7. *Margaret*, b. 29 May 1893; unm.

iii.   EVELYN SARAH (twin), b. at Bolivar, Tenn., 3 July 1848; m. (1) in Morehouse Parish, La., 2 Dec. 1868, JOHN HARVEY BRIGHAM; m. (2) JOHN HENDERSON PICKENS of Abilene, Tex., who d. 13 May 1905, grandson of Gen. Andrew Pickens of South Carolina. John Harvey Brigham was a lawyer, and occupied various positions of honor and trust. He was United States consul at Paso del Norte (now Juarez), Mexico, and was thence transferred to Kingston, Jamaica, B. W. I., where he died. Children by first husband (surname *Brigham*): 1. *Ophelia Polk*, b. at Bastrop, La., 30 Sept. 1869; d. at Fort Worth, Tex., 1 Aug. 1914; m. at Fort Worth,

15 Nov. 1905, Judge Truman H. Connor of the Supreme Judicial Court of Texas; no children. 2. *Annie Todd*, d. in infancy. 3. *Clara Caldwell*, d. in infancy. 4. *John Harvey*, of Atlanta, Ga., LL.B. (McDonald Institute, 1908), b. at Bastrop, La., 18 June 1878; m. at Cincinnati, Ohio, 28 June 1909, Ione Agnes Dagwell. He was graduated at the city schools of Abilene, Tex., in 1897, attended the Texas A. and M. College, 1897–98, was admitted to the Texas bar at Abilene in 1902, moved to Cincinnati, and was admitted to the Ohio bar in 1907; three children. 5. *Evelyn Davidson*, d. in childhood. 6. *Horace Polk*, b. 22 Jan. 1885; d. 26 Mar. 1896.

iv. THOMAS INDEPENDENCE (twin), b. at Bolivar, Tenn., 3 July 1848; d. in infancy.

v. CLARA BILLS, b. at Bolivar, Tenn., 4 Oct. 1850; m. there, 26 Jan. 1876, REV. CHARLES GRAY, a clergyman of the Protestant Episcopal Church, who d. 1 Apr. 1911 and was bur. at St. Petersburg, Fla., where his widow now resides. Children (surname *Gray*): 1. *Horace Polk*, d. in childhood. 2. *Charles Quintard*, b. 22 May 1878; d. 11 Jan. 1906. 3. *Arthur Rodefer*, b. 21 Mar. 1881; served in the World War as first lieutenant, Ordnance Department, United States Army, at Washington, D. C. 4. *Clara Polk*, b. 5 Aug. 1884. 5. *Charles McIlvaine*, paymaster, first-class yeoman, and chief petty officer, United States Navy, at Pelham Bay Training School and Princeton University, N. J., b. 5 Feb. 1889. 6. *Ophelia Wilson*, b. at Franklin, Tenn., 27 Nov. 1890; m. 6 June 1917 Lieut. Commander Louis Willard Strum, United States Navy, now stationed at Pago Pago, Tutuila, Samoa; one son.

vi. HORACE MOORE, of Spring Hill, Tenn., b. at Woodville, La., 12 Nov. 1852; m. near Spring Hill, 7 Dec. 1892, MARY LOUISA CAMPBELL, who d. 18 Mar. 1901, dau. of M. C. Campbell. Children: 1. *Campbell*,[9] d. in infancy. 2. *Allen Campbell*, b. 20 July 1895; served in the World War as a private in the Eighth Company, Fourth Recruiting Camp, Camp Greene, Charlotte, N. C. 3. *Horace Moore*, b. 5 Nov. 1897. 4. *Alice Ophelia*, b. 3 July 1899. 5. *Mary Lizinska Brown*, b. 23 July 1900.

vii. NEWTON NAPOLEON, b. at Woodville, La., 16 Nov. 1854; d. at Birmingham, Ala., 9 Sept. 1903; m. at Gadsden, Ala., 15 Nov. 1882, MINNIE TURRENTINE. He and his wife are buried at Gadsden. Children: 1. *Caroline*,[9] d. in infancy. 2. *Maj. Newton Napoleon*, b. at Tracy City, Tenn., 24 July 1888; unm.; he was graduated at the Birmingham (Ala.) High School in 1903, the Marion (Ala.) Military Academy in 1906, the Battleground Academy, Franklin, Tenn., in 1907, was a student at Vanderbilt University, Nashville, Tenn., 1907–1909, professor of science in the Ville Platte (La.) High School, 1909–10, and professor of mathematics at the Sewanee Military Academy, Sewanee, Tenn., 1910–11; on 3 Sept. 1911 he was examined in Washington, D. C., for appointment as second lieutenant, United States Army, and was commissioned as such in the Field Artillery, 26 Dec. 1911; in the World War he was major in the Thirteenth Field Artillery, serving at the School of Fire, Fort Sill, Okla., and in the American Expeditionary Forces, including the Army of Occupation.

viii. OPHELIA WILSON, b. 2 Dec. 1857; unm.

64. THOMAS MARSHALL[7] POLK (*Charles Clark*,[6] *Michael*,[5] *Capt. Charles*,[4] *William*,[3] *William*,[2] *Robert*[1]) was born in North Carolina 20 Mar. 1837. He married, 23 Dec. 1858, his first cousin, MARY LOUISA POLK, daughter of Michael[6] (11, i).
Children:

i. JAMES VERNON NOAH,[8] b. 25 Oct. 1860; m. 8 Dec. 1881 ELIZABETH CONGO.

ii. CYNTHIA CORNELIA, b. 16 May 1862; m. EDWARD VERNON.

iii. MARSHALL WESLEY, b. 18 June 1863; m. ALVA CHAMPION.

iv. JOSEPHINE ELIZABETH, b. 2 May 1866; d. 9 Sept. 1906; m. WIL-
LIAM HUTCHINSON.
v. FRANCES LETITIA, b. 25 Apr. 1867.
vi. EMMA LOUISA, b. 3 May 1870.
vii. JULIA BELL, b. 18 July 1872.
viii. CARRA LEE, b. 29 May 1874; m. GEORGE C. CHAMPION.
ix. LAURA EMMEONS, b. 18 Apr. 1877.
x. MARY MARVIN, b. 22 Aug. 1879.
xi. AMMIE DAISY, b. 18 Oct. 1882; m. 20 Dec. 1903 G. R. ANDERSON.

65. MICHAEL SANDERS[7] POLK (*Charles Clark,[6] Michael,[5] Capt.
Charles,[4] William,[3] William,[2] Robert[1]*), born near McDonough,
Ga., 12 Dec. 1848, died 26 Dec. 1904. He married at Alexander
City, Ala., 18 Oct. 1877, NARCISSA AUGUSTA GILBERT.
Children:
i. ELLA,[8] of Americus, Ga., b. 24 Feb. 1879; unm. She is chairman
(1922) of the Music Division of the Georgia Federation of Women's
Clubs.
ii. ALBERT CLARK, of Arcadia, Fla., b. 7 Aug. 1880; m. 14 Jan. 1912
LILLA BELLE LEE of Atlanta, Ga. Children: 1. *Albert Clark,[9]*
b. at Atlanta 3 Nov. 1913. 2. *Charles Michael*, b. at Atlanta 24
Aug. 1914. 3. *Annie Laurie*, b. at Arcadia, Fla., 1 Oct. 1917.
iii. BESSIE WESTERN, b. at Alexander City, Ala., 26 June 1887; m. 3
June 1906 WILLIAM RICHARDS HAMILTON of Nixburg, Ala. No
children.
iv. GILBERT, b. 31 Jan. 1889; m. 29 June 1914 SARAH LULU WICKER
of Warrenton, Ga. Children: 1. *Miriam Bessie,[9]* b. 18 Feb. 1916.
2. *A son*, d. in infancy. 3. *Lewis Gilbert*, b. 28 Oct. 1919.
v. OLGA, b. 30 July 1891; m. 1 Aug. 1921 JONATHAN CLARK MOUNTS
of Arcadia, Fla. Child (surname *Mounts*): 1. *Elizabeth Polk*, b. 3
Mar. 1922.

66. CHARLES CLARK[7] POLK (*Charles Clark,[6] Michael,[5] Capt. Charles,[4]
William,[3] William,[2] Robert[1]*) was born at Tallapoosa, Ga., 13
June 1856. He married, 1 Dec. 1875, MARY SUSAN PEARSON.
Children:
i. LENA,[8] b. 12 Dec. 1876.
ii. MAMIE, b. 18 Sept. 1878; d. 3 June 1888.
iii. ALICE IRENE, b. 17 Sept. 1880.
iv. WALTER MARCUS, b. 12 Nov. 1882.
v. CORINNE LUCILE, b. 16 May 1885.
vi. LAVINIA BONCILLE, b. 1 Apr. 1887; d. 3 June 1888.
vii. GEORGE CLARK, b. 10 Aug. 1890.
viii. AMANDA ELIZABETH, b. 24 June 1895; d. 19 June 1900.

67. CHARLES MARION[7] POLK (*Ezekiel,[6] Charles,[5] Capt. Charles,[4]
William,[3] William,[2] Robert[1]*), born in Campbell Co., Ga., in
1836, was killed in the Civil War while serving in the Confederate Army. He married first MITTIE CAIRNES; and secondly BRANTLY SHEFFIELD.
Child:
i. EMILY,[8] b. in Campbell Co., Ga., 2 Jan. 1862; m. JOSEPH A. WAL-
DROP, b. in 1863, d. in 1912. Children (surname *Waldrop*): 1.
Charles W., b. in Douglas Co., Ga., 9 Aug. 1883; m. Jimmie
Strawn. 2. *John Cleveland*, b. 1 Nov. 1885; m. Beulah Brooks.
3. *Jennie*, b. 26 Feb. 1887; m. Leonard Ward. 4. *Mary E.*, b.
26 Oct. 1890; m. Burnett Tyson. 5. *Rader*, b. 13 Mar. 1893;
m. 3 Nov. 1912 Eva Tyson. 6. *Margaret Elizabeth*, b. 22 Nov.
1895. 7. *Joseph Marvin*, b. 12 Jan. 1898; m. 19 Oct. 1919 Virgie
Lee. 8. *Ezekiel Polk*, b. 2 July 1904.

68. CHARLES THOMAS[7] POLK (*Charles Shelby,*[6] *Charles,*[5] *Capt. Charles,*[4] *William,*[3] *William,*[2] *Robert*[1]), born in Campbell Co., Ga., 23 Nov. 1850, died at Alabama City, Ala., 14 Aug. 1916. He married MARGARET ANN FREEMAN.

Children:

i.   ALMA,[8] b. in Douglas Co., Ga., 25 Dec. 1875; m. 18 Nov. 1900 WILLIAM McCAIN. No children.

ii. WILLIAM CHARLES, of Alabama City, Ala., b. in Douglas Co., Ga., 31 July 1877; m. 9 Aug. 1899 NORA LOYD. Children: 1. *Mary,*[9] b. 2 Oct. 1900; m. 26 Nov. 1920 C. J. Cargall; one daughter. 2. *Lucy,* b. 4 Apr. 1902. 3. *Charles Loyd,* b. 18 Feb. 1905. 4. *Douglas,* b. 10 Feb. 1907. 5. *William,* b. 2 Aug. 1914.

69. CHARLES GRANDISON[7] POLK (*John,*[6] *Charles,*[5] *Capt. John,*[4] *William,*[3] *William,*[2] *Robert*[1]), farmer, born in Maury Co., Tenn., 12 Mar. 1811, died at Bartlett, Shelby Co., Tenn., 27 Dec. 1899. He married, 28 Dec. 1837, MARY ANN MASSEY, who died at Bartlett 25 Feb. 1887, sister of Dr. William S. Massey, who married Margaret Benigna Polk (31, iii), sister of Charles Grandison Polk.

Children:

i.   LUCIUS JOSEPHUS,[8] b. 5 Dec. 1838; d. in infancy.

ii.   ELIZABETH EMILY, b. in Shelby Co., Tenn., 7 Mar. 1841; d. in 1876; m. ———. Four children.

iii. LOUISA, b. 30 Nov. 1842.

iv.   JOHN CROFFORD, b. 11 Aug. 1843; d. in infancy.

v.   CHARLES ARNOLD, b. 2 Nov. 1846; died at Corinth, Miss., in the Civil War, in 1861.

vi.   BENIGNA JANE, b. 22 Mar. 1852; d. unm. in 1883.

vii. WILLIAM EDDINGS, of Memphis, Tenn., b. at Bartlett 16 Jan. 1856; m. 19 Dec. 1877 LENA ELIZABETH WESSEN. Children: 1. *Dr. Charles Wessen,*[9] of Millington, Shelby Co., Tenn., b. near Bartlett 27 June 1880; m. 18 Dec. 1902 Thelma Maud Gladden; he was graduated at the Millington High School, attended the University of the South, Sewanee, Tenn., was graduated at the Memphis Hospital Medical College in 1902, practised medicine eight years at Henning, Tenn., moved to Millington, retired from practice, established a drug store there, and owns a farm; three children. 2. *Irving Kenneth,* b. in Nov. 1881; d. in infancy. 3. *Katie,* b. 1 Feb. 1883; d. in infancy. 4. *Dr. Lewis Reynolds,* of Memphis, Tenn., b. at Millington, Tenn., 8 Dec. 1886; m. 28 June 1907 Verlie Davidson; he was graduated at the Millington High School in 1905, attended the University of Tennessee, and was graduated at the Memphis Hospital Medical College in 1909; two children. 5. *Effie,* b. in Sept. 1889; d. in infancy. 6. *Evie,* b. in Shelby Co., Tenn., 12 Apr. 1893. 7. *Joseph,* b. 2 Aug. 1896; d. in infancy.

viii. THOMAS HAMILTON, b. 31 Jan. 1860; d. unm. in 1881.

70. ANDREW TYLER[7] POLK (*Judge Alfred,*[6] *Charles,*[5] *Capt. John,*[4] *William,*[3] *William,*[2] *Robert*[1]), born in Texas 21 Mar. 1846, was living in 1923. He married, 1 Oct. 1874, MARY ANN SIMMONS.

He served in the Confederate Army.

Children:

i.   SOPHIA LULU,[8] b. 25 Dec. 1877; d. 2 Feb. 1910; m. at San Augustine, Tex., in 1902, INLOE L. MILLER.

ii. JOHN SIMMONS, b. 29 Apr. 1879; m. 14 Nov. 1901 CATHERINE B. THOMAS. Children: 1. *Walter Earl,*[9] b. 26 Nov. 1903. 2. *Leland*

Thomas, b. 14 Dec. 1905. 3. *Annie May*, b. 13 Apr. 1908. 4.
Gladys, b. 4 Mar. 1912.

iii. TYLER VERNON, b. 28 May 1881; m. 14 Dec. 1902 MATTIE VIR-
GINIA THOMAS. Children: 1. *Aaron Gordon*,[9] b. 12 Jan. 1904.
2. *Annie Blanche*, b. 1 Sept. 1905. 3. *Margaret Ruth*, b. 22 Jan.
1909.

iv. SAMUEL CLARENCE, b. 7 May 1885; m. FRANKIE CARR of Kerrville,
Tex. Children: 1. *Eleanor Margaret*,[9] b. at Austin, Tex., 16 Dec.
1914. 2. *Samuel Clarence*, b. in Washington, D. C., 25 Mar. 1919.

71. WILLIAM VINCENT[7] POLK (*Evan Shelby*,[6] *John*,[5] *Capt. John*,[4]
William,[3] *William*,[2] *Robert*[1]), born 9 Mar. 1822, died 16 July
1893. He married, 23 Jan. 1844, ELIZABETH LONG, born
24 June 1826, died 11 Dec. 1895. Both are buried at Alabam,
Ark.

Children:

i. ARCHIBALD YELL,[8] b. 20 Apr. 1847; m. in Texas ———, and had
at least one son.

ii. MATILDA JANE, b. 15 Sept. 1849.

iii. MARY ELIZABETH, b. 30 May 1852; d. unm. 1 May 1898; bur. at
Huntsville, Ark.

iv. WILLIAM LONG, b. 19 Aug. 1854; d. 5 Aug. 1916; m. 9 Sept. 1877
FRANCES L. ARMSTRONG. Children: 1. *James Lafayette*,[9] of Alabam, Ark., b. 15 Aug. 1880; m. 8 Aug. 1907 Nellie Miller; four
children. 2. *Cora Ann*, b. 15 Dec. 1884; m. 18 Sept. 1899 Hill
Burns; residence, Alabam, Ark.; no children.

v. MARGARET ALICE, b. 6 Oct. 1856; m. MILLIE PARKS. Residence,
Ontario, Calif. No children.

vi. LAURA ANN, b. 11 Oct. 1862; d. in infancy.

72. JOHN SHELBY[7] POLK (*Evan Shelby*,[6] *John*,[5] *Capt. John*,[4] *William*,[3] *William*,[2] *Robert*[1]), born 9 Nov. 1827, died 18 Jan. 1884,
and is buried at Huntsville, Ark. He married, 5 Dec. 1852,
DORCAS LEAR ARMSTRONG, born 17 Mar. 1835, died 28 Aug.
1880.

Children:

i. OPHELIA JANE,[8] b. 4 July 1855; d. 16 Mar. 1893; m. (1) WILLIAM
P. HONEY, b. 24 Dec. 1847, d. 9 May 1869, bur. at Huntsville;
m. (2) 9 Apr. 1872 WILLIAM S. LOWRY of McMinnville, Tenn., b.
16 Sept. 1847, d. 11 Mar. 1893. Child by first husband (surname
Honey): 1. *Willie P.* (posthumous), b. 30 Oct. 1869; m. (1) in
1893 Edward Berry, by whom she had no children; m. (2) 10
Dec. 1897 Judge Houston Watson Johnston. Children by second
husband (surname *Lowry*): 2. *Clyde E.*, b. 14 June 1873; d. at
Houston, Tex., 21 Feb. 1914; bur. at Huntsville; m. 8 June 1896
Laura Rookwood of Montgomery Co., Mo.; he was a graduate of
the Lebanon (Tenn.) Law School. 3. *Cleo E.*, b. 20 July 1876;
m. 2 Sept. 1896 Mack C. Williams, b. in Kentucky 29 July 1868;
residence, Broken Arrow, Okla. 4. *Mamie Dorcas*, b. 11 Dec.
1879; m. 18 Apr. 1897 Samuel Nunneley of Madison Co., Ark., a
retired banker, b. 7 Feb. 1870; residence, Fayetteville, Ark. 5.
Virginia Polk, b. 7 Jan. 1881; m. 10 June 1903 George Edwin
Coffman; residence, Fayetteville, Ark. 6. *Estelle Gale*, b. 8 Nov.
1884; d. 25 Nov. 1911; bur. at Arcadia, La.; m. 8 Nov. 1906
Percy Kennedy, Sr., of Mineral Wells, Tex.

ii. BETTIE ANN, b. 25 Apr. 1858; d. 11 Dec. 1875.

iii. DORA, b. 10 Apr. 1861; d. 11 Dec. 1910.

iv. EDWARD, b. 26 Jan. 1868; d. in infancy.

v. LELIA, b. 11 Mar. 1873; m. (1) JOHN WILLIAMS; m. (2) ———
DONNELL. Residence, Dennison, Tex. Two children by first
husband, both of whom d. in infancy.

73. BENJAMIN RUFUS[7] POLK (*Evan Shelby,[6] John,[5] Capt. John,[4] William,[3] William,[2] Robert[1]*), born in Maury Co., Tenn., 3 June 1833, died at Ozark, Ark., 3 July 1869. He married, 20 Sept. 1853, FANNY BERRY, born 22 Nov. 1836, died at Ozark 30 May 1872, sister of Hon. James Henderson Berry, who was Governor of Arkansas in 1882 and a United States Senator from Arkansas, 1885–1907.
Children:

    i.   EVA JANE,[8] b. at Huntsville, Ark., 3 July 1855; d. at Dalton, Ga., 29 June 1889; m. 28 June 1870 STEPHEN BOONE FELKER, b. 16 Aug. 1845, d. 10 Jan. 1919. Children (surname *Felker*), b. at Ozark: 1. *Hester*, b. 5 June 1871; m. 18 Nov. 1890 William John Townley; no children. 2. *Fannie Flossia*, b. 15 Jan. 1878; m. 17 Sept. 1902 John Wallace Owens. 3. *Stephen Benjamin*, of Washington, D. C., b. 4 Aug. 1881; m. 23 June 1922 Coral Roberts. 4. *Bernice Berrien*, b. 29 Jan. 1884; m. 14 Nov. 1907 Thomas Stokely McCamy; residence, Dalton, Ga.

    ii.   BENJAMIN FRANKLIN, b. at Huntsville, Ark., 16 Feb. 1860.

    iii.   WILLIAM RUFUS, b. at Ozark 18 Sept. 1867; d. at Clarksville, Ark., 23 Apr. 1892.

74. JAMES KNOX[7] POLK (*Franklin Armstead,[6] John,[5] Capt. John,[4] William,[3] William,[2] Robert[1]*), born in Maury Co., Tenn., 23 May 1839, died at Guthrie, Okla., 15 Feb. 1921. He married, 9 Apr. 1861, FANNY ELIZABETH FOSTER.
He moved to Oklahoma from Carter's Creek, Tenn., in 1903, and remained there until his death.
Children:

    i.   MARY ELIZA,[8] b. in Lawrence Co., Ala., 23 May 1862; m. 23 Dec. 1880 ROBERT FLETCHER JACKSON. Residence, Franklin, Tenn. Children (surname *Jackson*): 1. *Eva Frances*, b. in Williamson Co., Tenn., 28 Feb. 1882; m. 3 June 1908 Neal House; no children. 2. *Andrew Vaughn*, of Franklin, Tenn., b. in Williamson Co., Tenn., 11 Dec. 1884; m. 2 Nov. 1914 Mary Currow, who d. 2 Oct. 1915; one son. 3. *John Armstead*, b. 22 Jan. 1886. 4. *Mary Louise*, b. at Nashville, Tenn., 1 Aug. 1892; m. 20 May 1913 Earl Toone; residence, Franklin, Tenn.; one son. 5. *Fannie Polk*, b. in Williamson Co., Tenn., 8 Nov. 1895; m. 20 May 1913 Henry Clay Ezell; residence, Franklin, Tenn.; one daughter. 6. *Roy Foster*, b. 22 Oct. 1898.

    ii.   ARGYLE FOSTER, of Frederick, Okla., b. 18 May 1866; unm.

    iii.   CHRISTINE HANCE, b. 28 Apr. 1868; m. (1) 15 Jan. 1894 ROBERT DARDEN LOCKRIDGE, who d. 8 Dec. 1900; m. (2) 24 June 1903 CHARLES COLLINS REDMAN. Residence, Newbern, Tenn. Children by first husband (surname *Lockridge*): 1. *Luther Polk*, of Catchings, Miss., cotton planter, b. in Maury Co., Tenn., 25 Dec. 1894; m. Hazel Boykin; he entered the Officers' Training Camp at Fort Oglethorpe, Ga., 29 Aug. 1917, after three months' training was attached to the Forty-fifth Infantry, of the Regular Army, at Louisville, Ky., as first lieutenant, in command of a machine gun company, and after about ten months was transferred to the National Army, to train replacement troops; after about two months he was promoted to a captaincy, serving in the Fourth Replacement Regiment at Camp Gordon, Ga., until the Armistice was signed; although he was recommended for a permanent captaincy in the Regular Army and passed the examination for that grade, he resigned his commission and returned to civil life; two children. 2. *Robert Darden*, b. 8 Nov. 1896; now a student of medicine in Vanderbilt University. 3. *Elizabeth Hill* (posthumous), b. 22 Feb. 1901; d. in infancy. Child by second husband (surname *Redman*): 4. *Christine Cornelia*, b. 29 Apr. 1904.

iv. JAMES KNOX, b. in Maury Co., Tenn., 21 Sept. 1869; d. 24 Nov. 1900; m. 2 Nov. 1897 MARY KILMARTIN, who d. at Nashville, Tenn., 9 July 1903. Children, b. at Nashville: 1. *Fanny Elizabeth*[9] (twin), b. 30 June 1899. 2. *Mary Lenora* (twin), b. 30 June 1899; d. in Maury Co. 25 Dec. 1902.

v. SARAH ARDELLA, b. in Maury Co., Tenn., 28 Oct. 1871; m. 8 Sept. 1904 GEORGE WASHINGTON FRITZE. Residence, Frederick, Okla. Children (surname *Fritze*): 1. *Leon George*, b. in Tillman Co., Okla., 25 Apr. 1906. 2. *James Knox*, b. at Shamrock, Tex., 12 Dec. 1908. 3. *Juanita Annie*, b. in Tillman Co., Okla., 19 Mar. 1912.

vi. FRANKLIN ARMSTEAD, of Frederick, Okla., b. in Maury Co., Tenn., 10 Mar. 1875; d. in Tillman Co., Okla., 18 Feb. 1920; m. (1) 8 Jan. 1904 JOHNNIE JACOBS, who d. in California 20 Aug. 1910 and is bur. at Trimble, Tenn.; m. (2) IDA FLORENCE MOORE, who d. in Tillman Co., Okla., 9 Aug. 1921. Children by second wife: 1. *Opal Frances*,[9] b. at Frederick 23 Dec. 1912; d. 9 Aug. 1921. 2. *Jessie* (twin), b. 6 Nov. 1914. 3. *Dessie* (twin), b. 6 Nov. 1914. 4. *Ida Florence*, b. 9 Feb. 1916. 5. *Bertha*, b. 1 July 1917.

vii. CURREN WHITTHORNE, of Grandfield, Okla., b. in Maury Co., Tenn., 17 Jan. 1878; m. 20 June 1906 ELVA LONA STONEBACH. Children: 1. *Lona Elizabeth*,[9] b. at Frederick, Okla., 30 Jan. 1908. 2. *Knox Sylvester*, b. at Grandfield, Okla., 16 Sept. 1910. 3. *Lois*, b. at Grandfield, Okla., 27 Oct. 1918. 4. *Minnie Louise*, b. at Grandfield, Okla., 4 Sept. 1921.

viii. BESSIE LEE (twin), b. in Maury Co., Tenn., 19 July 1880; d. in Tillman Co., Okla., 5 Jan. 1914; m. THOMAS PIERCE FULLER. Children (surname *Fuller*), b. in Tillman Co., Okla.: 1. *Whitthorne*, b. 27 Aug. 1906. 2. *Christine Martin*, b. 19 Apr. 1907. 3. *James Roe*, b. 8 May 1908. 4. *Cordez*, b. 18 Dec. 1911.

ix. FLORENCE HELEN (twin), b. in Maury Co., Tenn., 19 July 1880; m. 4 June 1905 THOMAS SPEED WARREN, who d. 15 Feb. 1911. Residence, Frederick, Okla. Children (surname *Warren*), b. in Tillman Co., Okla.: 1. *Katherine Elizabeth*, b. 27 Aug. 1906. 2. *Helen Florence*, b. 1 Jan. 1908.

x. ROBERT EVENDER, of Frederick, Okla., b. in Maury Co., Tenn., 29 Aug. 1882; m. 26 July 1909 EMILY HUFFHINES. Children: 1. *Theresa Carruth*,[9] b. 15 Jan. 1912. 2. *Robert Lee*, b. 7 Apr. 1914. 3. *Mary Frances*, b. 18 Feb. 1916.

Horace Moore Polk, Sr., son of Thomas Independence Polk &
Sarah Isham (Moore) Polk. *From Mrs. Alice Mitchum Fitts,
Oklahoma City.*

75. ANDERSON[7] POLK (*Taylor,*[6] *Taylor,*[5] *Capt. John,*[4] *William,*[3]
    William,[2] *Robert*[1]), born in the Valley of the Ouachita, in
    Arkansas, 14 Sept. 1824, died in Coryell Co., Tex., 15 Sept.
    1894. He married first ELIZA EPPERSON, sister of Capt.

George T. Epperson, the husband of Anderson Polk's sister Sarah Delaney (38, vii); secondly MARTHA MARTIN; and thirdly SUSAN LANGLEY.

Children by first wife, born in Arkansas:

i. HENRY,[8] m. ELLEN DETHROW. Two children.
ii. SARAH, m. JOHN HUDDLESTON. Four children.
iii. SYLVESTER, m. SARAH JUTZ. Two children.
iv. JANE, m. her first cousin, THOMAS HUDDLESTON (38, i, 5), s. of Daniel McKinley and Eleanor (Polk). Six children.

Children by second wife:

v. TEXANA, m. THOMAS WILLIAMSON. No children.
vi. MATILDA, m. JOSEPH JOPLIN.
vii. THOMAS, d. *s.p.*; m. ANNIE METLOCK.
viii. PRUDENCE, d. unm.
ix. ALMEDA, m. CHARLES CRUGER.

76. CUMBERLAND[7] POLK (*Taylor,[6] Taylor,[5] Capt. John,[4] William,[3] William,[2] Robert[1]*), farmer, was born 4 Nov. 1830. He married in Arkansas ALMEDA BLACKWOOD.

Children:

i. PRUDENCE,[8] m. JAMES STANFORD. Six children.
ii. TAYLOR, m. ELLEN GRIGGS. Four children.
iii. CALDONA, m. (1) ROBERT PRIEST; m. (2) WILLIAM BLACKWOOD. Seven children by first husband and one child by second husband.
iv. LUCINDA, m. JAMES HOUSTON. Two children.
v. LAWRENCE, m. PENELOPE ROSE. Two children.
vi. SARAH, m. ALONZO TRACY. Two children.
Also three sons, who d. young and unm.

77. HENRY CLAY[7] POLK (*Taylor,[6] Taylor,[5] Capt. John,[4] William,[3] William,[2] Robert[1]*), farmer, born near Mount Ida, Montgomery Co., Ark., 28 Jan. 1833, d. at Ben Lomond, Ark., 24 Nov. 1910. He married, 18 Sept. 1854, MARY ANN DICKSON, daughter of David S. and Rebecca (Bremer), born at Murfreesboro, Ark., 22 June 1837, d. at Murfreesboro 20 Apr. 1883.

He served in the Confederate Army in Arkansas.

Children, born at Murfreesboro, Ark.:

i. HENRY DICKSON,[8] b. 28 July 1855; m. ANNA GOULD.
ii. DAVID TAYLOR, b. 22 Oct. 1857; d. at Murfreesboro 17 Feb. 1859.
iii. EMMA AUGUSTA, b. 3 Jan. 1860; d. at Murfreesboro 30 Apr. 1862.
iv. MARY ALICE, b. 26 Nov. 1862; d. at Miller Grove, Tex., 31 May 1887; m. at Murfreesboro, 22 Feb. 1881, DR. G. B. GREEN. She left issue.
v. JOHN FLOYD, b. 2 Feb. 1866; m. SUSAN BROWN. He left issue.
vi. ANNA LOUISE, b. 17 Jan. 1869; m. at Miller Grove, Tex., 10 Dec. 1885, JOHN THOMAS HAWKINS. Children (surname *Hawkins*): 1. *George*, b. at Miller Grove 31 Oct. 1886; m. 30 Apr. 1917 Velma Garren. 2. *Irene*, b. at Miller Grove 28 Sept. 1890; m. 4 May 1921 A. L. Flowers. 3. *Dick*, b. 5 Nov. 1892; entered the Army 18 Dec. 1918, was trained at San Pedro, Calif., and was discharged in Mar. 1919. 4. *Don*, b. at Miller Grove 26 Aug. 1895. 5. *William Bryan*, b. at Miller Grove 18 Feb. 1897; volunteered for service in the spring of 1918, was trained at Fort Bliss, sailed for France in Nov. 1918, served in the American Expeditionary Forces, and returned in 1919. 6. *Mary*, b. at Sagerton, Tex., 25 Jan. 1903. 7. *John*, b. at Sagerton, Tex., 13 Aug. 1905.

78. SYLVESTER WALKER[7] POLK (*Taylor*,[6] *Taylor*,[5] *Capt. John*,[4]
William,[3] *William*,[2] *Robert*[1]), farmer, born in Montgomery
Co., Ark., 29 Jan. 1835, was living in 1921 at Mason, Tex.
He married in Coryell Co., Tex., 9 Jan. 1856, SARAH JANE
LARGE, daughter of Abraham and Drusilla (Latham).
He served four years in the Confederate Army, and moved
to Texas about 1866.
   Children:
   i.   ISAM WALKER,[8] of Streeter, Tex., farmer, b. in Arkansas 29 Oct.
        1856; m. in Mason Co., Tex., 7 June 1883, LUCY NARCISSA
        MILLER, b. at Springfield, Tex., 15 Mar. 1865, dau. of Thomas
        and Frances A. He came from Arkansas to Texas with his father's
        family in 1866. Children: 1. *Minnie Pearl*,[9] b. in Mason Co.,
        28 July 1884; m. there, 15 Nov. 1911, Henry Franklin Virdell;
        two daughters. 2. *Bessie Isadora Alice*, b. 8 Nov. 1886; m. 23
        Dec. 1915 James Monroe Fleming; one daughter, d. in infancy.
        3. *Janie Frances*, b. 8 Mar. 1889; m. 12 June 1908 James Dosy
        Wright; three children. 4. *Thomas Walker*, b. 8 Nov. 1891;
        m. 15 May 1912 Martha Sanders; three children. 5. *Laura Ellen*,
        b. 21 Jan. 1894; d. 31 Jan. 1894. 6. *Stella Maud*, b. 27 Mar.
        1895; m. 14 Oct. 1918 Alfred Lee Lemons; two sons. 7. *Lucy
        Prudence*, b. 13 Apr. 1899; unm. 8. *Elva Dee*, b. 26 Jan. 1903;
        unm.
   ii. VICTORIA, b. in Pike Co., Ark., 31 May 1860; m. 13 Dec. 1882
        HENRY OLIVER BROCKMAN, farmer, b. in Mason Co., Tex., 25
        Feb. 1858, s. of August and Elizabeth. Children (surname
        Brockman): 1. *Lula Helen*, b. 19 Sept. 1883; m. 20 Oct. 1912
        Fred E. Key; four children. 2. *Ruby Isadora*, b. 31 Mar. 1885;
        m. 12 Nov. 1914 Robert A. Leifeste; three children. 3. *Myrtle
        Jane*, b. 8 Feb. 1887; m. 15 Apr. 1908 Henry Holloway; four
        children. 4. *Grace Elizabeth*, b. 3 May 1889. 5. *Maud May*,
        b. 27 Nov. 1891; m. 19 Aug. 1914 August F. Simon; four children.
        6. *Iva Maria*, b. 11 May 1894; m. 6 Aug. 1921 Charles F. Bailey.
        7. *Hugh Oliver*, b. 1 Dec. 1896; d. 21 Nov. 1921. 8. *Clara Ellen*,
        b. 9 Mar. 1901; m. 20 Oct. 1921 Harold W. Millington.
   iii. ALFRED PASCAL, b. in Polk Co., Ark., 23 Oct. 1863; m. 30 Dec.
        1886 HANNAH JONES, dau. of B. M. and Minerva. Children:
        1. *Ranzy*,[9] b. 29 Oct. 1887; m. Cora Capps, dau. of John and
        Sally; seven children. 2. *Ethel*, b. 5 Sept. 1891; m. 3 Jan. 1905
        Ralph Carter; three children. 3. *Benjamin F.*, b. 19 Aug. 1885;
        m. Mae Mayo, dau. of Benjamin and Minnie; he enlisted at
        Mason, Tex., 19 Sept. 1917, as a private in Co. F, One Hundred
        and Forty-fourth Infantry, Thirty-sixth Division, and was
        wounded in the service. 4. *Alfred*, b. 8 Dec. 1893; m. Kate
        Gamel, b. 17 June 1902, dau. of James and Molly; he enlisted
        at Mason, Tex., 24 June 1918, sailed for France with the Ameri-
        can Expeditionary Forces 9 Sept. 1918, and returned in 1919.
        5. *Jewel*, b. 12 Sept. 1900; m. 12 Dec. 1917 Michael Miller.
   iv. ISADORA, b. 9 Jan. 1865; d. 24 Dec. 1912; m. (1) in 1880 WILLIAM
        R. CAPPS, b. in 1868; m. (2) RUFUS HAGE.
   v.   DAVID, b. in Navarro Co., Tex., 2 Aug. 1867; m. 28 Dec. 1887
        JANE BURNETT of San Antonio, Tex., dau. of William D. and
        Kizzie. Children: 1. *Lala*,[9] b. 15 Jan. 1889; m. 23 Jan. 1910
        Harry Leifeste, b. in Mason Co., Tex., 28 Apr. 1887; two chil-
        dren. 2. *Pascal*, b. 7 Oct. 1889; m. Stella Gipson, b. 27 Nov.
        1901, dau. of Beck and Emma. 3. *Robert*, b. 1 Nov. 1891; he
        enlisted in Aug. 1918 in the Balloon Division, in the World War,
        and returned in Jan. 1919. 4. *Lottie*, b. 18 Sept. 1894; m. 1 May
        1911 Hans Sells, b. in Germany 25 Nov. 1883; three children.
        5. *Ned*, b. 24 Sept. 1897; served in the World War in the Remount
        Division.

vi. LAURA, b. in Falls Co., Tex., 3 Feb. 1870; m. (1) 13 Nov. 1889 Dow BURNETT, farmer, b. 28 Nov. 1863, d. in Texas 28 July 1891, s. of William D. and Kizzie; m. (2) 5 Dec. 1906 WILLIAM THOMAS REED, farmer, b. in Coryell Co., Tex., 22 Aug. 1853, s. of Ace (b. in Hall Co., Ga.) and Margaret Dennie (Chaney). Child by first husband (surname *Burnett*): 1. *Ola*, b. 7 Sept. 1890; m. in Mason Co., Tex., in 1905, T. L. Payne. Children by second husband (surname *Reed*): 2. *Walter Jackson*, b. 23 Aug. 1907. 3. *Ace Walker*, b. 22 Jan. 1910.

vii. ALPHA, b. 18 July 1872; m. 11 Dec. 1889 JOHN H. LINDSAY of Lakewood, N. Mex., stockman, b. 12 Jan. 1872, s. of John, who came from Alabama to Texas. Children (surname *Lindsay*): 1. *Allan V.*, b. 4 Feb. 1891; he enlisted at Columbus, N. Mex., 6 May 1916, was mustered into the Federal service 13 June 1916, and served in the Mounted Police. 2. *Buck*, b. 5 June 1893; m. at Pecos, Tex., 1 May 1916, Hallie Moore; one daughter. 3. *Thomas*, b. 27 Oct. 1897; d. 14 Mar. 1898. 4. *Lewis*, b. 2 Feb. 1900. 5. *Lester*, b. 5 Jan. 1903. 6. *John Taylor*, b. 20 Aug. 1905. 7. *A. J.*, b. 5 Jan. 1911. 8. *A child*, b. 24 Dec. 1912; d. 1 Feb. 1913. 9. *Joseph*, b. 19 July 1914; d. in infancy.

viii. MAUD, b. in Texas 13 Dec. 1874; m. 16 Nov. 1893 LOUIS WILLIAM KOTHMAN, farmer, b. in Mason Co., Tex., 5 Sept. 1867, s. of William and Katherine. Children (surname *Kothman*): 1. *Emmett Floyd*, m. 13 Aug. 1914 Veda Bell Eaker; one son. 2. *Corda Jane*, b. 16 Oct. 1896; m. 1 Jan. 1920 Charles P. D. Leifeste; one daughter. 3. *Alpha Katherine*, b. 12 May 1899; m. 15 Dec. 1921 Andrew Clay Walker; one daughter. 4. *Howard Bert*, b. 6 Aug. 1902. 5. *Raymond David*, b. 13 Apr. 1905. 6. *Olen Ross*, b. 5 July 1908. 7. *Nellie Maude*, b. 27 Mar. 1911.

ix. CLAUD, farmer, b. 20 Sept. 1878; m. 6 Jan. 1904 BESSIE ARMES, b. 12 Aug. 1886, dau. of J. E. Armes. Children: 1. *Lydia*,[9] b. 5 Oct. 1904. 2. *Eva May*, b. 12 July 1908. 3. *Duke*, b. 11 Nov. 1911. 4. *Sylvester Wilkes*, b. 5 July 1921.

79. BENJAMIN FRANKLIN[7] POLK (*James*,[6] *Taylor*,[5] *Capt. John*,[4] *William*,[3] *William*,[2] *Robert*[1]), farmer, born in Arkansas 29 Jan. 1829, died in Texas 25 Nov. 1879. He married in Arkansas, in 1849, SARAH JANE RIDER, born in Arkansas 11 Oct. 1832, died in Texas 1 Feb. 1883.

He removed from Arkansas to Texas in 1856, and served four years in the Confederate Army.

Children:

i. PRUDENCE ANN,[8] b. in Montgomery Co., Ark., 1 Aug. 1851; d. in Montgomery Co. 30 Aug. 1851.

ii. JAMES MARTIN SYLVESTER, farmer, b. in Montgomery Co., Ark., 25 May 1852; d. on his home farm in Navarro Co., Tex., 21 Apr. 1881; m. at Richland, Navarro Co., in Sept. 1871, ALABAMA MORGAN, b. in Tennessee 21 Apr. 1854, d. in Navarro Co. 11 Nov. 1881. Children: 1. *A child*,[9] b. and d. on the same day. 2. *John Lee*, b. in Navarro Co. 16 Nov. 1875; m. at Abilene, Tex., 6 Mar. 1901, Dora J. Kelley, a graduate (1900) of Simmons College, Abilene, Tex., b. in Arkansas, dau. of James D. (stockman, of Gatesville, Tex., who d. in 1880) and Josephine (Coe); after his father's death he was raised by his uncle, John Lewallen Polk (79, iii) at La Junta, Colo., but returned to Texas in 1897 and engaged in livestock raising and farming on his ranch in Fisher Co.; in 1921 he went to New Mexico, where he now lives at Artesia, engaged in the livestock commission business and in insurance; four children. 3. *Eva Josephine*, m. at Sweet Water, Tex., —— Daniel. 4. *Rose Ella*, b. at Richland, Tex., 16 Oct. 1877; m. 14 Feb. 1895 Franklin Pierce Anderson, farmer, b. 20

Sept. 1872, s. of Francis Marion*; after her mother's death she was raised by her mother's sister, Mrs. Caroline (Morgan) Neill, wife of George Alfred Neill; nine children.

iii.   JOHN LEWALLEN, farmer, b. in Arkansas 11 Oct. 1854; d. at Roby, Tex., 25 Feb. 1906; m. at Muddyfork, Ark., 5 Apr. 1883, SUSAN WILLIAMS JONES, b. at Laurens, S. C., 30 Jan. 1868, living in 1921 at Royston, Tex., dau. of Dr. Benjamin Franklin (b. at Laurens 9 Aug. 1836, now living at Muddyfork, Ark.) and Susan Jane (Brooks) (b. at Laurens 19 Dec. 1841, now living at Muddyfork, Ark.). He lived for some years at La Junta, Colo., and afterwards moved to Texas, living later at Roby in that State. Children: 1. *Lillie,*[9] b. at La Junta 11 June 1885. 2. *Jones,* of Royston, Tex., farmer, b. at La Junta 2 Sept. 1887; m. at Roby, 15 May 1910, Bessie Olga Harris, b. at Copperas Cove, Tex., 11 Dec. 1891, dau. of Rev. William Hilliard (b. at Ringgold, Ga., 14 Oct. 1864, residing at Ovilla, Tex.) and Florence Ida (Johnson) (b. at Fairfield, Tex., 17 May 1866, d. 11 July 1892, m. in Sept. 1882); one daughter. 3. *Mart,* of Royston, Tex., b. at La Junta 16 Feb. 1891; unm. 4. *Clifford Allen,* of Royston, Tex., b. at La Junta 16 Mar. 1893; unm. 5. *Nellie Jane,* b. at Roby 29 Dec. 1899; m. at Hamlin, Tex., 22 Sept. 1919, Calvin Horace Carriker, b. 22 Sept. 1897, s. of Benjamin Lewis (b. in Mississippi 10 Mar. 1873) and Alice Armitice (Irby) (b. 24 Apr. 1875, m. 9 Sept. 1894); residence, Royston, Tex.

iv.   BENJAMIN FRANKLIN, b. in Montgomery Co., Ark., 5 Nov. 1856; d. unm. in Texas 21 Apr. 1877.

v.   LOUIS TAYLOR, b. near Corsicana, Tex., 27 June 1859; d. at Cheyenne, Okla., 5 July 1921; m. at Gail, Tex., 8 Sept. 1897, NETTIE LYONS, b. in Fayette Co., Tex., 3 Oct. 1878, living at Rankin, Okla., dau. of W. J. Lyons (b. near Lyonsville, Fayette Co., 16 Dec. 1847) and his wife Mary Ann (Criswell) (b. near Lyonsville 1 Dec. 1850). Children: 1. *Thomas Trammell,*[9] b. at Gail 4 Sept. 1898. 2. *Louis James,* b. at Gail 17 Jan. 1900. 3. *Pauline,* b. at Gail 31 Dec. 1901. 4. *Jack,* b. at Gail 21 Mar. 1904; d. near Roby, Tex., 22 Nov. 1905. 5. *Emmit Brit,* b. near Roll, Fisher Co., Tex., 22 May 1906. 6. *Hortense,* b. near Ralston, Tex., 22 Sept. 1909. 7. *Oleta Mae,* b. near Gem City, Hemphill Co., Tex., 22 July 1914. 8. *Frank Lyons,* b. at Gem City, Hemphill Co., Tex., 18 Dec. 1917.

vi.   WILLIAM FRANKLIN, of Royston, Tex., b. in Texas 25 Jan. 1862; m. 23 Aug. 1900 MINNIE UBBER.

vii.   MARY ELIZABETH, b. at Richland, Tex., 12 Sept. 1864; m. (1) 13 Jan. 1883 WAYNE BENNETT, who d. at Wortham, Tex., 21 Oct. 1895, s. of Francis Mason (b. in Tennessee) and Jane (White) (b. in Texas, m. in 1859); m. (2) at Durham, Tex., in 1909, JAMES A. LOCKLEAR. Residence, Norton, N. Mex. Children by first husband (surname *Bennett*): 1. *Willie,* b. at Richland 20 Sept. 1884; m. at Roby, Tex., 19 Aug. 1903, Thomas Perry Henry; seven children, b. at Royston, Tex. 2. *Dess.* 3. *Jane.* 4. *Wayne.* 5. *John Allen.*

viii. MARTHA ISABELLE, b. 22 Oct. 1866; m. at Richland, Tex., 20 Dec. 1887, WILLIAM MASTEN WHITE, farmer. Children (surname *White*): 1. *Mabel,* b. at Richland 24 Oct. 1888; m. there, 29 May 1910, Samuel Barron Goode, b. at Roby, Tex., in 1886; one son, b. at Eastland, Tex. 2. *Celia Elizabeth,* b. 4 July 1892; m. at Eastland, Tex., 21 Apr. 1917, Homer Paskel West, electrician, b. at Dallas, Tex., 4 July 1900; one daughter. 3. *Willie Ross,* b. at Roby, Tex., 13 Apr. 1906.

ix.   THOMAS TRAMMELL, b. 21 Aug. 1869; m. (1) in 1895 DELLA CAVE, who d. at Roby, Tex., 3 Mar. 1900; m. (2) in Ellis Co., Tex., in

*Francis Marion Anderson, born in South Carolina 24 July 1827, died in Texas 10 Apr. 1910. When two years of age he was taken by his parents to Missouri, and grew up there. He moved to Texas in 1863. In 1864 he joined the Rangers in Brown Co. He married (1) Elizabeth Smith, and by her had one son. On 29 Sept. 1864 he married (2) Mrs. Amanda Weeks, and by her had three sons and one daughter.

1904, MARIE HARRIS. Children by first wife, b. at Royston, Tex.:
1. *Allen.*[9] 2. *Wayne.* Children by second wife: 3. *Javita.*
4. *Linda.* 5. *Samuel Singleton.* 6. *Harris.*

x. FLOYD IDELLA, b. 1 Nov. 1871; m. at Purcell, Okla., in 1892, ARTHUR
ALEXANDER, who d. 14 Feb. 1919. Residence, Ardmore, Okla.

80. CUMBERLAND[7] POLK (*James,*[6] *Taylor,*[5] *Capt. John,*[4] *William,*[3]
William,[2] *Robert*[1]), of Prairie Lea, Tex., farmer, born in the
Valley of the Ouachita, Ark., 1 Apr. 1836, died at Prairie Lea
20 Sept. 1910. He married, 28 May 1861, LAURA JANE
KIRK.

His father died before he was born, and his mother died
soon after his birth; and he was raised by his uncle Cumberland Polk (40), whose wife, Nancy (Cox) Polk, was a sister
of his mother, Sarah (Cox) Polk. When his uncle moved to
Texas, he went with the family, and remained with them until
1857, when he went to California. He returned to Texas in
1859, and lived there until his death. After he was married,
he lived at Prairie Lea. He was a man of great intelligence
and character, and was much respected in his community,
where he was a prosperous farmer.

Children, born in Caldwell Co., Tex.:

i. JAMES KNOX,[8] b. 18 May 1863; m. at Luling, Tex., 27 Jan. 1897,
DOVIE JANE CONLEY. No children.

ii. ELIZABETH, b. 15 July 1865; m. (1) 19 June 1889 DE LAFAYETTE
NORMAN, who d. in Mar. 1894; m. (2) in 1897 E. H. ROBERTS
of Fentress, Tex. Children by first husband (surname *Norman*):
1. *Cecil Ray*, b. 22 Feb. 1890; m. Ella Shanklin. 2. *Ross Cumnor*,
b. 20 Dec. 1891; m. at Lockhart, Tex., 20 Nov. 1913, Sadie
Swearingin; one daughter.

iii. ANNIE, b. 1 July 1868. She was a teacher in the public schools of
Lockhart, Tex., later was appointed treasurer of Caldwell Co.,
Tex., and was then elected to the same office, which she still holds.
During the World War she was a member of the War Work Coun-
cil and was the only woman member of the County Council of
Defense. She was also chairman of the Women's Committee.

iv. FRANK, b. 8 Dec. 1870; d. 14 Mar. 1912.

v. MATTIE LENA, b. 20 Feb. 1874; m. at Prairie Lea, Tex., 4 Apr. 1894,
her first cousin once removed, JAMES PHILIP TRAMMELL, b. in
Navarro Co., Tex., 20 Nov. 1873, d. at Sweet Water, Tex., 20
Nov. 1913, s. of Thomas and Mary Jane (Newman) (cf. 39, ii, 2).
Children (surname *Trammell*): 1. *Thomas Gibson*, b. at Sweet
Water 24 Apr. 1896; m. at Roswell, N. Mex., 4 Jan. 1921, Marie
Gladys Jolly; he served in the Hospital Corps of the Navy in the
World War. 2. *Dorothy Elizabeth*, b. at Sweet Water 7 Sept. 1898.
3. *James Philip*, b. at Sweet Water 13 Nov. 1900. 4. *Annie
Laura*, b. 27 Mar. 1909; d. 23 Oct. 1910.

vi. LOUIS SHELBY, b. 1 Aug. 1876; m. at Sweet Water, Tex., in 1904,
MINNIE CONLEY, who d. 23 June 1912. Child: 1. *Marjorie*,[9] b.
at Sweet Water 25 Apr. 1906.

vii. MINNIE PEARL, b. 27 Jan. 1880; d. at Prairie Lea, Tex., 4 July 1908;
m. at Prairie Lea, in 1904, JOSEPH MUENSTER. Child (surname
Muenster): 1. *Josephine*, b. at Austin, Tex., 27 Mar. 1906.

81. JAMES ANDERSON[7] POLK (*Alfred,*[6] *Taylor,*[5] *Capt. John,*[4] *William,*[3]
William,[2] *Robert*[1]), farmer and stockman, born in Polk Co.,
Ark., 4 July 1841, died on his home farm near Belton, Bell
Co., Tex., 8 Oct. 1908. He married, 5 Aug. 1869, ZILPHA

SUTTON, born in Izard Co., Ark., 1 Sept. 1849, daughter of
Anderson and Rhoda, who moved from Arkansas to Texas in
1852.

He went with his father's family to Texas in 1851. He
served in Texas as a Ranger for two years, and in 1861 he
enlisted in the Confederate Army and served till the end of
the Civil War in 1865, when he returned home. He was enrolled in Co. K, First Texas Cavalry, which served in the
Trans-Mississippi Department. After his father's death he
owned the old homestead.

Children, born in Bell Co., Tex.:

i.   ROSE ETTA,[8] b. 13 Mar. 1871; m. 8 Jan. 1893 JAMES CHURCHILL
      COWAN, s. of James W. (b. in Georgia) and Mollie (Hood) (b. in
      Missouri). Children (surname *Cowan*), b. in Bell Co.:' 1. *Welborn
      Chester*, b. 18 Feb. 1894; m. Verdie Todd of Swisher Co., Tex.;
      one son, b. in Swisher Co. 2. *Ora Lea*, b. 15 Dec. 1897; m. Rich-
      ard Scott of Swisher Co., Tex.; one child, b. in Swisher Co.
      3. *James Churchill*, b. 28 June 1905.
ii.   PERRION YOUNG, b. 23 Apr. 1872; d. in July 1873.
iii. JESSE NEWTON, b. 3 Dec. 1873; d. 30 Nov. 1877.
iv.   WILLIAM CHARLES, of Belton, Bell Co., Tex., abstractor and deputy
      county clerk, b. 23 Nov. 1875; m. (1) 4 Dec. 1895 YETTIE TOBLER,
      who was drowned, with three of her children, in the flood at
      Belton, Tex., 2 Dec. 1913, dau. of Julius (of Belton, jeweler, a
      native of Zürich, Switzerland, who came to America in 1866) and
      Julia (Manning) (b. at Mobile, Ala., widow of ——— Cummins);
      m. (2) 7 May 1916 MARY PRICHARD, dau. of William Blue (b. in
      Missouri in 1853 and raised there) and Joan (Eaton) (b. at Shel-
      burn, Ind., in 1861, widow of Lewis Arman). Children by first
      wife: 1. *Yettie*,[9] b. 21 Sept. 1896; d. 2 Dec. 1913. 2. *Florence*,
      b. 16 Jan. 1899; d. 2 Dec. 1913. 3. *William Henry*, b. 13 Dec.
      1900; m. 10 Aug. 1920 Lillian Russell. 4. *George Marion*, b. 15
      Dec. 1902; d. 2 Dec. 1913. 5. *A child*, b. and d. 12 Mar. 1913.
      Children by second wife: 6. *Charles Eaton*, b. 26 Feb. 1918.
      7. *Rose Mary*, b. 2 Oct. 1920.

82. MITCHELL ALFRED[7] POLK (*Alfred*,[6] *Taylor*,[5] *Capt. John*,[4]
    William,[3] *William*,[2] *Robert*[1]), farmer, was born 24 Apr. 1845.
    He married, in 1873, MARY ELIZABETH CRABB, born 27 July
    1856.

    He served three years in the Confederate Army, being
    stationed on Galveston Island, Tex.

    Children:

i.   WILLIAM CARTEZ,[8] b. 8 Oct. 1875; m. EDNA JACKSON. Children:
      1. *Eva*.[9] 2. *Warren*.
ii.   MINNIE EVALINE, b. 7 July 1879; m. (1) WILLIAM FREEMAN; m.
      (2) WILLIAM BERNARD. Children by first husband (surname
      Freeman): 1. *Virgil*, who served in United States Navy in the
      World War. 2. *Mitchell*.
iii. RILEY MADISON, b. 11 Aug. 1883; m. BERTIE HANCOCK. Children:
      1. *Owen*.[9] 2. *Travis Wayne*.
iv.   LENA MAY, b. 20 Feb. 1887; m. (1) HENRY RILEY; m. (2) ARTHUR
      FREEMAN. Child by first husband (surname *Riley*): 1. *Lois*.
      Child by second husband (surname *Freeman*): 2. *Jewell*.
v.   PEARL, b. 1 Aug. 1896; m. FREDERICK TIBBS. Child (surname
      Tibbs): 1. *Duane*.
vi.   HARRIS, b. 17 Sept. 1898; m. (1) EDNA GOLD; m. (2) ROSA POLK.
      Child by first wife: 1. *Gloria Adell*.[9] He was called for service in
      the World War on the day of the Armistice, but returned home
      without training.

83. THOMAS BENJAMIN[7] POLK (*James Irvin,*[6] *Thomas,*[5] *Col. Ezekiel,*[4] *William,*[3] *William,*[2] *Robert*[1]), born in Robertson Co., Tenn., 6 July 1827, died at Cedar Hill, Tenn., 15 May 1896. He married at Cedar Hill, 2 Jan. 1850, ABIE LONG, daughter of James Henry.

Children, born at Cedar Hill, Tenn.:

i.   JAMES IRVIN,[8] b. 18 Dec. 1850; d. unm. at Cedar Hill 23 Sept. 1887.
ii. ELIZABETH ADLINE, b. 15 Sept. 1852; m. at Cedar Hill, 5 Nov. 1874, JAMES HENRY SMITH, s. of Abe and Mary (Long). Residence, Clarksville, Tenn. Children (surname *Smith*), b. at Clarksville: 1. *Thomas Polk*, b. 10 Sept. 1875; m. at Eddyville, Lyon Co., Ky., 15 Nov. 1899, Iola Gracey, dau. of William Robert and Laura (Scott); one daughter, b. at Clarksville. 2. *George Charlton*, b. 4 Apr. 1881; m. at Springfield, Tenn., 8 Mar. 1912, Maude Belle; no children. 3. *James Henry*, of Clarksville, b. 14 Nov. 1885; m. at Clarksville, 30 Dec. 1914, Elizabeth Barker; no children.
iii. WILLIAM KNOX, b. 5 Apr. 1854; d. 17 Dec. 1857.
iv. EMMA LOU, b. 25 Oct. 1855; m. at Springfield, Tenn., 19 Nov. 1901, G. A. LAPRADE. No children.
v.   THOMAS LUCIUS, of Gallatin, Tenn., b. 4 Sept. 1857; m. at Cedar Hill, 10 May 1894, NANNIE HENDERSON. He is entitled to membership in the Society of the Cincinnati by descent through the eldest male line from Col. Ezekiel Polk (8). No children.
vi. JOHN EDWARD, of Baker, Tenn., b. 15 Oct. 1860; m. at Baker's Station, Tenn., 25 Oct. 1888, MAGGIE MCCORKLE LUTON, dau. of William and Adelaide (Patton). Children, b. at Baker: 1. *Thomas Luton,*[9] of Evansville, Ind., b. 6 May 1890; m. at Guthrie, Ky., 22 Jan. 1914, Annie Penn Johnson, dau. of Samuel P. and Sarah Elizabeth (Penn); no children. 2. *Addie Blanche*, b. 23 May 1892; d. 7 Jan. 1898. 3. *John Edward*, b. 24 Sept. 1894. 4. *Nellie White*, b. 16 May 1897. 5. *Lucius Benjamin*, b. 14 Apr. 1899. 6. *Allie Elizabeth*, b. 3 Feb. 1901. 7. *Margaret Douglas*, b. 11 Mar. 1903. 8. *Emma Louise*, b. 30 Oct. 1904.
vii. ROBERT FRANKLIN, of Mount Pleasant, Tenn., b. 2 Nov. 1862; m. at Clarksville, Tenn., 14 Feb. 1895, SALLIE WATERS. No children.
viii. BLANCHE REBECCA, b. 25 May 1869; m. 28 Oct. 1890 GEORGE A. SMITH. Residence, Adairville, Ky. No children.

84. JAMES KNOX[7] POLK (*James Irvin,*[6] *Thomas,*[5] *Col. Ezekiel,*[4] *William,*[3] *William,*[2] *Robert*[1]), born at Adams, Tenn., 2 Aug. 1830, died there 23 July 1886. He married at Adams, 1 Oct. 1852, MIRANDA ANN BELL, daughter of Joel Egbert and Wilmoth Elizabeth (Edwards).

Children:

i. WILMOTH ELIZABETH,[8] b. at Adams 30 Nov. 1854; d. at Chillicothe, Mo., 12 Dec. 1881; m. at Adams, 25 Jan. 1880, WILLIAM HERSCHAL WILLETTE. Child (surname *Willette*): 1. *Thomas Carlton*, b. at Adams 16 Jan. 1881; m. at Springfield, Tenn., 28 Jan. 1904, Pattie Lou Alsbrook, dau. of Hiram David and Alice Eudora (Chambers); two children, b. at Adams.
ii. BELL VIRGINIA, b. at Springfield, Tenn., 25 July 1860; m. at Adams, 2 Jan. 1879, EPPA LAWSON FORT, s. of Iloi Metcalf and Charlotte Warren (Dancy). Residence, Springfield. Children (surname *Fort*): 1. *Combs C.*, b. at Adams 13 Mar. 1880; m. at Nashville, Tenn., 1 Jan. 1907, Ora Bell Moorehead, dau. of Robert Young and Betty Jane (Anthony). 2. *Mary*, b. at Chillicothe, Mo., 18 Sept. 1882; m. at Springfield, 23 Aug. 1899, Hubert Harry Woodard, s. of Moses Daniel and Leonora Polk (Johnson). 3. *Eppie Bell*, b. at Adams 5 Oct. 1884; living unm. at Springfield. 4. *Minnie Polk*, b. at Adams 19 Mar. 1889; m. at Springfield, 12 June 1912, Alford Broadus Waldrep, s. of Little Berry and Anna

Louise (Harris); residence, Verden, Okla. 5. *Margaret*, b. at
Adams 16 May 1891; m. at Springfield, 24 Sept. 1913, Isaac Wesley Shannon, s. of William Isaac and Emma Lincoln (McMurry);
residence, Tulsa, Okla.; no children.

iii. JAMIE KNOX, b. at Adams 28 Mar. 1863; m. at Springfield, Tenn.,
3 Jan. 1894, HARRY TINSLEY ENGLAND. Residence, Springfield.
No children.

85. CAPT. MARSHALL TATE[7] POLK (*Marshall Tate,[6] Samuel,[5] Col.
Ezekiel,[4] William,[3] William,[2] Robert[1]*), born at Charlotte,
N. C., 15 May 1831, died at Nashville, Tenn., 29 Feb. 1884.
He married at Bolivar, Tenn., 10 Jan. 1856, his second cousin,
EVELINA McNEAL BILLS, daughter of Maj. John Houston
and Prudence Tate (McNeal) Bills (cf. 8, vi, 3).

He was appointed in 1848 a cadet from Tennessee in the
United States Military Academy at West Point, was gradu-
ated there in 1852, and was commissioned a second lieutenant.
In the Sioux Expedition of 1855 he acted as aide-de-camp to
General Harney. He resigned from the Army in 1856. He
served as captain of Artillery in the Confederate Army.

Children, all except the last two born at Bolivar, Tenn.:

i.   EDWARD McNEAL,[8] b. 18 Nov. 1856; d. 19 Sept. 1858.
ii. CAPT. JAMES KNOX, of Nashville, Tenn., b. 26 Jan. 1859; m. at
Bolivar, 27 Jan. 1880, MARY FRANCES HIBBLER, who d. 26 Oct.
1920, dau. of Robert and Ann Kelsey. He was educated at the
University of Tennessee, and in the War with Spain served in the
Philippines, 1898–99, as first lieutenant and adjutant and later
as captain of Co. F, First Tennessee Volunteer Infantry. Children: 1. *James Knox,[9]* of Nashville, b. at Nashville 3 Mar. 1881;
m. at Nashville, 27 Jan. 1915, Virginia Gibson Prichard, dau.
of W. G. and Mary (Gibson); in the War with Spain he served in
the Philippines, 1898–99, in Co. A, First Tennessee Volunteer
Infantry; one daughter, b. at Nashville. 2. *Kelsey Hibbler*, of
Nashville, b. at Nashville 30 Dec. 1884; m. at Mount Pleasant,
Tenn., 18 Oct. 1910, Eleanor Frances Gregory, dau. of Edward L.;
one daughter, b. at Lawton, Okla. 3. *Albert McNeal*, b. at South
Pittsburg, Tenn., 12 Aug. 1888; unm.; in the World War he
enlisted in 1918 in the Fiftieth Infantry, was made first sergeant in
the Headquarters Company, served in the United States, and was
mustered out, with the regiment, in 1919. 4. *Edward Marshall*,
of Nashville, b. at Chattanooga, Tenn., 1 June 1891; m. at Nashville, 8 Dec. 1912, Olivia Winston Sharpe, dau. of Charles F. and
Olivia Winston (Scott); one daughter, b. at Nashville. 5. *Lawrence Norton*, b. at Nashville 17 Feb. 1896; unm.; in the World
War he enlisted 12 May 1917, attended the Officers' Training
School at Chickamauga, Ga., volunteered for the Aviation Section
in July 1917, and was ordered to Atlanta, Ga., for ground training;
in Oct. 1917 he was sent to France to be trained by the French;
in Feb. 1918 he was commissioned as first lieutenant, and served
chiefly in the Twenty-fifth Aero Squadron in France; he was
mustered out 6 Sept. 1919.

iii. MARY WILSON, b. 24 Aug. 1861; m. at Nashville, Tenn., 26 Nov.
1884, ALEXANDER HUMPHREYS KORTRECHT, s. of Judge Charles
and Augusta (Betts). Residence, Memphis, Tenn. Children
(surname *Kortrecht*), b. at Memphis: 1. *Charles Murray*, b. 13
Aug. 1886; unm. 2. *Humphreys*, b. 15 May 1888; unm. 3.
Evelyn Marshall, b. 30 Jan. 1890; m. at Nashville, 6 June 1914,
Edgar Morrison Richardson, s. of Edgar Morrison and Anna Black
(Price); residence, Memphis; one daughter, b. at Memphis.
4. *Eunice Polk*, b. 13 Jan. 1892; unm. 5. *Augustus*, b. 30 Jan.
1897.

iv. LAURA PRUDENCE, b. 4 Feb. 1865; unm.
v. EUNICE OPHELIA, b. 2 Aug. 1867; m. at Nashville, Tenn., 15 Nov. 1894, JESSE ROWLAND NORTON. Residence, Nashville. Children (surname *Norton*): 1. *Evelyn Polk*, b. at Chicago, Ill., 25 Aug. 1895. 2. *Frederick Rowland*, b. at Chicago, Ill., 6 Aug. 1897. 3. *Jesse Rowland*, b. at Nashville 29 Oct. 1900.
vi. CLARA ALLISON, b. 16 Nov. 1870; d. 21 Mar. 1872.
vii. MARSHALL TATE, of Nashville, Tenn., b. 8 Mar. 1873; m. at Nashville, 19 Apr. 1902, ANNIE SPERRY HILL, dau. of Robert and Ann (Patterson). Children, b. at Nashville: 1. *Robert Hill*,[9] b. 27 Apr. 1903. 2. *Marshall Tate*, b. 1 Nov. 1904. 3. *Prudence McNeal*, b. 8 Sept. 1906. 4. *Thomas Wilson*, b. 13 Dec. 1908. 5. *Anne Patterson*, b. 5 Apr. 1911. 6. *John Houston*, b. 14 June 1913. 7. *Evelina McNeal*, b. 15 Apr. 1916.
viii. EVELYN MCNEAL, b. 9 Dec. 1875; m. at Nashville, Tenn., 12 Jan. 1904, DIQUE ORSON ELDRED, s. of Orson and Delia (Harpendike). Residence, Princeton, Ky. Children (surname *Eldred*), b. at Princeton: 1. *George Orson* (twin), b. 14 Sept. 1904. 2. *Marshall Polk* (twin), b. 14 Sept. 1904. 3. *Mary Wilson*, b. 7 Aug. 1907.
ix. LEONIDAS, of Toledo, Ohio, b. at Nashville, Tenn., 27 Mar. 1878; m. at Toledo, 28 Mar. 1908, RACHEL MARIE SCOTT. In the War with Spain he was enrolled 20 May 1898 in Co. A, First Tennessee Volunteer Infantry, served in the Philippines, and was mustered out, with the regiment, at San Francisco, Calif., 23 Nov. 1899. Children, b. at Toledo: 1. *Elmer Scott*,[9] b. 24 May 1909. 2. *Dora Marie*, b. 12 Jan. 1911. 3. *Leonidas*, b. 3 July 1912. 4. *William McNeal*, b. 1 Aug. 1915. 5. *Eva Bills*, b. in Oct. 1916.
x. THOMAS ALLISON, b. at Nashville, Tenn., 13 June 1879; d. there 14 Sept. 1884.

86. CAPT. JAMES MONROE[7] POLK (*Thomas Marlborough*,[6] *William Wilson*,[5] *Col. Ezekiel*,[4] *William*,[3] *William*,[2] *Robert*[1]), born in Greene Co., Mo., 7 Oct. 1838, died in the Confederate Home at Austin, Tex., 15 Aug. 1920. He married at Galveston, Tex., 14 Feb. 1874, MARY IGLEHART, daughter of Michael and Lucinda (Steagal).

He migrated to Navarro Co., Tex., in 1859. In August 1861 he enlisted at Corsicana, Tex., in Capt. C. M. Winkler's company, which marched to Harrisburg, Tex., and was mustered into Hood's Texas brigade of the Confederate Army. Soon afterwards the organization was sent to Virginia. In the spring of 1862 he returned to Texas to enlist recruits for the Texas regiments in Virginia, but rejoined his company in Virginia in time to take part in the Battle of Seven Pines. He was wounded in the arm at Gaines's Mill on 27 June 1862, but rejoined his company in September in the Battle of Antietam. He participated in the Battles of Fredericksburg, Gettysburg, and Chickamauga, where he was desperately wounded, and was obliged because of his wound to spend several months in a hospital at Richmond, Va. In March 1864 he was commissioned a captain of Infantry, and was assigned to the Trans-Mississippi Department, joining General Price's army in Arkansas. In the summer of 1864 he was sent on several recruiting expeditions through the Federal lines into Missouri, whence he volunteered to go on a secret detail into St. Louis and Illinois, to secure arms and ammunition to be smuggled through the lines. He was captured, however, and confined for the remainder of the war. In 1888 he emigrated to Brazil, but returned to the United States in 1898.

Child:

i.   WILLIAM WILSON,[8] b. in Callahan Co., Tex., 10 Jan. 1879; m. (1) JENNIE STEWART; m. (2) at Austin, Tex., 27 July 1905, LYDIA BLANCHE SANDERS, dau. of George Walter and Hettie Florence (Grant). No children.

87. LIEUT. WILLIAM ALEXANDER[7] POLK (*Thomas Marlborough,*[6] *William Wilson,*[5] *Col. Ezekiel,*[4] *William,*[3] *William,*[2] *Robert*[1]), of Navarro Co., Tex., born in Lawrence Co., Mo., 14 Feb. 1844, died at Eureka Springs, Ark., 22 June 1908. He married at Hernando, Miss., 20 Dec. 1866, MATTIE MOSELEY, daughter of Judge John Thomas.

When seventeen years of age he enlisted in the first company of Confederate troops raised at Middleburg, Tenn., and was elected second lieutenant under Capt. W. B. Morrow. His company was attached to the Fourth Tennessee Infantry, and was stationed at Forts Randolph and Pillow during their construction. He took part in the campaign from New Madrid to Cape Girardeau, Mo., and later was transferred to Capt. Jack Neely's scout company, of the Seventh Tennessee Cavalry, under Gen. N. B. Forrest's command. In February 1865 he was captured while on scout duty in northern Mississippi, and was confined in the military prison at Camp Douglas, near Chicago, until the close of the war. In 1866 he moved with his father's family from Phillips Co., Ark., to Navarro Co., Tex., and settled about four miles south of Dresden. He was county commissioner, 1879–1883, and chairman of the Board of Trustees of the State Orphans' Home, 1903–1906.

Children, born in Navarro Co., Tex.:

i.   LULA IZA,[8] b. 22 Aug. 1868; d. *s.p.* at Waco, Tex., 23 May 1905; m. at Corsicana, Tex., 24 Nov. 1902, MALCOLM MCINTYRE EARLY, s. of Eugene and Patty (McIntyre).

ii.   THERESA, b. 5 Apr. 1870; m. at Corsicana, Tex., 25 Oct. 1894, ALBERT HENRY MILLER, s. of Daniel Jackson and Mary (Henry). Residence, Corsicana. No children.

iii. THOMAS EMMETT, of Chicago, Ill., b. 7 May 1872; m. at Corsicana, Tex., 25 Oct. 1894, STELLA FEWELL, dau. of Calvin L. and Mary (Jackson). Child: 1. *Thomas Emmett,*[9] b. in 1896; d. in 1901.

iv.   JUDGE, b. 10 Apr. 1873; d. 20 Feb. 1875.

v.   WILLIAM ARTHUR, of Fort Worth, Tex., C.E. (Agricultural and Mechanical College of Texas, 1895), b. 17 Dec. 1875; m. at Corsicana, Tex., 16 Nov. 1904, PEARL JOHNSON, dau. of Samuel Wistar. Children: 1. *Samuel Wistar,*[9] b. at Corsicana 29 Apr. 1907. 2. *Katherine,* b. at Dallas, Tex., 14 Feb. 1912.

vi.   EDWARD MONROE, of Corsicana, Tex., b. 11 Feb. 1878; m. at Corsicana, 19 Sept. 1900, ROSE LA VALLE BLAIR, dau. of James Robert and Harriet (Cushman). Child: 1. *Edward Monroe,*[9] b. at Corsicana 14 Feb. 1902.

vii. DAISY, b. 27 Aug. 1880; m. at Corsicana, Tex., 11 Nov. 1902, JOHN SMITH MURCHISON, s. of John and Josephine Augusta (Hale). Residence, Corsicana. Children (surname *Murchison*), b. at Corsicana: 1. *Martha,* b. 23 Sept. 1903. 2. *Josephine Augusta,* b. 9 Aug. 1905. 3. *William Polk,* b. 5 June 1908. 4. *Iza Polk,* b. 14 Aug. 1910. 5. *John Le Gory,* b. 17 Dec. 1913.

viii. LOUIE CERF, of Corsicana, Tex., b. at Corsicana 2 Feb. 1884; m. at Corsicana, 12 Feb. 1913, GRACE CHRISTIAN, dau. of Alexander Campbell and Julia (Jack). Child: 1. *Louis Christian,*[9] b. 13 Sept. 1915; d. 28 Oct. 1915.

ADDENDUM

ADDITIONS AND CORRECTIONS

VOL. 77

Page 134, line 4 and footnote. The compiler of this genealogy being at present (July 1924) abroad, it does not seem advisable to take up in the REGISTER at any length at this time the subject of the ancestry of Robert[1] Pollock or Polk, the immigrant, from whom the Polks of North Carolina and Tennessee are descended. It may be stated, however, that the authors of various published accounts of this family claim that Robert[1] Pollock or Polk belonged to an Irish branch of the ancient family of Pollok of Renfrewshire, Scotland. A Robert Pollok, of the Renfrewshire family, was created a baronet by Queen Anne in 1703, but the baronetcy is now extinct. The REGISTER will gladly publish any evidence that tends to prove or disprove the claims made by historians and genealogists about the ancestry of the founder of the American family. — EDITOR.

Page 143, line 45 (8, vi, 8), *for* Barry *read* Berry.
Page 266, line 44 (33), *for* 1800 *read* 1810.

VOL. 78

Page 39, line 21 (40, ii), *for* 28 May *read* 28 Mar.
Page 42, line 35 (40, ii, 9), *for* Tueuler *read* Tressler.
Page 46, line 7 (41, xii, 1), *for* 1920 *read* 1922.
Page 46, line 18 (42, i, 1), *for* Pleasant H. *read* Pleasant M.
Page 46, line 19 (42, i, 1), *for* eight *read* three.
Page 46, line 30 (42, i, 6), *for* 16 Feb. *read* 16 Sept.
Page 46, line 39 (42, iii), *for* LOUISE *read* LOUISA.
Page 46, line 52 (42, v, 1), *for* Irvin *read* Irvin Polk.
Page 46, line 60 (42, vi), *for* 22 Mar. *read* 22 May.
Page 47, line 3 (42, vi, 1), *for* seven *read* eight.
Page 47, line 6 (42, vi, 4), *for* Warner *read* Warren.
Page 47, line 15 (42, vii, 3), *for* Erving *read* Ewing.
Page 47, line 30 (42, xii), *for* LEONARD *read* LENNARD.
Page 47, line 46 (42, xiii, 2), *for* Finis *read* Finis Irvin.
Page 47, line 63 (42, xiv), *for* ANNA *read* ANNIE.
Page 48, line 18 (43, ii, 1), *for* 7 Apr. *read* 7 Aug.
Page 48, line 48 (45), *for* 16 Dec. *read* 15 Dec.
Page 48, line 50 (45), *for* 29 May *read* 29 June.
Page 52, lines 10–12 (47, xiii), *for* these three lines *read* South, serving first, for several years, in the West Tennessee Conference and later in the White River (Ark.) Conference. In Dec. 1882 he was transferred to the Texas Conference and about 1890 to the Northwest Texas Conference. Residence, Dallas, Tex.
Page 52, line 27 (47, xiii, 3), *for* Mineral Springs *read* Dallas.
Page 52, line 31 (47, xiii, 4), *for* Oliver *read* Olive.
Page 52, line 65 (third line from foot, in footnote), *for* 19 Jan. *read* 19 Dec.
Page 160, after line 49, *insert an additional child of No. 49, viz.,*

viii. ROBIN AP ALLEN, b. 8 June 1879.

Page 164. GEORGE WASHINGTON[7] POLK (54), of San Antonio, Tex., one of the collaborators in the preparation of this genealogy, died 18 May 1924, and was buried in St. John's Churchyard, Maury Co., Tenn. Mrs. Polk survives her husband.
Page 166, line 56 (57), *for* 24 June *read* 23 June.
Page 167, line 1 (57), *for* MARIE *read* MARIA.
Page 168, line 1 (57, ii), *for* 28 Feb. *read* 27 Feb.

Page 168, line 11 (57, ii), *for* 1907–1910 *read* 1907, 1910.
Page 168, line 22 (57, ii), *for* on *read* to 15 June 1920.
Page 168, lines 26–27 (57, ii), *for* On his retirement from public office at the close of the Wilson administration he resumed *read* After resigning from public office, 15 June 1920, he resumed.
Page 168, line 28 (57, ii), *after* Company *insert comma and dele* and.
Page 168, line 29 (57, ii), *dele the first* of *and before* a member *insert* the Park National Bank, the United States Trust Company, and the Mackay Companies, a trustee of the Cathedral of St. John the Divine, and.
Page 168, line 34 (57, ii), *for* 24 Nov. *read* 23 Dec.
Page 174, after line 12, *insert additional children of No. 68, viz.,*

 iii. MOLLIE, b. 9 Nov. 1879; m. 17 Mar. 1901 FRANK SAMPLES. Children (surname *Samples*): 1. *Lovella.* 2. *Jewell.* 3. *Mary.*
 iv. MATTIE J., b. 12 Feb. 1882; d. 4 Sept. 1884.
 v. TRANNIE, b. 16 Jan. 1884; d. 15 May 1905.
 vi. LOIS M., b. 28 June 1885; m. in 1901 HENRY WILLIAMSON. Children (surname *Williamson*): 1. *Mary.* 2. *Ruth.* 3. *A child,* d. in infancy.
 vii. JAMES FRANKLIN, b. 15 Feb. 1890; m. 23 Nov. 1911 BESSIE FROST. Children: 1. *Roy Alonzo,*[9] b. 23 Dec. 1912. 2. *James Elbert,* b. 7 July 1915; d. 31 Dec. 1916.
 viii. JOHN WESLEY, b. 3 Mar. 1893; m. BELLE CURRY. Children: 1. *Evelyn,*[9] b. 20 Feb. 1917; d. in infancy. 2. *Mary Helen,* b. 20 Mar. 1918.

Jane Knox Polk, wife of Samuel Polk and mother of President James K. Polk. *Portrait owned by Polk Memorial Association.*

President James Knox Polk. *Portrait owned by Polk Memorial Association.*

Sarah (Childress) Polk, wife of President James K. Polk. *Portrait owned by Polk Memorial Association.*

Tomb of President James K. Polk, now located on the Tennessee State Capitol Grounds, Nashville, Tenn.

Jane Maria (Polk) Walker, dau. of Samuel & Jane (Knox), wife of James Walker. *Portrait owned by Capt. Wm. Hine.*

James Walker, husband of Jane Maria Polk. *Portrait owned by Capt. Wm. Hine.*

Jane Clarissa Walker, dau. of James & Jane Maria (Polk) Walker, wife of Isaac Newton Barnett. *Portrait owned by Polk Memorial Association.*

Laura Wilson Polk, wife of Marshall Tate Polk. *From Marshall P. Eldred, Louisville, Ky.*

L. to R. Malvina, Laura, Amelia, and Maria Harris, daughters of Naomi Tate (Polk) and Adlai O. Harris. *From Fairfax Proudfit Walkup.*

Marshall Tate Polk; son of Samuel
Jane (Knox) Polk. *From Marshall .*
Eldred, Louisville, Ky.

Ophelia Clarissa Polk, dau. of Samuel & Jane (Knox) Polk, wife of Dr. John B. Hays. *Portrait owned by Polk Memorial Association.*

Brig. Gen. Thom
& Griselda Gile
Masterton, Chap

William Hawkins Polk, son of Samuel & Jane (Knox) Polk. *Portrait owned by Capt. Wm. Hine.*

Tasker Polk, son of Wm. Hawkins Polk & Lucy Eugenia (Williams) Polk. *From Mrs. James Marion Ross.*

Wm. Tannahill Polk, son of Tasker & Eliza Tannahill (Jones) Polk. *From Mrs. James Ross.*

Mc

Dr. William Julius Polk, son of Col. William and Grizelda (Gilchrist) Polk. *From Wm. Julius Polk, St. Louis, Mo.*

Samuel Washington
James K. Polk. *Port*
Wm. Hine.

Allen Jones Polk, son of Wm. Julius & Mary Rebecca A. (Long) Polk. *From Mrs. Ann McDaniels.*

Anne Clark Fitshugh, wife of Allen Jones Polk. *From Mrs. Ann McDaniels.*

Mary Jones Polk, dau. of Dr. Wm. Julius & Mary Rebecca (Long) Polk, wife of Joseph Branch. *From Mrs. Ann McDaniels.*

Gen. Lucius Eugene Polk, son of Dr. William J. Polk. *From Ann McDaniels, Nashville, Tenn.*

Grizelda Houston Polk Hargraves, dau. of Allen Jones Polk & Anne Clark (Fitzhugh) Polk & wife of D.T. Hargraves. *From Mrs. Ann McDaniels.*

Cadwallader Long Polk, son of Dr. Wm. Julius & Mary Rebecca A. (Long) Polk. *From Mrs. Ann McDaniels.*

Rufus Julius Polk, son of Dr. Wm. Julius & Mary Rebecca (Long) Polk. *From Mrs. Ann McDaniels.*

Grizelda Houston Polk Hargraves, dau. of Allen Jones Polk & wife of D.T. Hargraves. *From Richard Hargraves, Helena, Ark.*

Home of Grizelda Houston (Polk) Hargraves & husband Davis Thompson Hargraves, Helena, Ark. (razed). *From Richard Hargraves.*

Susan Huntington Polk Keesee, dau. of Allen Jones Polk & Anna Clark (Fitzhugh) Polk & wife of Thomas Woodfin Keesee II. *From Allen R. Keesee.*

William Julius Polk, Jr., St. Louis, Mo., son of Wm. Julius & Sarah (Chambers) Polk.

Rufus King Polk, son of Gen. Lucius Eugene Polk and Sally Moore (Polk) Polk. *From Mrs. J.L. Whiteside, Columbia, Tenn.*

Lucius Junius Polk, son of Col. William & Sarah (Hawkins) Polk. *Portrait owned by Dr. Harry Yeatman.*

Mary Eastin Polk (Mrs. Lucius J. Polk), Mary Lewis. Artist Ralph E.W. Earl. *Portrait owned by Mrs. J.L. Whiteside, Columbia, Tenn.*

Anne (Erwin) Polk, 2nd wife of Lucius Junius Polk. *Portrait owned by Mrs. Paul Shepard, Winston-Salem.*

Sarah Rachel Polk, dau. of Lucius Junius Polk & wife Mary (Easton) Polk, wife of Robin C. Jones. *Portrait owned by Mrs. J.L. Whiteside, Columbia, Tenn.*

Daisey (Cantrell) Polk, wife of Lucius Junius Polk. *From Mrs. Ann McDaniels.*

Lucius Junius Polk, son of Lucius Junius & Anne (Erwin) Polk. *From Mary Virginia Polk, Pharr, Tex.*

Hamilton Place, built by Lucius Junius Polk, 1832. (Picture taken ca. 1890.) *From Mrs. J.L. Whiteside, Columbia, Tenn.*

Frances Devereux Polk, wife of Bishop
Leonidas Polk. *From Mrs. Ann McDaniels.*

Bishop Leonidas Polk, son of Col. William & Sarah (Hawkins) Polk. *Portrait
at University of the South.*

William Mecklenburg Polk, son of Leonidas & Frances (Devereux) Polk. *From
Richard Ewell, Dennis, Mass.*

Ashwood Hall, built by Leonidas Polk, Maury Co., Tenn. (Burned.) *From Yeatman-Polk Collection, Tenn. State Library & Archives.*

Ida (Lyon) Polk, wife of Dr. Wm. Mecklenburg Polk. *From Frank L. Polk, Jr..*

Susan R. (Polk) Jones, dau. of Bishop Leonidas & Frances A. (Devereux) Polk & wife of Dr. Joseph Jones. *From Mrs. Ann McDaniels.*

Frank Lyon Polk, son of Dr. William Mecklenburg Polk. *From Frank Lyon Polk, Jr., Glen Head, N.Y.*

Elizabeth Sturgis (Potter) Polk, wife of Frank Lyon Polk, Sr. *From Frank L. Polk, Jr.*

Leighton, Home of Leonidas Polk in La Fourche Parish, Louisiana. (Burned.) *From University of the South.*

Captain James Hilliard Polk, son of
George W. & Sallie (Hilliard) Polk. *From
Gen. James H. Polk, Washington, D.C.*

George Washington Polk & sons. Seated L to R: James H., Geo. W., Rufus. Standing:
George Brevard Mecklenburg, Lucius Junius, Isaac Hilliard, William Hawkins. *From
Gen. James H. Polk (Ret.).*

Capt. Harding Polk, son of James Hilliard & Mary Demoville (Harding) Polk. *From Gen. James H. Polk, Washington, D.C.*

Gen. James H. Polk, son of Capt. Harding Polk & Esther (Fleming) Polk. *From Gen. Polk.*

Rattle and Snap, built by George Washington Polk, owned by Amon Carter Evans, Columbia, Tenn.

Antoinette Polk, Baronne de Charette, with son Antoine Polk Van Leer de Charette. Daughter of Andrew Jackson Polk. *From Brig. Gen. R.R. Van Stockum, Shelbyville, Ky.*

General Baron Athanase de Charette de la Contrie, husband of Antoinette Polk. *From Brig. Gen. R.R. Van Stockum, Shelbyville, Ky.*

Antoine Polk, Marquis de Charette, son of Antoinette Polk and Baron de Charette. *From Brig. Gen. R.R. Van Stockum, Shelbyville, Ky.*

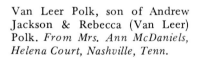

Van Leer Polk, son of Andrew Jackson & Rebecca (Van Leer) Polk. *From Mrs. Ann McDaniels, Helena Court, Nashville, Tenn.*

Mary Wood Hill, dau. of Benigna (Polk) and William Henry Wood. *From Sarah Wells Robertson, N.Y., N.Y.*

Napolean Hill, husband of Mary (Wood) Hill. *From Sarah Wells Robertson, N.Y., N.Y.*

ACKNOWLEDGMENTS

Our sincere appreciation goes to the New England Historic Genealogical Society for allowing the James K. Polk Memorial Association to reprint *The Polks of North Carolina and Tennessee.*

We are grateful to those who either furnished photographs for, or directed us to those who owned portraits and photographs.

Mrs. Evelyn Tate Buchanan, 505 N. Main St., Bolivar, TN 38008

Mrs. Faye Davidson, 608 Clifft St., Bolivar, TN 38008

Mr. Marshall P. Eldred, Brown, Todd & Heyburn, 16th Floor, Citizens Plaza, Louisville, KY 40202

Mrs. Vernell Lemons Endecott, P.O. Box 491, Drumright, OK 74030

Mr. Amon Carter Evans, Rattle and Snap, Rt. 1, Columbia, TN 38401

Mr. Richard Ewell, Dennis, MA

Mrs. Alice Mitchum Fitts, 8413 Sandpiper Rd., Oklahoma City, OK 73132

Mr. Richard H. Hargraves, 313 Plaza St., P.O. Box V, West Helena, AR 72390

Mrs. Valaree Hassell, 10609 S. Santa Fe Ave., Oklahoma City, OK 73170

Mr. Barnett Hine, Memphis, TN

Capt. William Hine, Memphis, TN

Mr. Allen R. Keesee, Ridgemont Rd., Helena, AR 72342

Mr. John Kiser, Reeves Rd., Antioch, TN 37013

Mrs. Matthew F. McDaniel, Helena Court, Nashville, TN 37205

Mrs. Robert Oliver, 1014 Rolling Fields Circle, Columbia, TN 38401

Mr. Frank L. Polk, Jr., 31 Old Wheatley Rd., Glen Head, NY 11545

General James H. Polk, Ret., 4355 Lowell St., N.W., Washington, DC 20016

Mary Virginia Polk, P.O. Box 1, Pharr, TX 78577

Mr. William Julius Polk, Jr., 4969 Pershing Place, St. Louis, MO 63108

Mrs. Margaret Y. Reeves, Eagledale Apts. 25, 5261 Eagledale Ave., Los Angeles, CA 90041

Sarah Wells Robertson, 210 W. 90th St., New York, NY 10024

Mrs. James Ross, 308 Woodlawn Ave., Greensboro, NC 27401

Mrs. Paul Shepard, Winston-Salem, NC

University of the South, Sewanee, TN

Brig. Gen. R.R. Van Stockum, Allen Dale Farm, Rt. 5, Box 388, Shelbyville, KY 40065

Miss Patricia L. Vincent, 212 W. Sycamore, Bolivar, TN 38008
Fairfax P. Walkup
Mrs. J.L. Whiteside, 1004 Hillcrest Ave., Columbia, TN 38401
Dr. Harry Yeatman, Sewanee, TN 37375
T.P. Yeatman, Nashville, TN

James K. Polk Memorial Association of Columbia, Tennessee

Mrs. Harold Lucas, President, 1982-1984
Mrs. William Stuart Fleming IV, President, 1984

ADDENDA AND ERRATA

Franklin Armistead Polk's daughter, Ophelia Elizabeth, was married to David Michael Kinnard (NOT David Mitchell Kennard).

(Correction from Kinnard Family Bible owned by Christine [Langsdon] Oliver, Columbia, Tenn.)

Evan Shelby Polk McReynolds' second wife was Martha Elizabeth Coffey (NOT Mary Elizabeth Coffey). Their only surviving daughter was Piccola McReynolds, b. 20 Sept. 1898 near Dallas, Texas, m. Alpha O. Waits 30 Nov. 1913 at Seymour, Baylor County, Texas.

(From Mrs. Valeree Hassell, Oklahoma City, Oklahoma.)

Page 259, para. 25 i

4th Line to read as follows:
"1877 General Baron Athanase de Charette de la Contrie,"

Page 260, para. 25 i

Top 5 lines (remainder of para. i) to read as follows:
"St. Patrick's Cathedral, New York City, 11 Nov. 1909, Susanne Henning of Louisville, Ky. dau. of James W. and Sue Thornton Meriwether Henning (direct descendant of Ann Pollock from Coleraine, Ireland who married Major John Allen in Carlisle, Pa. in 1760. In World War I Antoine de Charette served in the Tank Corps in the French Army, and was wounded on the Western Front. His daughter, Susanne was b. in Paris 12 April 1915.

(Corrections from Brig. Gen. R.R. Van Stockum.)

Home of Col. William Polk, Raleigh, N.C.

INDEX

Compiled by
Louise Clements Palmer
Texas City, Texas 77590

ADAMS, Emmie (Gilchrist)
66; George Grigg 66;
Jerry 66; Martha Ann 66
ADKINS, Rebecca Patton 10
AGEE, Annie T. 75; Christ-
opher 75; Polk Watkins
75
AKIN, Emma Winifred 54;
Franklin Eliezer 54;
Myrtle 54; William
Polk 54
ALBERTON, Annie 82
ALDERSON, Elizabeth 10,19
ALEXANDER, Abden Indepen-
dence 10; Adam 6,7,19;
Arthur 95; Benjamin 4;
Charles 4; Eliazer 10;
Eliza Eugenia 10; Floyd
Idella 95; Hezekiah 17;
Margaret 4,6,10; Mary
17; Mollie 46,51;
Nathaniel 6; Susan 4;
Susan Carter 25; Taylor
4; Thomas 4; William 4
ALKEA, Sumner 39
ALLEN, ___ 69; Ara Julian
(Sims) 52; Elizabeth 43;
Laura Sims 52; Margaret
Emma 40; Thomas 40;
William H. 52; Zane
Mira 69
ALSBROOK, Alice Eudora
(Chambers) 97; Hiram
David 97; Pattie Lou 97
AMES, Alexander Hogan 73;
Benjamin 59; Mary Ruff-
in 73
AMIS, Mary 30
ANN, Queen 101
ANDERSON, Abraham 21;
Amanda Weeks 94; Ammie
Daisy 85; Benjamin 21;
Bond 67; Eliza 21;
Elizabeth Smith 94;
Francis Marion 94;
Franklin Pierce 93;
Fanny 21; G. R. 85;
Hattie 47; Henry 21,54;
James 19,21,54; Jane
21; Jency 21; Jency
Polk 54; Minnie 19;
Mitchell 21,54; Pru-
dence 21,54; Rose Ella
93; Ruth 57; Sarah 21,
54; Stacy 21; Taylor
21; Theresa 21; Will-
iam 57
ANGELLOTTI, Emma Teressa
58; Frances Louise 59;
Frank M. Mrs. 1,14,29,
59,90; Frank Marion 58;
Geltruda 58; Giuseppe
58; Jose 58; Joseph 58;
Lois Frances 58; Lois
Frances (Osgood) 58;
Marion Polk 59
ANTHONY, Betty Jane 97
ARMAN, Joan (Eaton) 96;
Lewis 96
ARMAND, Anna W. 17
ARMES, Bessie 93; J. E. 93
ARMSTRONG, Clinton Adol-
phus 28; Dorcas Lear
87; Eugenia 28; Fran-
ces L. 87; Frank 76;
Margaret 28; Robert

ARMSTRONG (cont.) Cowden
28; Roddy 76
ARNOLD, Cattie 22; Clar-
issa Adaline 21; Emily
21; Jane 22; Jim 22;
John H. 21,22; Richard
K. 22; Rufus 22; Susan
Josephine Parr 22;
Thomas Polk 22
ASHE, John 29; John Bap-
tist 29; Mary (Moore)
29; Samuel 29
ATKEISON, Agnes (Griggs)
67; Elizabeth Griggs
67; Richard Drewery 67
ATKINS, Adeline Elizabeth
64; Joseph Willis 64;
Thomas 64; Virginia 64
ATTWOOD, Mary Catherine
12; William Woods 12
AUSTIN, Mary 18; Wilson 18
AVERY, Alexander Hamilton
40; Charles Polk 40;
Ebenezer Root 40;
Harriet 40; Herbert 40;
Lora Belle 40; Minnie
Fisher Pullen 40; Nor-
man LeNoir 40; Sarah
Henrietta 40; Walter
Hamilton 40
BABCOCK, Deodatus 58;
George 58; Mrs. George
56; James 58; Job 58;
John H. 58; Louise
Elizabeth 58; Margaret
Bull 58
BADGER, George Edmund 16;
Katherine Mallon 16;
Mary Brown 16; Sally
Polk 16
BAGGETT, Cornelia 43;
Curley 43; Minnie 42;
Stephen 42
BAGLEY's brigade 60
BAILEY, Charles F. 92;
Iva Maria 92
BALDWIN, Benjamin Joseph
69; Fannie Tabitha 69;
William Saunders 69;
Willie Catherine
(Saunders) 69
BALL, Florence (Gill) 77;
George Gill 77; George
Homer 77; Jane Jackson
77; Jane Polk 77;
Louisa 27
BALTIMORE, Lord 3
BANKHEAD 79
BARFIELD, Ina 46
BARKER, Elizabeth 97
BARNES, Bartel 57; Betty
57; Charles 57; Eliza-
beth 57; George 57;
Isabell 57; John 57;
Lydia 57; Martha 57;
Mary 56,57; Peter 57;
Polly 57; Rachel 57;
Ruben 57; Ruth 57;
Sallie 57; Solomon 57
BARNETT, Isaac Newton 23;
Jane Clarissa 23
BARRETT, Martha 43
BARTLETT, Frances 55,56
BASS, James Weston 27;
Olivia Polk 27
BAXTER, Margaret 19; Mar-

BAXTER (cont.) garet Polk
50
BEACH, Emily 78
BEARD, Martha Jane Polk 49;
Mary E. 46; Young 49
BEARDSLEY, Edna Sarah 69;
Ezra Marvin 69; Maggie
Olive 69; Maggie Olive
(Miller) 69; Maggie
(Lemmon) 69; William
Lincoln 69
BEASLEY, Elizabeth 43;
James 43
BEESON, Jessett 44
BELL, Adela Clarissa 12;
James 12; Joel Egbert
97; Marshall 70; Mir-
anda Ann 97; Nellie
Watts 70; Vivian 70;
Wilmoth Elizabeth
(Edwards) 97
BELLE, Maude 97
BENARD, Minnie Evaline
Polk 96; William 96
BENNETT, Dess 94; Elijah
68; Francis Mason 94;
Jane 94; Jane (White)
94; John Allen 94; Mary
Elizabeth Polk 94;
Mattie Barnett 68;
Mattie Belle (Grant) 68;
Wayne 94; Willie 94
BERRY, Benjamin 26; Christ-
inia Theresa 27; Clar-
issa 26; Daniel Dorsey
27; Edward 87; Elizabeth
Dodd 26; Elizabeth (Dor-
sey) 26; Elizabeth Shel-
by 27; Elizabeth Walker
11; Ellen Dupuy McKinney
27; Fanny 88; James
Handerson 88; John Thom-
as 27; Laura Juliette
26; Louise Matilda 27;
Lutie 49; Mary Eliza 27;
Mary Gordon 27; Olivia
Marbury 26; Olivia Polk
27; Sarah Meredith 12;
William Benjamin 27;
William Polk 26; Willie
P. 87
BESTIE, Josephine (Cahill)
64; Lillie 64; William
64
BETTS, Augusta 98
BILLINGTON, Bertie Jackson
60; Blanche Starnader
60; Daisy Blanche Star-
nader 60; Ezekiel Jack-
son 60; Julia Angeline
60; Louisa Jane 60;
Mary Lucretia 60; Nancy
(Wadsworth) 60; Penn-
iuel 60
BILLS, Elizabeth 53; Eve-
lina McNeal 98; Isaac
11; John Houston 11,83,
98; Lillias 11; Lillias
Olivia 13; Ophelia Jane
83; Prudence Tate 11;
Prudence Tate (McNeal)
83,98
BIRCH, ___ 22; Cattie 22
BIRDWELL, Charles Grandi-
son 44; Mary Gorman 44;
Victoria Polk 44; Will-

JOHNSON (cont.) Pearl 100; Samuel 100; Samuel P. 97; Sarah Elizabeth 97; William W. 48
JOHNSTON, Eugenia Morris 64; Houston Watsen 87; John Henry 64; Joseph E. 35; Martha Emaline (Reed) 64; Matthew 68; Willie P. 87
JOLLY, Marie Gladys 95
JOPLIN, Matilda 91; Joseph 91
JONES, Alice Tannahill 66; Allen 30; Amanda Bowen 45; B. M. 92; Benjamin Franklin 94; Cadwallader 32; Calvin 13; Caroline 36; Charles J. 66; Eliza 43; Eliza Tannahill 66; Elizabeth 26; Ellen Nesbit 45; Emiline 45; Etha Lee 64; Fanny 36; Frances Elizabeth 61; Frederick P. 60; George Martin 26; Hamilton Polk 36; Hannah 92; Henry Tandy 26; James 26; Jane Emily 60; Jency (Walker) 61; Joseph 36; Kate 45; Laura 45; Laura Maxwell 36; Lucius Polk 45; Lucy Cadwallader 32; Lily 45; Marshall Branch 45; Martha 14,30; Mary 30; Mary Edwards 26; Mary Haynes 30; Mary Polk 32; Mary Rebecca 30; Meady 61; Minerva 92; Mollie 45; Octavia Rowena 13; Peter B. 45; Prudence Polk 60; Rebecca Edwards 30,32; Robert 14; Robin 32; Robin A. P. Cadwaller 32; Sarah 30; Sarah Polk 32; Sue 45; Susan 50; Susan Jane (Brooks) 94; Susan R. 36; Susan Williams 94; Virginia Spencer 45; William 61
JORDAN, Mary 41
JUTZ, Sarah 91
KAY, Della 44; Emma 45; J. S. 44; Willie Allen Birdwell 44
KEAN, Elizabeth Hazyline 82
KELLEY, Dora J. 93; James D. 93; Josephine Coe 93
KELSEY, Ann 98
KEMP, John 43; Minnie 43
KENNARD, Anna Laura 54; David Della Morgan 54; David Mitchell 53; Eliza Adilene 54; James Knox Polk 54; Mary Elizabeth 54; Michael 54; Ophelia Elizabeth Hines 53; Sallie Foster 54;Rebecca Novaline 54
KENNEDY, Bettie 42,43; Estelle Gale 87; Percy, Sr. 87
KENT, Joseph 27; Joseph Jackson 27; Margaret 78; Olivia Polk 27; Sarah Roach 27; William 2
KEARBY, _____ 56
KERLY, Absalom 57; Chloe 57; Clemond 57; Eliza-

KERLY (cont.) beth 57; Elizabeth Teague 57; Elijah 57; John 57; Joseph 57; Larkin 57; Lucy 57; Martha 57; Martha Carter 57; Rachel Neal 57; Sarah 57; William, Jr. 56; William, Sr. 56; Wilmoth 57
KERCHEVAL, Margaret 28
KESEE, Allen Polk 72; Sarah Gladys Key 72; Susan Huntington 72; T. W. 72; Thomas Woodfin 72; Zelda Polk 72
KESMIRE, Okie 61
KEY, Anna 67; Fred E. 92; Lula Helen 92; Sarah Glayds 72
KEYLICH, Anna 62; Fedor 62; Lila M. 62
KILMARTIN, Mary 89
KIMBALL, Martha 19
KING, Cora 65; Fanny 41; Isham 41; Jane 41; Kate Burleson 51; Mary Ellen 41; Rufus 73; Sarah Moore (Jackson) 73
KIRBY, Ethelbert 20; Nancy 20; Susan 63
KIRK, Laura Jane 95
KIRKPATRICK, Ann Eliza 63
KIRKSEY, Margaret M. 44; W. S. A. Dr. 44
KNOX, James 22; Jane 22; Joanna 2; Nancy 2
KORTRECHT, Agusta (Betts) 98; Alexander Humphreys 98; Augustus 98; Charles 98; Charles Murray 98; Eunice Polk 98; Evelyn Marshall 98; Humphreys 98
KOTHMAN, Alpha Katherine 93; Corda Jane 93; Emmett Floyd 93; Howard Bert 93; Katherine 93; Louis William 93; Maud 93; Nellie Maude 93; Olen Ross 93; Raymond David 93; Veda Bell 93; William 93
LABOUISSE, Frances Devereux 36; Henry Richardson 36
LAFAYETTE _____ 5,29
LAMAR, Mirabeau Buonaparte Lucius Quintus Cincinnatus 71
LAMB, Charles 9
LANE, _____ 27; Emeline Winifred 53
LANIER, Lucy 39; Susie 67
LANGLEY, Susan 91
LANGSDON, Isaac 54; Rebecca Novaline 54
LANSING, Robert 80
LAPRADE, Emma Lou Polk 97; G. A. 97
LARGE, Abraham 92; Drusilla (Latham) 92; Sarah Jane 92
LATHAM, Drusilla 92
LAUDERDALE, Annie M. 25; Benjamin Winchester 25; Frank 25; Mary 25; Mary Caroline 25; Mary H. 25; Samuel Holmes 25
LAURENCE, Lelia 69
LAWS, _____ 4; Charles 3; Elizabeth 57; Elizabeth

LAWS (cont.) Williams 3; John 3; Joseph 3; Magdalen 3; Polly 57
LEA, Charles 12; Elizabeth 12; John M. 12
LEACH, Eugenia 17; Susan Sophia 58
LEE, Beatrice 18; Catherine 12; Cornelia 18; Debora 18; E. F. 24; Edna Mae 42; Elizabeth Colclough 18; Irene Debora 18; James F. 18; Jane Virginia 24; Lilla Bell 85; Margaret 18; Margaret J. 18; Marion 34; Mary 18; Nannie 76; Susanna 18; Theressa 18; Thomas Virgil 42; Virgie 85; Virginia 18
LEFESTE, Charles P. D. 93; Corda Jane 93
LEIFESTE, Harry 92; Lala Polk 92; Robert A. 92; Ruby Isadora 92
LEGH, Pier Capt. 32; Sarah 32
LEMMEN, Eva Frank 37; Sarah 69; Susan Polk 37
LEMONS, Alfred Lee 92; Stella Maud Polk 92
LENNARD, Eliza 22; Lecie 22; Lucius 22
LE NOIR, Sarah John 81
LESTER, Emily 45; S. P. Dr. 45
LEWIS, Emma Margaret 46
LIMEBAUGH, Mary Elizabeth 65
LINDSAY, A. J. 93; Allen V. 93; Alpha Polk 93; Buck 93; John 93; John H. 93; John Taylor 93; Joseph 93; Lester 93; Thomas 93
LINTON, Blanche 77
LITTLEJOHN, Lavinia Polk 73; Margaret 73; Margaret Wallace 73; Mary Rebecca 73; Thomas 73; W. W. 73; William Whitson 73
LITTRELL, Ada Octavia 81
LOCKE, Francis 7
LOCKLEAR, James A. 94; Mary Elizabeth Polk 94
LOCKRIDGE, Christine Hance 88; Elizabeth Hill 88; Hazel Boykin 88; Luther Polk 88; Robert Darden 88
LONG, Abie 97; Anne 30; Bessie Pasture 30; Elizabeth 87; Frances Quintard 30; Gabriel 30; George Washington 30; James Henry 97; John Joseph 30; Lemuel McKinney 30; Lunsford 30; Martha 30; Mary 30,97; Mary Amis 30; Mary Rebecca A. 17,30; Mary Reynolds 30; Nicholas 30; Rebecca Edwards 30, 32; Rebecca Jones 30; Richard 30
LORING, Benjamin 58; Caleb 58; Caleb Gould 58; David Webster 58; Des Thomas 58; Emma Teresa 58; Harold Angellotti 58; Harriet (Tuttle) 58; Jane 58; Marjorie

POLK (cont.) Alice L. 45;
Alice Ophelia 84; Alice
Potter 80; Allen 95;
Allen Campbell 84;
Allen Cucula 78; Allen
Jones 71,72; Allie
Elizabeth 97; Alma 86;
Almeda 62,91; Almonte
Lee 53; Alpha 93;
Alphonso 7; Althea Mc
Knight 46; Alva Champ-
ion 84; Amanda 43,45;
Amanda Elizabeth 85;
Amanda M. 43; Amanda
Pauline 42; Ammie
Daisy 85; Anderson 54,
90,91; Andrew 5,19;
Andrew Jackson 17,38;
Andrew Tyler 47,86;
Ann 2,3; Ann Eliza 27;
Ann Elizabeth 41,46,47;
Anna 2,3; Anna Clark
Fitzhugh 72; Anna Eliza-
beth 66; Anna Gould 91;
Anna Lee 72; Anna Leah
38; Anna Louise 91;
Anne (Erwin) 32; Anne
Leroy 78; Anne Patter-
son 99; Annie 95; Annie
Alberton 82; Annie
Blanche 87; Annie Cecil
82; Annie Goodwin 67;
Annie Holt 82; Annie
Laura 85; Annie May 87;
Annie McNeal 83; Annie
Metlock 91; Annie Penn
Johnson 97; Annie
Sperry Hill 99; Annie T.
75; Antoinette Van Leer
38; Archibald Yell 87;
Argyle Foster 88;
Arkansas Almeda Black-
wood 91; Armour Cantrell
77; Atlas Ewing 64;
Augusta 55; Belinda G.
Dickinson 65; Bell
Virginia 97; Belle
(Hughs) 40; Benigna 13;
Benigna Jane 86; Ben-
jamin 21,62; Benjamin
Carlo 53; Benjamin D. A.
47; Benjamin F. 48,92;
Benjamin Franklin 55,88,
93,94; Benjamin Rufus
49,88; Bertha 89; Ber-
tie Hancock 96; Bessie
Armes 93; Bessie Davis
8; Bessie Isadora Alice
92; Bessie Lee 89;
Bessie Olga Harris 94;
Bessie Stitt 75; Bessie
Western 85; Betsey
Gillis 4; Bettie Ann
87; Betty Cottman 4;
Betty Georgiana 53;
Beverly Porter 55;
Birdie Douglas 64;
Blanche Linton 77;
Blanche Rebecca 97;
Brantly Sheffield 85;
Buck 93; Burt 55;
Cadwallader Long 75;
Cadwallander Long 75;
Cadwallder Long 75;
Caldona 91; Campbell
84; Caroline 26,38,62,
73,75,84; Caroline
James 82; Caroline
Lowry 75; Carra Lee 85;
Carry May 75; Cather-
ine 7; Catherine B.
Thomas 86; Charles 1,2,
4,6,7,8,17,18,19,21,27,

POLK (cont.) 39,40,41,42,
43,45,50,51,81,82,83,
84,85,86; Charles
Arnold 86; Charles
Bingley 39,81,82;
Charles Clark 40,41,84,
85; Charles Eaton 96;
Charles Edwin 27;
Charles Grandison 43,
86; Charles H. 7;
Charles Isaac 45,46;
Charles James 17,40;
Charles Junius 17;
Charles King 49;
Charles Loyd 86;
Charles Marion 42,85;
Charles Martin 76;
Charles Michael 85;
Charles N. 62; Charles
Perry 13; Charles
Shelby 19,42,86;
Charles Taliaferro 40;
Charles Thomas 43,86;
Charles Wesley 46;
Charles Wesson 86;
Charlotte H. Zimmerman
78; Charlotte Patricia
78; Charlotte Payne 77;
Christine Hance 88;
Clara 27; Clara Allison
99; Clara Bills 84;
Clarence 82; Clarissa
25; Clarissa Adaline
21; Clark Fitzhugh 72;
Claud 93; Cleora
Lawrence 75; Clifford
Allen 94; Clyde 62;
Cora Ann 87; Cora Annie
Murphy 64; Cora Capps
92; Corinne Lucile 85;
Cornelia 27; Cornelia
Jane 41; Cornelia Lowry
75; Cornelia Lowry
75; Cumberland 21,54,
55,56,91,95; Curren
Whitthorne 89; Curry
Young 62; Cynthia
Cornella 84; Cynthia
Harkness 17; Cynthia
Martin 76; Cynthia
Springs 19; Cynthia
Spring Polk 50; D. A.
20; Daisy 100; Daisy
Cantrell 77,78; Daisy
Ellen 78; David 2,3,4,
92; David Taylor 91;
Deborah 4,6,18; Delilah
(Tyler) 4; Della Cave
94; Dessie 89; Dicy 5;
Dora 87; Dora J. Kelley
93; Dora Maria 99;
Dorcas Lear Armstrong
87; Douglas 86; Dovie
Jane Conley 95; Dow 40;
Drew Smith 46; Drusilla
Williams 49; Duke 93;
Edmond 4; Edna 48; Edna
Gold 96; Edna Jackson
96; Edward 87; Edward
Marshall 98; Edward
McNeal 98; Edward Mon-
roe 100; Edward Win-
field 75; Edwin Fitz-
hugh 13; Edwin Moore
75; Effie 65,86; Elea-
nor 7,8,91; Eleanor
(Ellen) 54; Eleanor
Margaret 87; Eleanor
Shelby 18; Elias Rector
60; Eliza Eastin 33;
Eliza Epperson 99;
Eliza Tannahill Jones
66; Elizabeth 3,4,5,10,
19,20,43,55,65,95;

POLK (cont.) Elizabeth
Adline 97; Elizabeth
Allen 43; Elizabeth Ann
48; Elizabeth Bills 53;
Elizabeth Blackburn 61;
Elizabeth Bonds 65;
Elizabeth Congo 84;
Elizabeth Devereux 36;
Elizabeth Dodd 24;
Elizabeth Emily 86;
Elizabeth Hayne 19;
Elizabeth Hazylin Kean
82; Elizabeth Jane 68;
Elizabeth Jerome 51;
Elizabeth Kinchin Wilson
63; Elizabeth Long 87;
Elizabeth Parmelia 67;
Elizabeth Sturgis Potter
80; Elizabeth Williams
3; Ella 71,82,85; Ella
Baillio Hayes 71; Ella
Dee 92; Ella Martha
Cook 81; Ella Wood 51;
Ella Word Burleson 46;
Ellen 27; Ellen Dethrow
91; Ellen Griggs 91;
Ellen Harrell 78; Ellen
Matilda 27; Ellie 68;
Ellis Rivere 75; Ellon-
er 7; Elmer E. 49; Elmer
Scott 99; Elsie Warren
83; Elva Lona Stonebach
L. 89; Elvira Juliette
34; Emeline Winifred
(Lane) Hancock 53;
Emiline 45; Emily 29,85;
Emily Beach 78; Emily
Donelson 33; Emily
Hamilton 78; Emily Huff-
hines 89; Emma 81; Emma
Agusta 91; Emma Grier
74; Emma Lou 97; Emma
Louisa 85; Emma Louise
97; Emma M. 41; Emma
Octavia 39; Emma Thomas
65; Emmit Brit 94;
Ephriam 23; Erasmus 53;
Esther Fleming 80;
Esther Pool 6; Esther
Woodward 60; Ethel 92;
Eugene 64; Eugene Adams
Yates 78; Eugene LeNoir
81; Eugenia 13,27,52;
Eunice Ophelia 98; Euola
Greenleaf 73; Eva 96;
Eva May 93; Eva Bills
99; Eva Jane 88; Eva
Josephine 93; Evan 7;
Evan Shelby 20,48,51,
80,87,88; Evelina Mc-
Neal Bills 98; Evelyn
McNeal 99; Evelyn Sarah
83; Evie 86; Ezekiel 1,
5,6,7,8,9,11,15,18,20,
21,22,24,27,41,56,63,
65,66,67,85,97,98,99,
100; F. A. 53; Fannie
62; Fannie Douglas 64;
Fannie Elizabeth 89;
Fannie Tabitha Foster
68; Fanny Berry 88;
Fanny Elizabeth Foster
88; Fessonia 53; Flor-
ence 67,96; Florence
Helen 89; Floyd Idella
95; Frances Anne 33;
Frances A. Devereux 34;
Frances Devereux 36;
Frances J. 40; Frances
L. Armstrong 87; Fran-
ces Letitia 85; Francis
2,3; Francis Devereux
78; Frank 45; Frank 95;

POLK (cont.) Frank Dever-
eux 78; Frank Lyon 79,
94; Frankie Carr 87;
Franklin 48; Franklin
Armstead 20; Franklin
Armstead 48,53,88;
Franklin Ezekiel 24;
George Beach 78; George
Brevard Mecklenburg 37;
George Clark 85; George
Donnell 75; George Mar-
ion 96; George R. 64;
George Washington 1,6,
7,17,18,32,34,37,76,77,
80,81; Georgia Darnell
42; Gilbert 29,85; Glor-
ia Adell 96; Grace 62;
Greenfield Quarles 75;
Griselda 73; Griselda
Gilchrist 14,30; Gri-
selda Houston 72; Ham-
ilton R. 78; Hannah 5,
18; Hannah Elizabeth
41; Hannah Jones 92;
Harding 80; Harris 95,
96; Harrison Jackson
77; Harry K. 46,51;
Henrietta 43; Henry 3,
55,91; Henry C. 43;
Henry Clay 54,91; Henry
Dickson 91; Henry M. 7;
Horace Moore 39,83,84;
Horace Moore, Jr. 84;
Hortense 94; Hulett
Clinton Merritt, Jr. 81;
Ida A. Lyons 78; Ida
Cornelia 41; Ida Flor-
ence 89; Ida Florence
Moore 89; Iola 67;
Iredell D. 46; Irene
82; Irene Debora 18;
Irene Florence Rollow
64; Irin 65; Irving
Kenneth 86; Issac 7;
Isaac Carlo 51; Isaac
Hilliard 38,81; Isaac
Shelby 19; Isabel Grier
74; Isabella 45,47;
Isadora 92; Isam Walker
92; Jack 94; James 2,3,
4,6,7,21,55,56,65,93,95;
James Anderson 61,95;
James C. 32; James
Cecil 82; James D. 62;
James E. 43; James H.
53; James Hillard 37,
80; James Irvin 21,63,
64,97; James K. 55,62;
James Knox 1,10,25,57,
29,41,43,49,54,61,63,
66,75,88,89,95,97,98;
James Lafayette 87;
James Martin Sylvester
93; James Monroe 88,99;
James Moore 48; James
Potter 80; James V. 46;
James Vernon Noah 84;
Jane 2,3,4,19,45,54,91;
Jane Bouchelle 29; Jane
Burnett 92; Jane Eliza-
beth 40; Jane Jackson
76,77; Jane Knox 22;
Jane Margaret 48; Jane
Maria 23; Jane Miller
48; Janie 62; Janie
Frances 92; Javita 95;
Jency 20,21,54,60;
Jency (Tweedle) 55;
Jency Walker 20; Jennie
Stewart 100; Jesse Lee
Forest 45; Jesse Newton
96; Jessie 89; Jessie
Irene 82; Jewel 92;

POLK (cont.) Jimmie Belle
41; Joanna Knox 2; Job
5; Joel 21; John 2,3,5,
6,7,8,10,14,19,20,43,
45,47,48,50,53,54,55,
61,65,68,81,86,88,90,
91,92,93,95,96; John A.
18; John Crofford 86;
John D. 46; John de
Kalb 53; John Edward
97; John Floyd 91; John
Hale 41; John Hawkins
16; John Horace 83;
John Houston 83,99;
John Jackson 27,66,67;
John Kenneth 46; John
Lee 24,93; John Lewal-
len 93,94; John McGowan
67; John Metcalfe 80;
John P. 7; John R. 43;
John Shelby 49,87; John
Simmons 86; John Thad-
deus 48; John Wilson
64; Johnnie Jacobs 89;
Jones 94; Joseph 2,86;
Josephine Elizabeth 85;
Josiah L. 62; Judge
100; Julia 60; Julia
Anne 68; Julia Bell 85;
Kate 43,48; Kate Gamel
92; Kate Jackson 77;
Kate Lillian 82; Kath-
erine 36,100; Katie 86;
Katie McLarty 42; Kel-
sey Hibbler 98; Keziah
Prior 6; Knox Sylvester
89; Lafayette Smith 82;
Lala 55,92; Lamar 71;
Laura 55,93; Laura Ann
87; Laura Ellen 92;
Laura Emmeons 85; Laura
Jane Kirk 95; Laura Lee
Sharp 67; Laura Prud-
ence 98; Laura T. Wilson
65; Laura Weston 24,25;
Laurentine S. 45; Lavin-
ia Boncille 85; Lavinia
C. 72; Lawrence 91;
Lawrence Norton 98;
Lecie Amelia 46; Lecie
Norwood 22; Lee 55;
Leland 86; Leland Thom-
as 87; Lelia 87; Lena
85; Lena Elizabeth
Wessen 86; Lena May 96;
Lenora Maude 82; Leon-
idas 1,16,32,34,35,36,
38,55,76,78,79,99;
Leonidas Rev. 16; Leon-
idas Charles 78; Leon-
idas Napoleon 82;
Leonidas Tennessee 65;
Leontine Adele 78; Levi
21; Lewis Bradbury 81;
Lewis Gilbert 85; Lewis
Reynolds 86; Lila M.
Keylich 67; Lillian
Russell 96; Lillie 94;
Lillie Belle Lee 85;
Linda 95; Lizzie Rob-
erts 55; Lois 89; Lois
James 94; Lona Eliza-
beth 89; Lonzy Frances
49; Lottie 92; Lottie
Isabel Pafford 64;
Lottie Schwartz 75;
Louis Christian 101;
Louis Shelby 95; Louis
Taylor 60,94; Louisa
27,86; Louisa Adeline
63; Louisa Blount 22;
Louisa Jane 60; Louise

POLK (cont.) Cerf 101;
Louise Elizabeth 56;
Louise Von Isberg 66;
Lucia 36; Lucille
Quarles 75; Lucinda 56,
91; Lucinda Davis 16;
Lucinda Younger 67;
Lucius 48,64; Lucius
B. 48; Lucius Benjamin
97; Lucius Eugene 73,
74,75,76; Lucius Jose-
phus 86; Lucius Junius
16,17,31,34,35,38,76,
77,78; Lucretia 56,57;
Lucy 86; Lucy Blount
65; Lucy Eugenia Wil-
liams 65; Lucy Fairfax
66; Lucy Narcissa 92;
Lucy Nicholson Cocke
82; Lucy Prudence 92;
Ludie Gertrude 46; Lula
Ella 68; Lula Gilmer
82; Lula Iza 100; Lulu
Donnell 75; Lula 93;
Lydia Eliza 24,25;
Mabel 55; Mabel Vander-
bogart 38; Madeline
Tasker 73; Mae Mayo 92;
Magdalen Tasker 78;
Maggie Coopwood 45;
Maggie McCorkle Luton
97; Maggie Miller 48;
Malissa Jane 41; Mamie
85; Mamie Sims 46;
Margaret 62,67,83;
Margaret A. Rose 78;
Margaret Alice 87;
Margaret Ann Freeman
86; Margaret (Baxter)
19,50; Margaret Benigna
43,86; Margaret Calla-
way 78; Margaret Cath-
erine 46; Margaret
Douglas 97; Margaret
Emma 40; Margaret Ethel
Worthington 78; Margaret
Jane 48; Margaret Olivia
51; Margaret Phillips 81;
Margaret R. Moore 47,48;
Margaret Ruth 87; Mar-
garet Taylor 4; Margaret
Viana 42; Margaret Wen-
dell 78; Maria 78; Maria
H. Dehon 79; Marie
Harris 95; Marion Deveux
82; Marjorie 65,95;
Marshall Alexander 60;
Marshall T. 11; Marshall
Tate 24,65,98,99; Mar-
shall Wesley 84; Mart
94; Martha 3,6,7,21;
Martha Ann 42,43,63;
Martha Barrett 43; Mar-
tha Isabella 94; Martha
Jane 49; Martha Kimball
19; Martha Martin 91;
Martha Rebecca 40; Mar-
tha Robinson 61; Martha
Sanders 92; Martha
Washington 7; Marvin 65;
Mary 3,5,6,62,65,72,86;
Mary Abigail 63; Mary
Adelaide 29; Mary Alex-
ander 17; Mary Alice 91;
Mary Ann 39,61; Mary
Ann Dickson 91; Mary
Ann Eastin 31; Mary Ann
Massey 86; Mary Ann
Petty 54; Mary Ann Sim-
mons 86; Mary Bell 55;
Mary Border 48; Mary
Brown 16,32; Mary Carol-
ine 67; Mary Clark 6;

POLK .(cont.) Mary Clend-
ennin 72; Mary Cottman
4; Mary Cynthia 46;
Mary Delphine 76; Mary
Demoville Harding 80;
Mary E. 40; Mary Eliza
54,83,88; Mary Eliza
Stevens 53; Mary Eliza-
beth 48,81,83,87,94;
Mary Elizabeth Coffee
49; Mary Elizabeth
Crabb 96; Mary Eliza-
beth Walton 81; Mary
Ellen 41; Mary Eloise
29,71; Mary Frances 89;
Mary Frances Hibbler
98; Mary Gertrude 80;
Mary Hilliard 37; Mary
Hurt Gossett 65; Mary
Jane 41,62; Mary Jordan
41; Mary Kilmartin 89;
Mary L. Corse 65; Mary
Lenora 89; Mary Lillian
82; Mary Lizinska Brown
84; Mary Louisa 41,65,
84; Mary Louisa Camp-
bell 84; Mary Marvin 85;
Mary McIlhenny 50; Mary
Murfree 37; Mary (Polly)
18; Mary Prichard 96;
Mary Ophelia 48,82;
Mary Rebecca 73,74,75;
Mary Rebecca (Long) 17,
30; Mary Runnels 48;
Mary S. 7; Mary Shelby
5; Mary Stilwell 40;
Mary Susan Pearson 85;
Mary Tasker 66; Mary
Thomas 46; Mary Virgin-
ia 78; Mary Virginia
Nichols 78; Mary W. 21;
Mary Walton 81; Mary
Williams 3; Mary Wilson
8,26,98; Mathew 48;
Matilda 9,91; Matilda
Golden 9,20; Matilda
Jane 87; Matta 68;
Mattie Catherine (Pike)
64; Mattie E. Moore 45;
Mattie Lena 95; Mattie
Moseley 100; Mattie
Virginia Thomas 87;
Maud 93; Melvina 20;
Michael 6,17,40,84,85;
Michael Sanders 41,85;
Milbry Catherine 81;
Minerva J. Bradbury 81;
Minerva Josephine 81;
Minnie 19,65; Minnie
Conley 95; Minnie Eva-
line 96; Minnie Louise
89; Minnie Murphy 76;
Minnie Pearl 92,95;
Minnie Turrentine 84;
Minnie Ubber 94; Mir-
anda Ann Bell 97;
Miriam Bessie 85;
Mitchell Alfred 62,96;
Mitchell Anderson 54;
Mittie Cairnes 85;
Mollie 48; Moses 7;
Myrtle 55; Nancy 20,42,
44; Nancy (Cox) 95;
Nancy (Knox) Owens 3;
Nancy McIvor 45;
Nancy Newsom 50; Nancy
Petty 45; Nancy Tram-
mell 55; Nannie Hen-
derson 97; Nannie Lee
76; Naomi Tate 24;
Narcissa Augusta Gil-
bert 85; Ned 72; Nellie
Jane 94; Nellie Miller

POLK (cont.) 87; Nellie
White 97; Nettie Lyons
94; Newton Napoleon
39,82,84; Nichols
Beach 78; Nora 62; Nora
Loyd 86; Octavia 13;
Octavia Rowena Jones
13; Oleta Mae 94; Olga
85; Olivia 68; Olivia
Marbury 26; Olivia
Winston Sharpe 98; Oll-
ie Massie 49; Opal
Frances 89; Ophelia
Clarissa 24; Ophelia
Elizabeth Hines 53;
Ophelia Jane 87;
Ophelia Wilson 84;
Oscar Bowles 67; Owen
96; President 22; Pas-
cal 92; Patricia Jane
60; Patsy 5; Pattie 28;
Pauline 13,94; Pearl
96; Pearl Johnson 100;
Pearl Margaret 67;
Peggy 6; Penelope Rose
91; Perrion Young 96;
Perry 27,28; Phebe 7;
Philemon Hawkins 17;
Philopena Helms 6;
Phoebe Wolf 40; Polly
Campbell 8; Porter
Grier 74; Priscilla 21,
83; Priscilla McNeal
83; Priscilla Roberts
2; Prudence 55,60,91;
Prudence Ann 93; Pru-
dence McNeal 99; Rachel
Marie (Scott) 99;
Ralph Bingley 82; Ranzy
92; Rebecca Evaline
Lamar 71; Rebecca Mayes
33; Rebecca Van Leer 38;
Richard 21,29; Richard
Edward 64; Richard
Tyler 61,62; Richard
Watson 64; Riley Madi-
son 96; Robert 1,2,3,4,
5,6,7,8,14,17,18,19,20,
21,22,24,27,29,30,31,34,
37,38,39,40,41,42,43,45,
47,48,50,53,54,55,61,63,
65,66,67,71,72,73,75,76,
77,78,80,81,82,83,84,85,
86,87,88,90,91,92,93,95,
96,97,98,99,100,101;
Robert Bruce 49; Robert
Evender 89; Robert
Franklin 97; Robert
Green 48; Robert Hicks
64; Robert Hill 99;
Robert LeNoir 82;
Robert Lee 61,62,89;
Rosa 62,97; Rose Ella
93; Rose Etta 96; Rose
LaValle (Blair) 100;
Rose Mary 96; Roxana
Eugice Ophelia 65;
Rufus Eugene 76; Rufus
Julius 76; Rufus King
16,32,37,74,81; Rufus
Walter 75; Sallie Ann
54; Sallie Clymer 81;
Sallie Hawkins 37;
Sallie Hilliard 81;
Sallie L. Hilliard 37;
Sallie Waters 97; Sally
Abigail 65; Sally
Moore 16,73; Samuel 9,
22,62,65,98; Samuel
Clarence 37; Samuel
McNeal 83; Samuel Sin-
gleton 95; Samuel T.
62; Samuel Walker 28;

POLK (cont.) Samuel Wilson
24; Samuel Wistar 100;
Sarah 3,4,17,68,82,91;
Sarah Ardella 89; Sarah
(Cox) 95; Sarah (Sally)
Cox 55; Sarah Delaney
54,91; Sarah E. 42;
Sara E. Chambers 76;
Sarah Elizabeth 63;
Sarah Ella 82; Sarah
Evelyn 41; Sarah Glass
75; Sarah H. 36; Sarah
Hawkins 14; Sarah Hen-
rietta 40; Sarah Irene
Chandler 61; Sarah
Isham 39; Sarah Jane
Large 92; Sarah Jane
Rider 93; Sarah John
LeNoir 81; Sarah Jutz
91; Sarah Lulu Wicker
85; Sarah Moore 74;
Sarah Moore Jackson 16;
Sarah R. 48; Sarah
Rachel 32; Sarah Roach
27; Sarah Robina 48;
Sarah Wilson 55; Serena
Devereux 80; Shelby 5,8;
Silas Gelaspy 46; Silas
William 25; Sophia 27;
Sophia (Neely) Lennard
8; Sophia Lulu 86;
Stella Fewell 100;
Stella Gipson 92; Stel-
la Maud 92; Sue Louise
Powell 75; Susan 4,65;
Susan Brown 91; Susan
Elizabeth 40; Susan
Huntington 72; Susan
Langley 91; Susan R.
36; Susan Rebecca 34;
Susan Spratt 17,37;
Susan Williams Jones
94; Susanna 7,17;
Susanna Amelia Caroline
22; Susanna Pryon 17;
Susanna Spratt 5;
Sylvester 55,91; Syl-
vester Walker 54,92;
Sylvester Wilks 93;
Tabitha 7; Tabitha
Josephine 41; Tandy 20;
Tandy, Jr. 21; Tasker
66; Taylor 8,20,21,54,
55,61,90,91,92,93,95,96;
Texana 91; Thelma Maud
Gladden 86; Theresa 67,
100; Theresa Carruth 89;
Theressia Bowles 66;
Thomas 1,4,5,6,9,14,17,
19,21,29,30,31,34,37,38,
39,40,45,47,60,63,65,71,
72,73,75,76,77,78,80,81,
82,83,91,97; Thomas
Allison 99; Thomas Ben-
jamin 63,97; Thomas Cal-
vin 48; Thomas Emmett
100; Thomas Gilchrist
16,29,71,72; Thomas
Hamilton 86; Thomas
Independence 17,39,81,
82,83,84; Thomas James
40; Thomas Jefferson
22,65; Thomas Julian
82; Thomas Lucius 97;
Thomas Luton 97; Thomas
Marlborough 27,67,99,
100; Thomas Marshall 40,
84; Thomas Richard 39,
82,83; Thomas Trammell
94; Thomas Walker 92;
Thomas Wilson 99; Thur-
ston 82; Tillie Walling
62; Travis Wayne 96;

POLK (cont.) Tyler Vernon 87; Verlie Davidson 86; Victoria 44,92; Victoria Thomas 45; Viola Catherine 48; Viola Tranquilla 49; Virginia Adeline 65; Virginia Gibson Prichard 98; Virginia Green 67; Walter Earl 86; Walter Marcus 85; Warren 96; Wayne 95; Will 65; William 1,2,3,4,5,6,7, 8,9,14,17,18,19,20,21, 22,24,27,29,30,31,33,34, 37,38,39,40,41,42,43,45, 47,48,50,53,54,55,61,63, 65,66,67,71,72,73,75,76, 77,78,80,81,82,83,84,85, 86,87,88,90,91,92,93,95, 96,97,99,100; William Alexander 68,100; William Alfred 47; William Allen 43; William Arthur 82,100; William C. 45; William Cartez 96; William Charles 43,86,96; William D. 67; William Eddings 86; William Epps 66; William Ezekiel 64; William Franklin 94; William Hale 42; William Harrison 1; William Hawkins 24,38, 65,66; William Henry 96; William I. 45; William Jackson 60; William Julius 16,17, 30,71,72,73,75,76; William Knox 19,45,97; William Lee 76; William Long 87; William McNeal 99; William Mecklenburg 36,78; William Port 62; William (Robert) 3,4; William Rufus 88; William S. 7; William Tannahill 66; William Vincent 48,87; William Wilson 24,66,67,99,100; William Wood 28; Willie May Glass 75; Willie Rodgers 67; Wilma 67; Wilmoth Elizabeth 97; Wilport Alfred 62; Winifred Colburn 5; Winnie Elizabeth 62; Wylie Amanda Moseley 82; Yettie 96; Yettie Tobler 96; Young C. 62; Zipha Sutton 95,96;
POLLETT, Martha Polk 3; Thomas 3
POLLITT, Thomas 2
POLLOCK, Ann 3; Frances 34; James 3; Joseph 2, 3; Magdalen 2; Robert 2,3,101; Thomas 34; Zephaniah 3
POPE, Adelia Clarissa 12; Charles Henry 58; John Col. 12
PORCHER, Annie Robert 46; John W. 47; Joseph H. 46; Margaret Isabella 47
PORTER, Colonel____ 2; Emma 74; Lily Jones 45; Magdalen Taskee 2,3; Melvina 20; W. D. 45
POTTER, Elizabeth Sturgis 80; James 80

POTTS, Amanda 45; Cleland 82; Edgar Nelson 39; F. F. Helmich 39; Horace B. 39; Jane 19; John 19; John J. 39; Laura 45; Layfette 45; Lafayette Brown 82; Lucy Lanier 39; Mary Ann Polk 39; Mary Octavia 39; Mary Ophelia 82; Missoni 19; Pauline 82; Sumner Alkea 39; Thomas 39; Van H. 45; William 39;
POWELL, Frank 44; Margaret Benigna Childers 44; Sue Louise 75
PRESSER, Elise 31; Theodore 31
PRICE, General ____ 10, 99; Anna Black 98; Annie Cecil 82; Ernest E. 82; Fannie B. 47
PRICHARD, Ada Theressia 67; Joan (Eaton) 96; Mary 96; Mary (Gibson) 98; Nathaniel (Reddick) 67; Virginia Gibson 98; W. G. 98; William Blue 96
PRIEST, Caldena 91
PRIOR, ____ 11; Keziah 6; Olivia Mary 11
PRITCHETT, John C. 48; Sarah Robina 48
PRYON, Susanna 17
PUCKETT, Clemmie 42
PULLEN, Benjamin King 40; Minerva Anner (Smith) 40; Minnie Fisher 40
PULLIAM, Joel L. 66; Tymoxena 66
PUTNAM, Eben 59
QUARLES, Lucille 75
QUEEN, Ann 101
QUINTARD, Frances 30
RAGSDALE, Lulu 17
RAMEY, Anna Kate 67; Anna (Key) 67; William Nathaniel 67
RANDAL, Eliza 48
RANEY, Aurora McCellan 42
RAPE, John 17; Martha 18; Mary E. 18; Susan P. 18; Susanna 17; W. Clark 18
RAY, Ann Crenshaw 40; George W. 40; Marshall Gaines 40; Samuel Turner 40; Susan Elizabeth Polk 40
RAYNER, Anna Armand 17; Eliza Nelms 17; Eugenia Leach 17; Fanny 17; Hamilton Polk 17; Henry A. 17; Kenneth 17; Lulu 17; Mary 17; Sallie Polk 17; Susan Polk 17; William Polk 17
READE, Sarah Ann 12
REARDON, Frank J. 62; Nora 62
REAMS, David Crockett 69; Fannie Bates 69; Louise (Moss) 69
REDMAN, Charles Collins 88; Christine Cornelia 89; Christine Hance 88
REDFORD, Henrietta Polk 40; Leonard Warren 40; Lucy Jane (Holmes) 40; Moncure Warren 40

REED, Ace 93; Ace Walker 93; Benigna Ellen 13; Charles Henry 13; Laura Polk 93; Margaret Dennie 93; Martha Emaline 64; Walter Jackson 93; William Thomas 93
REILEY, Eliza 68; Frances 25
RENSHAW, Ann Polk 3; John 3
REYNOLDS, Frank Edward 58; John Williams 58; Julia 59; Mabel Velma 58; Marjorie Angellolli 58; Mary 30; William Stowell 58
RICHARDS, Margaret 52
RICHARDSON, Anna Black (Price) 98; D. F. 18; Edgar Morrison 98; Edgar Morrison, Jr. 98; Evelyn Marshall Polk 98; Susan 18
RICHMOND, Edmonia 24; Edward 24; Lydia Eliza 24
RICKETTS, Belle A. 61; E. J. 61; Elizabeth Blackburn 61; James Knox 61; Mary 61
RIDER, Sarah Jane 93
RIGGAN, Ann Eliza 27; S. W. 27
RILEY, Henry 96; Lena May Polk 96; Lois 96
RING, Frances 36; Frank W. 36
ROACH, Catherine 19; William 19
ROBERTS, Ann Polk 2,3; Coral 88; E. H. 95; Edward 2,3; Elizabeth Polk 95; Eliza 27; Francis 3; Jessie 34; Lizzie 55; Mark R. 11; Mary Eliza 11; Prisella 2,3
ROBERTSON, Sarah 25
ROBINSON, Martha 67
RODDY, General 76
RODGERS, Frank B. 27; J. Ferdinand 27; Louise Matilda 27; Mary 27; Olivia Polk 27; Willie 67
ROE, Addison J. 81; Adelaide E. 80; Jennie H. (Scranton) 81
ROGERS, Arthur Graham 69; Charles Thomas 68,69; Cleora May Harris 70; Edna Beardsley 70; Edna Sarah (Beardsley) 70; Effie Eleana 69; Elizabeth (Hutton) 68,69; Ernest Crockett 69; Ethel Olivia 69; Eunie Edwards 69; Fannie Bates (Reams) 69; Fannie Tabitha 69; Herman Titus 69; Leonidas Gideon 68, 69; Leonidas Winfield 69; Lewis Galloway 70; Lula 69; Lula Ella 68; Lula May 70; James William 69; John Henry 69; John Matthew Freeman 69; Marcia Butts 69; Mark Washington 68, 69; Sarah Tabitha (Mitchell) 68,69; Theodore Pressley 69;

STRICKLAND, Mary Amanda 18; Williamson Parks 18
STROUD, Della Walker 68; Ethan Beden 68; Mandred 68; Napoleon 68; Narcissus (Oliver) 68; Olivia Polk 68; Ora 68; Roderick 68; Thomas Mandred 68
STRUM, Louis Willard 84; Ophelia Wilson 84
SUMPTER, Mary Wardlow 26; Volney Edward 26
SURRATT, Elizabeth 28
SUTTON, Anderson 96; Rhoda 96; Zilpha 96
SWAIN, Polly 57; Sallie 57
SWIFT, Francis Montgomery 67; Katherine Elnora 67; John Julian 67; Susie (Lanier) 67
SWINK, George W. 25; Olivia Polk 25
SWOPE, Abraham Lee 62; Ira Abraham 62; Mary Allie 62; Winnie Elizabeth Polk 62
SWOR, Anne 46
TABB, Augusta T. 23
TALLEY, Clarke B.; Eliza (Clark) 63; Eliza (Martin) 25; Emily 25; Jesse 63; Martin 25; Sarah Frances 63
TANDY, Nancy 20
TANNAHILL, Alice 66
TASKEE, Colonel 2; Magdalen 2
TASKER, Colonel 2; Barbara 2
TAPPAN, J. C. 73
TAYLOR, Abner 24,25; Abner Cunningham 25; Adeline Davy 63; Amanda Jackson (Thompson) 63; Amanda Pauline 42; Andrew 25; Ann Elizabeth 25; Benjamin Franklin 25; Charles 4; Clarissa 25; Clarissa Sarah 25; Frances (Reiley) 25; Frank 25; General 51; Henry Sanford 63; Isaac 25; James S. 45; Jane Elizabeth 25; Jesse Baggett 63; John Adams 25; John Jackson 25; John Lewis 25; Laura Theressia 25; Laura Weston 24; Margaret 4; Mary Caroline 25; Mary Elizabeth 25; Mattie Bowen 45; Olivia Berry 25; Olivia Polk 25; Rebecca Williams 25; Sarah Jane 24,25; Thomas Le Roy 25; William 4,42; William Polk 25
TEAGUE, Elizabeth 57; Isabell 57
TEEL, George 46; Margaret Jane 48; Ollie 46; Rebecca 46; Wyatt F. 48
TERRY's Rangers 53
THOMAS, Catherine B. 86; Colonel 9; Iredell D. 45; Ludie Gertrude 46; Mary 46; Mattie Virginia 87; Murray B. 46; Penelope (Edwards) 45;

THOMAS (cont.) Victoria 45,46
THOMPSON, Amanda Jackson 63; Colonel 8; William Col. 15
THORNTON, Susan 39
TIBBS, Duane 96; Frederick 96; Pearl Polk 96
TILGHMAN, _____ 4
TOBLER, Julia 96; Julius 96; Yettie 96
TODD, Verdie 96
TOONE, Earl 88; Mary Louise 88
TORT, Frances 67
TOWNLEY, Hester 88; William John 88
TOWNSEND, Martha Jane 63
TRACY, Alonzo 91; Sarah Polk 91
TRAMMELL, Annie Laura 95; Dorothy Elizabeth 95; James Phillip 95; Marie Gladys Jolly 95; Mary Jane 55; Mary Jane (Newman) 95; Mattie Lina 95; Nancy 55; Thomas 55,95; Thomas Gibson 95
TRESSLER, Jane 59
TROTTER, Mary Louise 29; Richard 29
TROWBRIDGE, George 37; Sarah Camilla 37
TRYON, William 8
TUCKER, Bettie 43
TULL, Martha Polk 3; Richard 3
TURNER, Clara B. 33; Henrietta (Garrett) 66; Kenneth Garrett 66; Midicus Joel 66; Paris 25; Susan Carter 25; Theressa 66
TURRENTINE, Minnie 84
TUTTLE, Harriet 58
TWEEDLE, Jency Fielding 55; William 55
TYLER, Delilah 4; President 66
TYRON, Governor 15
TYSON, Burnett 85; Eva 85; Mary E. 85
UBBER, Minnie 94
UTLEY, Susan Alexander 25
VANCE, Mary 29
VAN DAVETTE, Anna 43; James, Jr. 43
VANDERBOGART, Mabel 38
VANDERGRIFT, Ann 41; Peck 41
VANDERSICKLE, Laura S. 48
VAN DORN, Earl 31
VAN LEER, Rebecca 38
VANSANT, Mantell 42; Sarah E. 42
VERNON, Cynthia Cornelia 84; Edward 84
VESEY, Ann Eliza 27; Ellen Elizabeth 27; M. L. 27
VIRDELL, Henry Franklin 92; Minnie Pearl 92
VON ISBERG, Louise 66
WADE, D. F. 33
WADDINGTON, Alexander 18; Alexander Green 18; Amanda 18; Charles William 18; Campie 19; Catherine 19; Hannah 18; Jane 18; Jennie Watson 18; Louisa Blanchard 18; Martha Elizabeth 18; Polly

WADDINGTON (cont.) Ann 18
WADSWORTH, Nancy 60
WALDREP, Alford Broadus 97; Anna Louise Harris 98; Little Berry 97,98
WALDROP, Beulah Brooks 85; Charles W. 85; Eva Tyson 85; Ezekiel Polk 85; Jennie 85; Jimmie Strawn 85; John Cleveland 85; Joseph A. 85; Joseph Marvin 85; Margaret Elizabeth 85; Mary E. 85; Rader 85; Virgie Lee 85
WALKER, Alexander 20; Alpha Katherine 93; Andrew Clay 93; Andrew Jackson 24; Annie Maria 23; Augusta T. Tabb 23; Celestine Garth 23; Della 68; Eleanor T. 23; James 23; James Hayes 23; James Knox 61; Jane Clarissa 23; Jane Maria 23; Jane Rutherford 20,23; Jency 20,21, 61; Joe; 21; John 20,23; Joseph Knox 23; Leonidas Polk 24; Lucius 23; Martha 61; Martha Robinson 61; Mary 21,26; Mary Eliza 23; Mary Orme 29; Mary Vance 29; Okie Kesmire 61; Ophelia Lazinska 24; Samuel Polk 23; Sarah Naomi 23; Sophy Davis 23; Susan Wilcox 24; Sylvester 21; Tandy 20,26; Tandy, Jr. 21; Thomas D. 29; William 20; William Hardy 61
WALKERS, _____ 20
WALL, Bune 48; Kate 48
WALLACE, Margaret 73
WALLING, Elizabeth 62; J. H. A. 62; Tillie 62
WALTERS, Nora 65
WALTON, Mary Elizabeth 81; Sarah Willis 63
WARD, Hattie 42; Jennie 85; Julia 42; Leonard 85
WARDWELL, Elizabeth 59
WARDWICK, Hallie (White) 60; Julia Angeline 60; Robert William 60; Samuel 60
WARREN, Florence Helen Polk 89; Helen Florence 89; Katherine Elizabeth 89; Thomas Speed 89
WASHINGTON, George 30; President 15
WATERS, Sallie 97
WATTERS, _____ 16
WATSON, Jennie 18; Alfred Bacon 44; Amanda M. 43; Emily B. 44; Eudora Harr 44; Jennie Noble 44; Jesse 44; Jesse Allen 44; John Polk 44; Laura Murchison 44; Larena McCallum 44; Mary Elizabeth 44; Morphia Collins 44; Ray Richard Overton 43; Richard Overton 44; Robert Smith 44; William Archiball 44
WATTS, Nellie 70; Susan 24; Susan Wilcox 24; Thomas 24

James Knox Polk & wife Fanny Elizabeth (Foster) Polk. Son of Franklin Armistead Polk & Mary Eliza (Stevens) Polk. *From Mrs. Robert Oliver, Columbia, Tenn.*

Ophelia Elizabeth Hines (Polk) Kinnard, dau. of Franklin Armistead Polk & Mary Eliza (Stevens) Polk and wife of David Michael Kinnard. *From Mrs. Robert Oliver, Columbia, Tenn.*

Eliza Adeline (Kinnard) McGaughey, dau. of David Michael Kinnard & Ophelia Elizabeth (Polk) Kinnard & wife of Felix Polk McGaughey. *From Mrs. Robert Oliver, Columbia, Tenn.*

Sylvester Walker Polk, son of Taylor & Prudence (Anderson) Polk. *From Vernell Endecott, Drumright, Okla.*

Jency Polk Anderson, dau. of Taylor & Jency (Walker) Polk & wife of Mitchell Anderson. *From Vernell Endecott, Drumright, Okla.*

Mitchell Anderson, husband of Jency Polk. *From Vernell Endecott, Drumright, Okla.*